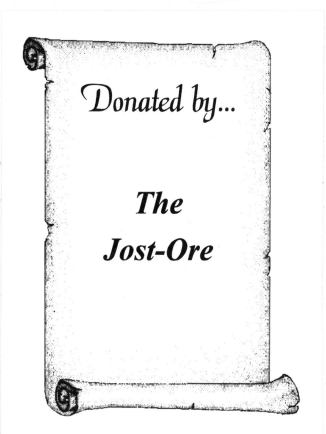

Donated by...

The

Jost-Ore

The Symbolic Meaning

D. H. LAWRENCE

The Symbolic Meaning

The uncollected versions of
Studies in Classic American Literature

Edited by
ARMIN ARNOLD
with a Preface by
HARRY T. MOORE

CENTAUR PRESS LIMITED

First published in 1962 *by the Centaur Press Ltd. of Fontwell, Arundel, and printed in Great Britain by T. J. Winterson, London, in* 11 *on* 13*pt. Baskerville*

Contents

Acknowledgments

For locating, purchasing and copying manuscripts the editor is indebted to Prof. Dexter Martin, Harrisonburg, Va.; Dr. Warren Roberts and the Humanities Research Center, University of Texas; Frances Hamill, Hamill and Barker, Bookdealers, Chicago; Mrs. Barbara Arnold-Apollony; and Dr. E. W. Tedlock, Jr., University of New Mexico. The publication of this book would not have been possible without the active help of Jon Wynne-Tyson, director of the Centaur Press, London, and without the friendly consent of Laurence Pollinger, representative of the D. H. Lawrence estate. The Essay on Dana is reprinted with the permission of Laurence Pollinger, Literary Executor to the Estate of the late Mrs. Frieda Lawrence, and the publishers, William Heinemann, Ltd., London, and the Viking Press, New York.

The editor wishes to express his gratitude to Dr. Ernest Reinhold, University of Alberta; the University of Alberta Library; the staff of the Redpath Library, Montreal; the Research Fund of the University of Alberta; and the Canada Council; he is also grateful to Mrs. Barbara Surman Meisner for a careful comparative analysis of Lawrence's styles of writing in the three versions of the *Studies in Classic American Literature;* and to Dexter Martin for many useful suggestions.

Preface

By HARRY T. MOORE

D. H. Lawrence's most impressive book, after his major novels and his finest poems, is *Studies in Classic American Literature,* published in 1923. Earlier versions of parts of that work, the essays printed in full for the first time in the present volume, were written toward the end of the First World War, shortly after Lawrence had completed his greatest novel, *Women in Love.* He was at the peak of his ability and yet, after finishing the novel in 1916, he wrote little in the imaginative vein until after he left England late in 1919. In the interim, his creative energy went into these essays.

The war had from the first embittered Lawrence, who knew Germany and despised its militarism. On the other hand, he found that he could not support the British cause, and he resented the attempts of patriotic bullies, in the excitement of the moment, to force conformity upon everyone. Lawrence's position in England was all the more difficult because he had a German wife. When his novel *The Rainbow* was suppressed in 1915, the ostensible reason for the action was that the book was indecent, but Richard Aldington and others familiar with the circumstances at the time have suggested that there was a military influence in the suppression: in that autumn of 1915, British morale was low, and the heroine of Lawrence's story jeered at the uniform of her lover, an officer in the Boer War.

Whatever the cause, *The Rainbow* was taken out of circulation. Lawrence and Frieda had passports, and their passage to America was booked—America, toward which his thoughts had been turning, a country not yet involved in the war. When the authorities suppressed his novel, Lawrence believed that the English literary world was going to help him fight for it, and he postponed his westward journey. But nothing was done to help *The Rainbow* beyond the asking of a few questions in Parliament

which were squelched. Later, when Lawrence again tried to go
to America, he and his wife were forbidden to leave England.

It was in this dark time that he completed *Women in Love,* in
Cornwall. It had to wait four years before he could find a
publisher for it. Meanwhile, because Lawrence and his wife were
apparently suspected of being in contact with enemy submarines,
they were put out of Cornwall and ordered not to go into any
coastal area. Lawrence developed a dislike of his fellow-country-
men; he got out of England after the war ended and, because
his antagonism lasted, he could never bring himself to live there
again; on the few visits he made after 1919, he stayed only
briefly. It was in the period before he finally left that he began
writing the American-literature essays, whose full history Dr.
Armin Arnold traces in the Introduction which follows. It is Dr.
Arnold who has collected the early versions of them which
appeared in magazines towards the end of the war and soon
after it, and he has added some hitherto unpublished material.

These essays are not merely the result of Lawrence's wartime
dissatisfaction with England and his desire to go to America.
He had from childhood been an ardent reader, and Cooper and
some of the other "classic" Americans had long appealed to him;
Whitman, who often antagonized him, had profoundly influenced
his own writings. During the war, Lawrence found Melville's
books about the Pacific particularly moving, as his letters of the
time demonstrate. Indeed, he was one of the discoverers of
Melville, and in the *Studies* was one of the first to treat him as
the great writer that he is.

In turn, it was these American-literature essays which helped
bring about American recognition of Lawrence's own greatness
after the Second World War. At that time, following a long
period of neglect of Lawrence in the United States, a paperback
reprint of the *Studies* was published there; American literature
had become the fashion, and commentaries on it were read
avidly. American-literature scholars found the *Studies* to be
irreverently colloquial and sometimes just vulgar, but they also

noted Lawrence's insights, of the kind perhaps possible only in such vigorously iconoclastic writing. These scholars discussed Lawrence seriously as a critic and helped make his name better known. Meanwhile, other readers in America were rediscovering Lawrence's novels, and his books began coming back into print there.

His critical ability is now recognised along with his creative powers. Lawrence was one of those readers untrained in formal criticism who make their judgment on books directly from life rather than from aesthetic imperatives. He did not regard life as the instrument of books. Nor was he ever so one-sided anti-rationalistic as those who try to belittle him pretend: he emphasized the importance of what he called blood-consciousness because he felt that mankind was stifling it; he strongly wanted to bring it into balance with what he called mind-consciousness. All this is inspired commonsense, which is just what the reader will often find underneath the brashness of Lawrence's criticism. And he will find, too, that Lawrence, in pursuing these ideas and others which he explains as he goes along, usually says just the right thing about the books and authors he discusses.

These earlier versions of *Studies in Classic American Literature* are an important contribution to studies of Lawrence himself. I disagree with much that my friend Dr. Armin Arnold says about these essays, but, as all readers of Lawrence should be, I am extremely grateful to him for making this significant collection available.

Southern Illinois University
October 12, 1961

Introduction

I

On January 9, 1917, Lawrence wrote to his agent J. B. Pinker: "I want to go to New York and write a set of essays on American literature, and perhaps lecture. It is no use my sitting cooped up here any longer . . . I have got in my head a set of essays, or lectures, on Classic American literature. But I can't write for America here in England. I must transfer myself."[1] Lawrence hated England at the time. He and his wife were treated as German spies; his novel *The Rainbow* had been suppressed, and Lawrence had suddenly found himself without publisher and without money. Desperately he tried to obtain visas for America, but all attempts, in spite of Cynthia Asquith's help, were fruitless. Nevertheless, he decided to go ahead with the lectures, in the hope of selling them as essays to periodicals in England or America.

On August 30th, 1917, he wrote to Pinker again: "I am doing, in the hopes of relieving my ominous financial prospects, a set of essays on *The Transcendental Element in American Literature.* You may marvel at such a subject, but it interests me. I was thinking of speaking to Amy Lowell about it. Her brother is principal of Harvard, and she can touch the pulse of the *Yale Review* and things like that. We might get the essays into a periodical here in England . . . " On March 12, 1918, the essays were almost complete. He wrote to Cecil Grey: "I ebb along with the American essays, which are in their last and final form." On June 3, 1918, he told Mrs. S. A. Hopkin: "I am writing a last essay on Whitman—then I have done my book of American essays . . . " Lawrence had them typed between July

---

[1] If not indicated otherwise, all the letters quoted appear in *The Letters of D. H. Lawrence,* edited by Aldous Huxley, 1932. Page references are to the English edition.

1

and September. On August 3, 1918, he sent two copies of the first one, "The Spirit of Place", to his agent, telling him that six or seven more would arrive the following week. Lawrence suggested to Pinker that Austin Harrison, the editor of the *English Review*, might be interested in publishing the essays. "The Spirit of Place" appeared in the *English Review* for November, 1918.

Lawrence had written twelve essays in all, as he told Harriet Monroe on February 1, 1919. Only eight appeared in the *English Review* between November, 1918 and June, 1919. Of these the one on Nathaniel Hawthorne was published in a very mutilated form. The eight essays are: "The Spirit of Place", "Benjamin Franklin", "Hector St. John de Crèvecoeur", "Fenimore Cooper's Anglo-American Novels", "Fenimore Cooper's Leatherstocking Novels", "Edgar Allan Poe", "Nathaniel Hawthorne", and "The Two Principles". Why did Harrison not publish the rest? We have no evidence. The complete manuscript on Hawthorne is still extant; approximately sixty per cent of it appeared in the *English Review*.

In January, 1920, Lawrence dispensed with the services of his English agent, J. B. Pinker. Already on December 27, 1919, Lawrence had written to Pinker: "I think there is not much point in our remaining bound to one another. You told me when we made our agreement that we might break it when either of us wished. I wish it should be broken now. What bit of work I have to place, I like to place myself." On January 10, 1920, the break was made complete. Lawrence wrote to Pinker: "Thank you for your letter. Yes, I am grateful to you for all you have done for me in the past. But I am an unsatisfactory person, I know. And therefore it would be best for me to act just on my own responsibility. So do please let us conclude our agreement.

"What things you have to return to me, please tell me. But don't send any more MS. to me here. I will arrange with my sister, or a friend, to keep the things for me."

In the summer of 1920, Lawrence revised the essays in Sicily.

He wrote to Cecil Palmer on June 26th : "The *Studies in Classic American Literature* I finished revising ten days ago. They make a book about 70-80 thousand words."[2] Lawrence sent the essays to his American agent, Robert Mountsier, who was in Paris at the moment. The diary entry for August 2, 1920, reads : "Post Studies in Cl. Am. Lit. to Mountsier in Paris for America."[3]

It appears that he had no English agent till April, 1921, when Curtis Brown replaced Pinker. The friend who kept the manuscripts received from Pinker was Barbara Low. She handed them over to Curtis Brown in April, 1921. In his first letter to Curtis Brown, Lawrence mentions several manuscripts at hand, but no manuscript of the American essays.[4] Mountsier probably brought these along with him on his 1921 trip to Europe. He arrived in Paris on May 10, 1921 : from there he proceeded to London in order to meet Curtis Brown. At that time Mountsier delivered several manuscripts (or copies of manuscripts) to Curtis Brown, among which probably were the essays not published in the *English Review* and revised by Lawrence in 1920.

Curtis Brown succeeded in publishing the essay on Whitman in *The Nation and The Athenaeum* (July 23, 1921). The Dana-manuscript is missing, but the three other essays, the two on Melville and the one on Hawthorne (printed herein as "Hawthorne II"), are extant. They carry the name and address of Robert Mountsier at the bottom of the title-page, and, stamped in later, the name and address of Curtis Brown (the stamp is lacking on the title-page of the essay on Melville's *Typee* and *Omoo*).

We do not have enough evidence to determine the extent of Lawrence's revision of each of the original essays. In one instance, however, one can see how far this revision went, e.g.,

    [2] Harry T. Moore: *The Intelligent Heart,* London, 1955, p. 267.
    [3] Diary in E. W. Tedlock: *The Frieda Lawrence Collection of D. H. Lawrence Manuscripts,* Albuquerque, 1948.
    [4] Letter to Curtis Brown, April 4, 1921.

by comparing the essay "Hawthorne II" (version 2) to the second part of "Hawthorne I" (version 1). The chances are that he only slightly touched the essays published in the *English Review,* but revised the rest extensively. The essays on Dana and *Moby Dick*—both full of quotations—were probably less subjected to change.

Lawrence radically revised the essays once more in America. They were finally published in New York by Thomas Seltzer in August, 1923 and in London by Martin Secker in June, 1924. The American edition carried a preface which does not appear in the English edition.

II

We have then three versions of Lawrence's *Studies in Classic American Literature*: Version 1: The twelve original essays written in Cornwall in 1917-1918. Eight of these were published in the *English Review,* the one on Hawthorne in mutilated form. In addition the complete manuscript of the essay on Hawthorne —which had been only partly published—is extant. Version 2: The essays as revised in Sicily in 1920; the only published example is the essay on Whitman in *The Nation and The Athenaeum* of July 23, 1921. In addition three typescripts are extant: "Herman Melville's *Moby Dick*", "Herman Melville's *Typee* and *Omoo*", and the essay herein entitled "Hawthorne II". Version 3: Twelve essays written in the winter of 1922-1923 in America, including two essays on Hawthorne, but "The Two Principles" left out.

III

What distinguishes these three versions from each other? Lawrence had originally planned to write purely literary essays which he would be able to use as lectures in America. But, as always with Lawrence, he had to write about the problems which occupied him most at the moment. And what really was on his mind in 1917-1918 was his "philosophy". In 1915 he had intended to lecture in London, together with Bertrand Russell and J. M. Murry, Russell "on Ethics, I on Immortality."[5] Long and confused essays like "The Crown" and "Education of the People" were the results. Thereupon he started out to write a study of Thomas Hardy, but he ended up in another hundred pages of philosophy. The same happened, to a lesser extent, in the first version of the American essays. Long passages about Lawrence's philosophy appear in most essays in the *English Review*, and the last one, "The Two Principles", has lost all contact with American literature. We are, therefore, not surprised when we find Lawrence writing to Cecil Grey : In the "American essays . . . I have got it all off my chest. I shall never write another page of philosophy—or whatever it is—when these are done."[6]

Lawrence's solar-plexus-theories had already occurred in "Education of the People".[7] Now he repeated and enlarged them. Typically he changed the theories from essay to essay. He starts out with two "centres of consciousness" in the essay on Crèvecoeur, but changes them to four later on. Lawrence did not keep his promise : he continued to write down his philosophy, first in *Psychoanalysis and the Unconscious* (1921), and then, when the critics had poked fun at him, in *Fantasia of the Unconscious* (1922). It is possible that, when revising the essays in Sicily, he left most of the solar-plexus-philosophy out; he probably knew that he was going to write a separate volume about it. Of course, Lawrence did not reintroduce the philosophical parts in version 3.

Version 1 is, to a small extent, marred by this philosophy. Lawrence tried to do two things at once : to produce approving essays on American literature to be used as lecture-material, and

[5] *Letters,* p. 239 (American edition, p. 243).
[6] Letter to Cecil Grey, March 12, 1918.
[7] In *Phoenix,* ed. by E. McDonald, 1936.

B

secondly, to jot down reflections about his solar-plexus-theories. But it must be said that the surprising originality, the vital quality of the essays in their first version could not exist without Lawrence's philosophical passion. Nobody has ever expressed it better than E. M. Forster who defended Lawrence against an attack from T. S. Eliot: Lawrence "was both a preacher and a poet, and some people, myself included, do not sympathize with the preaching. Yet I feel that without the preaching the poetry could not exist. With some writers one can disentangle the two, with him they are inseparable."[8] Version 1 is more objective and more impersonal, as far as literary criticism is concerned. America was, for Lawrence, in 1917-1918, a refuge, a paradise compared with England (although he had no illusions about American materialism and industrialism). Version 1 is written in a very moderate, explanatory tone. Quotations are more frequent than in version 3. The procedure is scientific; Lawrence is more at ease. What he says is logical, intelligent, and well-observed. All this is still true of version 2. America was still a paradise, and version 2 of the essay on Whitman concludes with Lawrence's ecstatic exclamation: "Ave America." In version 3 this would have been impossible. Still, the four extant essays in version 2 have lost something compared to version 1. They are less vital, less original; Lawrence is less concerned, they are "well-behaved", "neat", but something has gone out of them.

The factor that completely spoilt version 3 was not philosophy—it is too much absent this time—but the hysterical tone. Lawrence was living at Lobo Ranch near Taos. His violent hate against Mabel Dodge and Toni Luhan was at its peak; he was in a state of extreme nervous tension resulting in almost insane outbreaks against his wife, his friends, his animals, against America as a whole.[9] This is reflected in version 3 of the essays. Most American reviewers, of course, did not understand the reasons for Lawrence's hysterical outbreaks and severely criticized the exag-

[8] Letter to *The Nation and Athenaeum,* April 26, 1930.
[9] See Knud Merrild: *A Poet and Two Painters,* 1938.

gerated, shrieking style of the book which had appeared in
August, 1923. H. I. Brock, for instance, found that Lawrence's
sympathy for Dana's captain who flogs Sam, the sailor, is perverse; he also said that Lawrence's hysterical style "contrives in
the long run to become intolerably tiresome."[10] Even the sympathetic Stuart P. Sherman wrote: " . . . I suspect that our
younger *literarti* will tell him that this coal-heaver style was quite
the thing ten years ago, but it is now regarded as rather out of
date." Sherman perfectly analyses Lawrence's state of mind when
he says: "It may be safely assumed also that his attack upon
American intellectualism and idealism proceeds from a reaction
for the recovery of his own balance."[11] Kurt L. Daniels makes
some very sound criticisms of version 3: "Lawrence is full of
ideas, but he lets them fly half-fledged. His positive, staccato,
repetitious style is effective when it isn't exasperating . . . Again
and again he falls a victim to his own metaphors, and too frequently seems to have made the argument fit the phrase."[12]

The reactions in England were similar. Here is Conrad Aiken
who chose for his review the title "Mr. Lawrence: Sensational-
ist": Lawrence "behaves like a man possessed, a man who has
been assured by someone (perhaps an Analyst) that restraint is
nonsense, that nothing is of importance save a violent, unthinking
outpouring of feelings and perceptions; unselected, unarranged,
and expressed with a conscious disregard for personal dignity.
Perhaps it is Whitman's barbaric yawp which has so disturbed
him."[13] The review in the *Times Literary Supplement* is even
more severe: "Mr. Lawrence the critic is vehemently, even
wearysomely, didactic; wearysomely because he is at the same
time bent on teaching and disdainful of the world for being so
foolish as to need to be taught." The critic credits Lawrence
with genius in every paragraph, but he finds "obstinacy, compla-

---

[10] *New York Times Book Review,* September 9, 1923.
[11] *New York Evening Post, The Literary Review,* October 20, 1923.
[12] *New Republic,* October 24, 1923.
[13] *The Nation and The Athenaeum,* July 12, 1924.

cency, and perversity" as well; " . . . the whole team is driven
too hard."[14] The criticisms of the early reviewers were repeated
later. Hugh Kingsmill poked fun at the essay on *Moby Dick*.[15]
Even Edmund Wilsom said that the essays "have shots that do
not hit the mark and moments that are quite hysterical,"[16] and
Thornton Wilder wrote to Harry T. Moore that "there are
passages of nonsense in it."[17]

These remarks are true enough of version 3, but they could not
be said of version 1 and 2. Lawrence was rarely content to revise
by merely exchanging a word for a better one or by crossing
a superfluous adjective out. He usually rewrote the entire story
or book from beginning to end. *Lady Chatterley's Lover*, for
instance, was revised twice; each of the three versions represents
a different novel. He did exactly the same with most of the
essays on American literature. Nobody thought of looking the
original essays up, and that is why nobody found out that they
are completely different from the essays in the book of 1923.
"The Two Principles" should have been included in Edward
McDonald's *Phoenix*, an almost complete collection of
Lawrence's miscellaneous writings which had not previously been
published in book-form. No anthologist was aware that there
are earlier and, in many ways, better versions in existence.[18] The
only one who ever noticed the difference between version 1 and
3 was Frederic Carter whom Lawrence had met in England in
the winter of 1923-24. Carter says: Lawrence's solar-plexus-
theories "appear in the original chapters on 'Classic American

[14] *Times Literary Supplement,* July 24, 1924.
[15] Hugh Kingsmill: *D. H. Lawrence,* 1938, p. 146.
[16] Edmund Wilson: *The Shock of Recognition,* 1943, p. 906.
[17] Harry T. Moore: *The Intelligent Heart,* p. 267.
[18] Edmund Wilson included the whole of *Studies in Classic American
Literature* in *The Shock of Recognition* (1943); anthologies containing
one or more of Lawrence's essays on Classic American Literature are: the
Everyman's Library volume of *Stories, Essays and Poems,* edited by
Desmond Hawkins (1939); *The Portable D. H. Lawrence,* edited by Diana
Trilling (1947); *Selected Essays,* edited by Richard Aldington (Penguin
Books, 1950); *Selected Literary Criticism,* edited by Anthony Beal (1956).

Literature' when they appeared as magazine articles. Later, in book form, he cut them down, and explaining his reason for deletion he said that he felt 'the esoteric parts should remain esoteric.' He was not satisfied with his previous scheme of interacting centres, they were difficult to get at and stayed obscure."[19]

IV

Lawrence is not only a great novelist and poet, he is also a very perceptive literary critic. Herbert J. Seligmann was probably the first to point out the critical qualities in Lawrence.[20] F. R. Leavis called Lawrence "the finest literary critic of our time —a great literary critic if ever there was one;"[21] and Martin Turnell compared Lawrence to T. S. Eliot: " .. *Studies in Classic American Literature* and *Phoenix* are not simply great criticism; they show that Lawrence, with his immense emphasis on life, possessed incomparably the most powerful personality among modern European critics and that from an artistic point of view his criticism is satisfying in a way that Mr. Eliot's is not."[22] There is no doubt that *Studies in Classic American Literature* is Lawrence's major work of literary criticism. Edmund Wilson calls the essays "one of the few first-rate books that have ever been written on the subject."[23] It is, therefore, all the more important to go back to the original essays and to point out that the essays in their first version are completely different and in many ways superior to those published in the book of 1923. The present collection of version 1 and 2 of the essays represents a hitherto unknown new book by Lawrence.

---

[19] Frederic Carter: *D. H. Lawrence and the Body Mystical,* 1932, p. 25.
[20] H. J. Seligmann: *D. H. Lawrence; an American Interpretation,* 1924.
[21] F. R. Leavis: *The Common Pursuit,* 1952, p. 233.
[22] Martin Turnell: "An Essay on Criticism", *Dublin Review,* 1948, No. 444.
[23] Edmund Wilson: *The Shock of Recognition,* p. 906.

V

A word about the title of this collection : in all three versions, specifically in the first one, Lawrence sets out to find the hidden meaning in the American classics. He explains this in version 1 of "The Spirit of Place" : "Art-speech is . . . a language of pure symbols. But whereas the authorized symbol stands always for a thought or an idea, some mental *concept,* the art-symbol or art-term stands for a pure experience, emotional and passional, spiritual and perceptional, all at once." The two tendencies in every work of art are : 1. "The didactic import given by the author from his own moral consciousness," and 2. "The profound symbolic import which proceeds from his unconscious or sub-conscious soul." In version 3 this distinction is made in the following terms : "The artist usually sets out—or used to—to point a moral and adorn a tale. The tale, however, points the other way, as a rule. Two blankly opposing morals, the artist's and the tale's. Never trust the artist. Trust the tale." This method of interpretation, the search for the symbolic meaning, for the meaning which the author had unconsciously put into his tale, was quite original. Lawrence explains his method in version 1 of "The Spirit of Place", taking Hawthorne as an example : "What Hawthorne deliberately says in *The Scarlet Letter* is on the whole a falsification of what he unconsciously says in his art-language. And this, again, is one of the outstanding qualities of American literature : that the deliberate ideas of the man veil, conceal, obscure that which the artist has to reveal."

Kurt L. Daniels wrote that Lawrence's book "gets its origin-ality from the playing of psycho-analytically derived methods on old familiar (and hence unknown) subjects . . . "[24] Edmund Wilson means something very similar when he says : "To an Ameri-can, American Literature is a part of his native landscape, and so veiled with associations that he cannot always see what the

[24] *New Republic,* October 24, 1923.

author is really saying. D. H. Lawrence has here tried to do
what it would be difficult for an American to do : read our books
for their meaning in the life of the western world as a whole."[25]

VI

A few notes about the editing : Every essay is preceded by a
short preface, pointing out where it was published, or which
version the manuscript is likely to be. Footnotes have been
avoided; wherever it was considered necessary, comments appear
in the prefaces. Misprints in the *English Review, The Nation
and The Athenaeum,* and the typescripts have been silently corrected. Lawrence was fond of using dashes and hyphens; they
have occasionally been left out. Lawrence's quotations from the
American authors are frequently inaccurate; they have not been
corrected.

When a preface to an essay mentions that a manuscript is
"lost", this means that the manuscript has never been discovered,
and that its location is unknown to Lawrence-scholars such as
E. W. Tedlock, Warren Roberts, and Harry T. Moore. In a
letter to Armin Arnold dated December, 1954, Frieda Lawrence
said that no manuscripts of the American essays were extant
except the ones mentioned in E. W. Tedlock's book, *The Frieda
Lawrence Collection of D. H. Lawrence Manuscripts.*

ARMIN ARNOLD

[25] Edmund Wilson: *The Shock of Recognition,* p. 906.

" . . . to criticise American books, to discover their symbolic meaning, we must first trace the development of the orthodox European idea on American soil; because there is always a dual import in these works of art: first, the didactic import given by the author from his own moral consciousness; and then the profound symbolic import which proceeds from his unconscious or subconscious soul . . . "

(*D. H. Lawrence*: "*The Spirit of Place*", *Version* 1)

1. THE SPIRIT OF PLACE

1. The Spirit of Place

This version of "The Spirit of Place" appeared in the
English Review *for November, 1918. Version 2, if it existed,
is lost. The third version in the book of 1923 differs vastly
in content and extent from this version. Version 1 is twice
as long as version 3. The most interesting part of version 1,
corresponding to about the first fifty per cent of the present
essay, has been left out in version 3. There the reasons why
the Pilgrim Fathers left their country are simplified to this :
"They came largely to get* away—*that most simple of
motives. To get away. Away from what? In the long run,
away from themselves. Away from everything. That's why
most people have come to America, and still do come. To
get away from everything they are and have been." Version
3 is quite hysterical; words like "democracy", "liberty",
"Whitman", and "idealist" throw Lawrence into fits of
hysterical shrieking. The repetitions are more than tiresome.
Version 3 is written rapidly, in the white heat of anger and
excitement. There would be no use in looking for any kind
of logic there. "Democracy is Slavery" would be a more
adequate title for the essay. Version 1, which follows here,
is, on the other hand, written in a logical, quiet, didactic
style; the arguments are original, but carefully arranged and
may be followed easily. Lawrence sticks to the theme and
explains the method which he intends to use in the essays
on the classic American authors.*

15

I T IS NATURAL that we should regard American literature as a small branch or province of English literature. None the less there is another view to be taken. The American art-speech contains a quality that we have not calculated. It has a suggestive force which is not relative to us, not inherent in the English race. This alien quality belongs to the American continent itself.

All art partakes of the Spirit of Place in which it is produced. The provincial Latin literature ferments with a foreign stimulus. It is Africa, and the mysterious religious passion of Lybia, which, voicing itself in Latin, utters the infant cry of Tertullian, Augustine, Athanasius, the great saints of the African Church. These are not Romans. They are the prelude to a new era. It is not only that they utter the *ideas* which made Europe. Chiefly in them is felt the first throb of the great mystic passion of mediaeval life. And in Apuleius, decadent and sensuous, we feel the last throb of the old way of sensuality, Babylon, Tyre, Carthage. Africa, seething in Roman veins, produces these strange pulses of new experience, incipient newness within the old decadence.

In the same way America, the new continent, seething in English veins, has produced us the familiar American classics, of Hawthorne, Poe, Whitman, or Fenimore Cooper, for example. We read the English utterance without getting the alien American implication. We listen to our own speech in American mouths, but our ears have been shut to the strange reverberation of that speech. We have not wanted to hear the undertone, the curious foreign, uncouth suggestion, which is in the over-cultured Hawthorne or Poe or Whitman. Augustine and Apuleius are both writers of the Roman decadence. The orthodox Romans, no doubt, saw mainly the decadence, and objected to it. They could not see that the qualities which *they* called decadence, judging from the standards of Virgil and Cicero and Tacitus, were perhaps the incipient realities of a whole new era of experience.

It is time now, for us, who have always looked with indulgence on the decadent or uncouth or provincial American literature, to open new eyes, and look with respect, if not with fear. It is time for us now to see that our great race experience is surpassed and exceeded. Our race *idea* may apparently hold good in the American mind. What we have to realise is that our way of feeling is superseded, just as Cicero's way of feeling was superseded in Apuleius. It is the quality of life-experience, of emotion and passion and desire, which has changed in the Romans of Africa, and in the English-speaking Americans. Life itself takes on a new reality, a new motion, even while the idea remains ostensibly the same.

And it is this change in the way of experience, a change in being, which we should now study in the American books. We have thought and spoken till now in terms of likeness and oneness. Now we must learn to think in terms of difference and otherness. There is a stranger on the face of the earth, and it is no use our trying any further to gull ourselves that he is one of us, and just as we are. There is an unthinkable gulf between us and America, and across the space we see, not our own folk signalling to us, but strangers, incomprehensible beings, simulacra perhaps of ourselves, but *other,* creatures of an other-world. The connection holds good historically, for the past. In the pure present and in futurity it is not valid. The present reality is a reality of untranslatable otherness, parallel to that which lay between St. Augustine and an orthodox senator in Rome of the same day. The oneness is historic only.

The knowledge that we are no longer one, that there is this inconceivable difference in *being* between us, the difference of an epoch, is difficult and painful to acquiesce in. Yet our only hope of freedom lies in acquiescing. The change has taken place in reality. And unless it take place also in our consciousness, we maintain ourselves all the time in a state of confusion. We must get clear of the old oneness that imprisons our real divergence.

It is the genuine American literature which affords the best approach to the knowledge of this othering. Only art-utterance

reveals the whole truth of a people. And the American art-speech
reveals what the American plain speech almost deliberately con-
ceals. What Hawthorne deliberately says in *The Scarlet Letter*
is on the whole a falsification of what he unconsciously says in
his art-language. And this, again, is one of the outstanding
qualities of American literature : that the deliberate ideas of the
man veil, conceal, obscure that which the artist has to reveal.
This quality of duplicity which runs through so much of the art
of the modern world is almost inevitable in an American book.
The author is unconscious of it himself. He is sincere in his own
intention. And yet, all the time, the artist, who writes as a som-
nambulist, in the spell of pure truth as in a dream, is contravened
and contradicted by the wakeful man and moralist who sits at
the desk.

The occultists say that once there was a universal mystic language, known to the initiated, or to the adept, or to the priesthood of the whole world, whether Chinese or Atlantean or Maya
or Druid—a language that was universal over the globe at some
period, perhaps before the Flood. This must have been a written
rather than a spoken language, and must have consisted in symbols or ideographs. It is conceivable, perhaps even probable, that
at one time the priesthoods of all the world—Asiatic, African,
European, American, Polynesian—held some common idea of
the creation of the Cosmic universe, and expressed this idea in
the same symbols or graphs. It is quite easy to conceive that the
circle should be a universal symbol for the All, and the rosy
cross, and the ankh, the Egyptian so-called symbol of life, may
have been used by all the wise men on the earth to express
certain cosmological ideas. And it may be possible, as the scientists of the subtler psychic activities desire and need to do, to
discover a universal system of symbology : for practically the
whole of psychometry and psycho-analysis depends on the
understanding of symbols.

But art-speech, art-utterance, is, and always will be, the
greatest universal language of mankind, greater than any esoteric

symbolism. Art-speech is also a language of pure symbols. But whereas the authorized symbol stands always for a thought or an idea, some mental *concept,* the art-symbol or art-term stands for a pure experience, emotional and passional, spiritual and perceptual, all at once. The intellectual idea remains implicit, latent and nascent. Art communicates a state of being—whereas the symbol at best only communicates a whole thought, an emotional idea. Art-speech is a use of symbols which are pulsations on the blood and seizures upon the nerves, and at the same time pure percepts of the mind and pure terms of spiritual aspiration.

Therefore, when we reduce and diminish any work of art to its didactic capacity—as we reduce a man to his mere physical-functional capacity in the science of medicine—then we find that that work of art is a subtle and complex *idea* expressed in symbols. It is more or less necessary to view man as a thing of various functions and organs. And in the same way, for certain purposes, it is necessary to degrade a work of art into a thing of meanings and reasoned exposition. This process of reduction is part of the science of criticism.

But before we can undertake to criticise American books, to discover their symbolic meaning, we must first trace the development of the orthodox European idea on American soil; because there is always a dual import in these works of art : first, the didactic import given by the author from his own moral consciousness; and then the profound symbolic import which proceeds from his unconscious or subconscious soul, as he works in a state of creation which is something like somnambulism or dreaming. Also we must wake and sharpen in ourselves the subtle faculty for perceiving the greater inhuman forces that control us. It is our fatal limitation, at the present time, that we can only understand in terms of personal and conscious choice. We cannot see that great motions carry us and bring us to our place before we can even begin to know. We cannot see that invisible great winds carry us unwitting, as they carry the locust swarms,

and direct us before our knowledge, as they direct the migrating
birds.

We ask ourselves, How was it that America became peopled by
white men at all? How, in the first place, did Europeans ever get
across the great blank ocean? The Greeks and Romans turned their
backs on space, and kept their breasts landwards as if magnetised.
How was it, then, that fifteenth-century Europe looked space-
wards? Was it just the attraction of space? Or was it that
Spanish and Venetian sailors were determined to fill in the great
blank on the Atlantic Ocean which confronted them?

It was something more positive. Every people is polarised in
some particular locality, some home or homeland. And every
great era of civilisation seems to be the expression of a particular
continent or continent region, as well as of the people concerned. There is, no doubt, some peculiar potentiality attaching
to every distinct region of the earth's surface, over and above the
indisputable facts of climate and geological condition. There is
some subtle magnetic or vital influence inherent in every specific
locality, and it is this influence which keeps the inhabitant stable.
Thus race is ultimately as much a question of place as of hered-
ity. It is the island of Great Britain which has really determined
the English race, the genius of Place has made us one people.
The place attracts its own human element, and the race drifts
inevitably to its own psychic geographical pole.

We see this in Roman history. We see the city of Rome
gradually losing its psychic-magnetic polarity, the Roman individuals gradually loosed from the old stay, and drifting like
particles absolved from the original influence, falling impercep-
tibly into two currents—one setting northwards towards Milan
and Gaul, one setting east towards Constantinople and Asia.
Africa had always been connected with Rome herself—Rome
and Carthage were the positive and negative poles of a stable,
vital current, as were Athens and Sardis or Ecbatana.

After the removal of the Empire to the east a new circuit
began, the circuit of Rome and Treves, or, better, of Italy and

Germany. There is, and has been, since the break of the old Roman-African circuit, a natural and inevitable balance between Rome and Germany.

England, France, and even Spain lay within the great German-Italian circuit of vital magnetism, which subsisted all through the Middle Ages. We can see Spain caught in another influence, from Africa again, and Germany influenced from the great Slavonic field. But the main polarity of Europe, from the time of Diocletian to the Renaissance, lay between Italy and Germany.

About the time of the Renaissance, however, this circuit exhausted itself, as the Italian-African circuit had been exhausted a thousand years before. Italy suddenly scintillated, and was finished in her polar potentiality. The old stability of Europe was gone, the old circle of vital flow was broken. It was then that Europe fell directly into polar unison with America. Europe and America became the great poles of negative and positive vitalism.

And it was on the wings of this new attraction that Europe discovered America. When the great magnetic sway of the mediaeval polarity broke, then those units which were liberated fell under the sway of new vital currents in the air, and they were born helplessly as birds migrate, without knowing or willing, down the great magnetic wind towards America, towards the centrality in the New World. So the first individuals were caught up and swept overseas in the setting of the great current. They had no choice, because the influence which was upon them was prior to all knowledge and all option.

Some races of Europe, moreover, seem never to have been included in the great Latin-Germanic circuit of cultural vitalism. Among these are the Iberian and the Celtic. The strange early flowering of Celtic Christianity would be found, on examination, to be quite apart from the whole Italian-Germanic Christianity which has prevailed in Europe. Its first principle was individualistic, separatist, almost anti-social, a recoil of the individual into

C

a mystic isolation, quite the contrary of the European religious principle, which was the fusing into a whole.

And these separate races located themselves on the sea-board, under the influence of the Atlantic Ocean; Spain, Ireland, Scotland, England, Brittany, these have lain from the beginning under the spell of the great western sea. And the people of Spain, dissociated from the circle of Italian-German culture, felt most distinctly the pull of the American magnetism. And they answered the pull as the needle answers the pull of the magnetic north. Spain moved across-seas in one great blind impulse, which was not primarily a desire for wealth. Desire for wealth never shifted a nation which was attached to its home, or vital in its own home-life.

If we are to understand the Celtic and Iberian races at all, we must realise that they have always remained outside of the European circuit of life—that they have always been excluded and subjected, never incorporated; and that their principle has been one of mystic opposition, even hatred, of the civilising principle of the rest of Europe. These races have remained true to some principle which was contained in the African and the Druid realities, but which has had no place in the European Christian-social scheme. Therefore they placed themselves in a polarity with the great invisible force of America, they looked to their positive pole into the west, the land of the setting sun, over the great sea to the unknown America. Their heaven was the land under the western wave, the Celtic Tir na Og.

They knew of no America. And yet, in the most immediate sense, they knew America. They existed in the spell of the vital magnetism of the unknown continent. The same is more or less true of Spain and of Scandinavia. These great sea-board countries are inevitably controlled by the pull of America. It is inevitable that the Vikings should sail to Greenland and Labrador.

This unconscious reaction to the vital magnetism of the far-off unknown world is perhaps sufficient to have given rise to the Atlantis myth. If it gave rise to the land of Tir na Og, which

lies under the western wave, why not to Atlantis? If the great
magnetic pole of the Celtic and Iberian psyche was away in the
west, would it not follow that, as in a dream, the myth should
interpret the unconscious experience? The same would be true
of the Norse myths—their polarity is westwards, towards
America.

It follows, also, that if the Atlantic sea-board of Europe lies
under the spell of the far-off American vital magnetism, the
Atlantic sea-board of America must lie under the spell of Europe.
And so, when Cortes lands in Mexico, he finds the subtle and
pathetic Montezuma, the priest-emperor, who receives him with
mystic sympathy, mystic desire. In America a similar break in
the circuit of vitalism, a similar shifting of the great mystic-mag-
netic polarity must have taken place, in the fifteenth century, as
it took place in Europe. And as Europe fell under the spell of
America, America fell under the spell of Europe. So Montezuma
embraced the Spanish as the fulfilment of the legend of the
white, bearded strangers, who would come as gods across the
east. Legend is supposed to be race-memory. But surely it is just
as likely to be a kind of race-clairvoyance. Montezuma, a priest,
a decadent and sensitive character, was filled with mystic
apprehension. The Aztecs, subject to the fine vibrations in the
ether, given off by vital Europe, highly religious and mystical in
their natures, only expressed in their legend of the coming of the
white stranger that which their innermost, sensitised souls knew
beforehand as a fact. If we can understand the sending of wireless messages from continent to continent, can we not much more
readily understand that the unthinkably sensitive substance of
the human intelligence could receive the fine waves of vital
effluence transmitted across the intervening space, could receive,
and, as in a dream, plainly comprehend? It was not even in
symbols that the Aztecs knew the future; but in plain, direct
prescience. They knew the white, bearded strangers hundreds of
years before they could see them. And they knew so perfectly
because, in their semi-barbaric state, their consciousness was

fluid, not mechanically fixed, and the rarest impressions upon the physical soul, from the invisible ether, could pass on occasionally into uninterrupted consciousness.

Prophecy, the mystery of prophecy, is no absurdity. It is no more absurd than the sending of a wireless message. A people, or an individual, need only most delicately submit to the message which is being received all the time upon its own finest tissue, and it will be able to prophesy. But it is easier for us to invent sensitive machines than to avail ourselves of our own extreme and marvellous sensibilities.

We may see, then, how Spain was called across the Atlantic, in the spell of the positive magnetism of the great western continent. And we may understand better the departure of the Pilgrim Fathers. It is not enough, it is never enough, upon an important occasion to accept the plausible explanation offered by the protagonist. The protagonist will always assert that he moves of his own intention. The Pilgrim Fathers sailed off in an enthusiastic, stern vigour of desire for religious freedom. They sailed to find freedom of worship—so they say. But it is a palpable fiction. Because at once they instigated the most cruel religious tyranny in America, equivalent to the Spanish-American Inquisition. Nay, it even seems as if the impulse to religious cruelty *came* to the Spaniards from America, and was exercised secondarily by them in Europe.

The Pilgrim Fathers did not sail to America in search of religious freedom. The Pilgrim Fathers, if they had wanted this freedom, would have stayed and fought for it, with Cromwell. Religious liberty was with them a phrase that covered complex motives. For the deepest human soul all the while offers specious reasons for her own movement, covering beyond all knowledge the true motive. The Pilgrim Fathers sternly believed themselves that they sailed in search of purer Christian worship and the liberty to that worship. It was the innermost soul offering a sufficient pretext to their stubborn, self-righteous minds.

For, if we consider the early American colonies, the Pilgrim

Fathers were not Christians at all—not in any reasonable sense of the word. They were no more Christians than the dark and violent Spaniards of the Inquisition were Christian. At the close of the fifteenth century Spain fell back from Christian Europe and became a thing apart. In the same way the first Americans departed from the Christian and the European vital mystery. They became dark, sinister, repellent. They seemed to seek, not liberty, but a gloomy and tyrannical sense of power. They wanted to have power over all immediate life. They had a gloomy passion, similar to that of some of the African sects of the Early Christian Church, to destroy or mutilate life at its very quick, lusting in their dark power to annihilate all living impulses, both their own and those of their neighbour. For all of which the Christian religion served as a word, a weapon, an instrument: the instrument of their dark lust for power over the immediate life itself, as it stirred to motion in the breasts and bowels of the living.

This lust is latent in all religious passion. So long as a people is living and generous, it fulfils its religious passion in setting free the deep desires which are latent in all human souls. Bernard of Clairvaux, St. Francis of Assisi, Martin Luther, these were liberators. They made it possible for every man to be more himself, more whole, more full and spontaneous than ever man had been before.

But into Puritanism and Calvinism had already entered the dangerous *negative* religious passion of repression, this passion which so easily becomes a lust, a deep lust for vindictive power over the life-issue. It was on the hard recoil of this destructive religious passion that the Pilgrim Fathers left Europe. America, dark, violent, aboriginal, would lend them force to satisfy their lust of anti-life.

It is absolutely necessary to realise once and for all that every enthusiasm, every passion, has a dual motion: first a motion of liberation, of setting free; and secondly a motion of vindictive repression of the living impulse, the utter subjection of the living,

spontaneous being to the fixed, mechanical, ultimately insane
will.

When at the Renaissance the great religious impulse of Europe
broke, these two motions became separate. We see the Calvinists,
the Puritans, the Spaniards of the Inquisition, all filled with a
wild lust for cruelty, the lust for the power to torture, to dominate
and destroy the mysterious body of life. It is the will of man
rising frenzied against the mystery of life itself, and struggling
insanely to *dominate*, to have the life-issue in unutterable control, to squeeze the mystic thing, life, within the violent hands
of possession, grasp it, squeeze it, have it, have unspeakable power
over it.

Whereas, if we have one spark of sanity, we know that we can
never possess and direct the life-mystery. The utmost of our
power is to possess and destroy. The life-mystery precedes us.
Our simplest spontaneous movement *precedes* all knowing and
willing. Secondly, and afterwards, we are conscious, we have
voluntary control. Our knowing is always secondary and subsequent to our being, which is an issue of the creative unknown.
And our volition is always subsidiary to our spontaneous arrival.

But there lies latent in the soul of man, at all times, the desire
to reverse this order. In every man lies latent the passion to control and compel the issue of creation, by force of the self-
conscious will. We have a latent craving to control from our
deliberate will the very springing and welling-up of the life-
impulse itself. This craving, once admitted, becomes a lust. This
lust, once established and dominant, carries mankind to unthinkable lengths in the frenzied, insane purpose of having the
life-issue utterly under human compulsion.

The Jews of old became established in this lust: hence their
endless purifications, their assertion of control over the natural
functions; hence also the rite of circumcision, the setting of the
seal of self-conscious will upon the very quick of bodily impulse.
The frenzied, self-mutilating Christians, the fakir-like saints, such
as St. Simeon Stylites, the St. Anthony frenzied in celibacy, these

men do but assert the utter tyranny of deliberate will over every spontaneous, uncontrollable motion. There must be a measure of control, that every deep desire may be fulfilled in its own fulness and proportion. But there must never be control for control's sake.

The great field for the lust of control in the modern world is America. Whether we read the history of Spanish America or of English-speaking America, it is the same, a disheartening, painful record of the lusting triumph of the deliberate will. On the one hand, the Spaniards in America, following the Spaniards of the Inquisition, lusted in the overweening sensual desire for repression of freedom in the spiritual self, whereas the North Americans lusted spiritually for utter repression in the sensual or passional self.

The New Englanders, wielding the sword of the spirit backwards, struck down the primal impulsive being in every man, leaving only a mechanical, automatic unit. In so doing they cut and destroyed the living bond between men, the rich passional contact. And for this passional contact gradually was substituted the mechanical bond of purposive utility. The spontaneous passion of social union once destroyed, then it was possible to establish the perfect mechanical concord, the concord of a number of parts to a vast whole, a stupendous productive mechanism. And this, this vast mechanical concord of innumerable machine-parts, each performing its own motion in the intricate complexity of material production, this is the clue to the western democracy.

It has taken more than three hundred years to build this vast living machine. It has taken just as long to produce the modern Mexican, a creature of incomprehensible sensual reactions, barely human any longer.

But North America has proceeded in one line wonderfully. After only two generations in New England the first Yankees noticed that their stock had changed. The sturdy, ruddy, lusty English yeoman had disappeared, the long-jawed, sallow

American took his place, with a pale, nervous women-folk such as England has only lately begun to reckon with.

Uprooted from the native soil, planted in strong aboriginal earth, this thing happened to the English stock. The natural impulsive being withered, the deliberate, self-determined being appeared in his place. There was soon no more need to militate directly against the impulsive body. This once dispatched, man could attend to the deliberate perfection in mechanised existence. This is what makes good business men. And in this the American is like the Jew : in that, having conquered and destroyed the instinctive, impulsive being in himself, he is free to be always deliberate, always calculated, rapid, swift, and single in practical execution as a machine. The perfection of machine triumph, of deliberate self-determined motion, is to be found in the Americans and the Jews. Hence the race talent for acting. In other races the impulsive mystery of being interferes with the deliberate intention of the individual. In these not. Only, Americans and Jews suffer from a torturing frictional unease, an incapacity to rest. They must run on, like machines, or go mad. The only difference between a human machine and an iron machine is that the latter can come to an utter state of rest, the former cannot. No living thing can lapse into static inertia, as a machine at rest lapses. And this is where life is indomitable. It will be mechanised, but it will never allow mechanical inertia. Hence the Orestes-like flight of unrest of Americans and Jews.

And yet it cannot be for this alone that the millions have crossed the Ocean. This thing, this mechanical democracy, new and monstrous on the face of the earth, cannot be an end in ʾitself. It is only a vast intervention, a marking-time, a mechanical life-pause. It is the tremendous statement in negation of our European being.

This sheer and monstrous reflection of Europe, Europe in negative reality, reflected to enormity on the American continent, will surely vanish swiftly, like one of the horrifying dreams. This is not the reality of America. It is only the reality of our

own negation that the vast aboriginal continent reflects back at
us. There will come an America which we cannot foretell, a new
creation on the face of the earth, a world beyond us. The early
Christianity produced monstrous growths, monstrous reflections
of the world then dying, distorted and made huge by the new
spirit. These monstrosities, like enormous horrifying phantoms
that men do not care to remember, disappeared, leaving the new
era to roll slowly on to the European summer. So the mechanical
monstrosity of the west will presently disappear.

It was not for this that myriads crossed the seas, magnetically
carried like birds in migration, without knowing why or whither,
yet conducted along lines of pure magnetic attraction, to a goal.
Spaniards, Puritans, Jews, Celts, they went in recoil of negation
from Europe. They went in the lust for deliberate control of the
living issues: lust for sensual gratification in pride or power or
slave-tyranny on the part of the Spaniards and perhaps the
Celts; lust for spiritual gratification on the ethical control of all
life on the part of Jews and Puritans. But this was not the final
motive for departure. This was the negative impulse. The
positive is more unsearchable.

They went like birds down the great electric direction of the
west, lifted like migrating birds on a magnetic current. They
went in subtle vibration of response to the new earth, as animals
travel far distances vibrating to the salt-licks.

They walked a new earth, were seized by a new electricity,
and laid in line differently. Their bones, their nerves, their
sinews took on a new molecular disposition in the new vibration.

They breathed a savage air, and their blood was suffused and
burnt. A new fierce salt of the earth, in their mouths, penetrated
and altered the substance of their bones. Meat of wild creatures,
corn of the aboriginal earth, filled and impregnated them with the
unknown America. Their subtlest plasm was changed under the
radiation of new skies, new influence of light, their first and
rarest life-stuff transmuted.

Thus, through hundreds of years, new races are made, people

slowly smelted down and re-cast. There is the slow and terrible process of transubstantiation. Who can tell what will come at the negative crisis of this reduction? What monstrosity? And, much more, who can tell what will come when the new world sets in?

For every great locality has its own pure daimon, and is conveyed at last into perfected life. We have seen Asia, and North Africa, and a good deal of Europe. We know the white abstraction of the Arctic and Antarctic continents, the unspeakable immortality of the ice, where existence is and being is not. There remains America, and, beyond, the even farther-off Australia.

Every great locality expresses itself perfectly, in its own flowers, its own birds and beasts, lastly its own men, with their perfected works. Mountains convey themselves in unutterable expressed perfection in the blue gentian flower and in the edelweiss flower, so soft, yet shaped like snow-crystals. The very strata of the earth come to a point of perfect, unutterable concentration in the inherent sapphires and emeralds. It is so with all worlds and all places of the world. We may take it as a law.

So now we wait for the fulfilment of the law in the west, the inception of a new era of living. At present there is a vast myriad-branched human engine, the very thought of which is death. But in the winter even a tree looks like iron. Seeing the great trunk of dark iron and the swaying steel flails of boughs, we cannot help being afraid. What we see of buds looks like sharp bronze stud-points. The whole thing hums elastic and sinister and fatally metallic, like some confused scourge of swinging steel throngs. Yet the lovely cloud of green and summer lustre is within it.

We wait for the miracle, for the new soft wind. Even the buds of iron break into soft little flames of issue. So will people change. So will the machine-parts open like buds and the great machines break into leaf. Even we can expect our iron ships to put forth vine and tendril and bunches of grapes, like the ship of Dionysos in full sail upon the ocean.

It only wants the miracle, the new, soft, creative wind: which

does not blow yet. Meanwhile we can only stand and wait,
knowing that what is, is not. And we can listen to the sad, weird
utterance of this classic America, watch the transmutation from
men into machines and ghosts, hear the last metallic sounds.
Perhaps we can see as well glimpses of the mystic transubstantiation.

2. BENJAMIN FRANKLIN

2. Benjamin Franklin

This essay appeared in the English Review, *December, 1918. Version 2, if it existed, is lost. Again, this version is longer than version 3. In both versions Lawrence points out the absurdity of Franklin's belief in "the Perfectibility of Man"; in this version by logical arguments, in version 3 by some dozens of exclamations. Version 3 is tinged with subjectivity from beginning to end. For instance, "The perfectibility of the Ford car!" expresses Lawrence's disgust with the little Ford belonging to the Danish painters which had, to his annoyance, broken down once or twice (see Knud Merrild;* A Poet and Two Painters, 1938). *Version 3 contains a humorous seven-point creed and a funny list of Lawrence's thirteen virtues; both are absent in version 1. But it would be useless to look for too much reason in the third version of the essay. Lawrence had hardly arrived in America and had only just seen San Francisco and Santa Fe, yet he already felt competent to condemn the whole of the United States and to point out to the Americans what a happy homeland Europe, and England specifically, had been. A lot of version 3 is hysterical, but Franklin is, astonishingly enough, more highly rated in version 3 than in version 1 : the only time that version 3 is more appreciative.*

T HE IDEA of the perfectibility of man, which was such an inspiration in Europe, to Rousseau and Godwin and Shelley, all those idealists of the eighteenth and early nineteenth century, was actually fulfilled in America before the ideal was promulgated in Europe. If we sift the descriptions of the "Perfect Man", and accept the chief features of this ideal being, keeping only to what is possible, we shall find we have the abstract of a character such as Benjamin Franklin's.

A man whose passions are the obedient servants of his mind, a man whose sole ambition is to live for the bettering and advancement of his fellows, a man of such complete natural benevolence that the interests of self never obtrude in his works or his desires—such was to be the Perfect Man of the future, in the Millennium of the world. And such a man was Benjamin Franklin, in the actual America.

Therefore it is necessary to look very closely at the character of this Franklin. The magicians knew, at least imaginatively, what it was to create a being out of the intense *will* of the soul. And Mary Shelley, in the midst of the idealists, gives the dark side to the ideal being, showing us Frankenstein's monster.

The ideal being was man created by man. And so was the supreme monster. For man is not a creator. According to the early creed, the only power that the Almighty Creator could *not* confer upon His created being, not even upon the Son, was this same power of creation. Man by his own presence conveys the mystery and magnificence of creation. But yet man has no power over the creative mystery. He cannot *make* life—and he never will.

This we must accept, as one of the terms of our being. We know we cannot make and unmake the stars or the sun in heaven. We can only be at one, or at variance with them. And we should have the dignity of our own nature, and know that we cannot ordain the creative issues, neither in ourselves nor beyond ourselves. The ultimate choice is not ours. The creative mystery precedes us.

This has been the fallacy of our age—the assumption that we, of our own will, and by our own precept and prescription, can create the perfect being and the perfect age. The truth is, that we *have* the faculty to form and distort even our own natures, and the natures of our fellow men. But we can *create* nothing. And the thing we can make of our own natures, by our own will, is at the most a pure mechanism, an automaton. So that if on the one hand Benjamin Franklin is the perfect human being of Godwin, on the other hand he is a monster, not exactly as the monster in *Frankenstein*, but for the same reason, viz., that he is the production or fabrication of the human will, which projects itself upon a living being, and automatises that being according to a given precept.

It is necessary to insist for ever that the source of creation is central within the human soul, and the issue from that source proceeds without any choice or knowledge on our part. The creative gesture, or emanation, for ever precedes the conscious realisation of this gesture. We are moved, we *are,* and then, thirdly, we *know.* Afterwards, fourthly, after we know, then we can *will.* And when we *will,* then we can proceed to make or construct or fabricate—even our own characters. But we can never construct or fabricate or even change our own *being,* because we have our being in the central creative mystery, which is the pure present, and the pure Presence, of the soul—present beyond all knowing or willing. Knowing and willing are external, they are as it were the reflex or *afterwards* of being.

Fairly early in life Franklin drew up a creed, which, he intended, "should satisfy the professors of every religion, but which should shock none." It has six articles.

"That there is One God, who made all things."

"That He governs the world by His Providence."

"That He ought to be worshipped with adoration, prayer, and thanksgiving."

"But that the most acceptable service of God is doing good to man."

D

"That the Soul is immortal."

"And that God will certainly reward virtue and punish vice, either here or hereafter."

Here we have a God who is a maker and an employer, whose one business is to look after the smooth running of the established creation, particularly the human part of it—Benjamin is not afraid to "but" the Lord his impertinent "buts"—who makes each man responsible for the working of the established system; and who reserves for Himself the right of granting a kind of immortal pension, in the after-life, to His praiseworthy mechanics of creation, or of condemning the unworthy to a kind of eternal workhouse.

Such a God is, of course, only the inventor and director of the universe, and not a God at all. In order to shock none of the professors of any religion, Benjamin left out all the qualities of the Godhead, utterly dispensed with the mystery of creation. The universe once set up, it has only to be kept running. For this purpose it has an efficient manager in Providence. Providence sees that the business of the universe—that great and complicated factory of revolving worlds—is kept profitably going. The output of human life increases with each generation, and there is a corresponding increase in the necessities of life. Providence is then entirely successful, and the earthly business is a paying concern.

Such is the open, flagrant statement which America makes, a hundred and fifty years after the religious arrival of the Pilgrim Fathers. The process of the will-to-control has worked so swiftly, in its activity of mystic destructive metabolism, that in a hundred and fifty years it has reduced the living being to this automatic entity.

The religious truth is the same now as it ever has been : that preceding all our knowledge or will or effort is the central creative mystery, out of which issues the strange and for ever unaccountable emanation of creation : that the universe is a bush which burns for ever with the Presence, consuming itself and yet never consumed; it burns with new flowers and with crumpling leaves that fall to ash; for ever new flowers on the way out of the mystic center of creation which is within the bush—central and omnipresent; for ever old leaves falling. We cannot know where the quick of next year's roses lies, within the tree. In what part, root or stem or branch, is to be found the presence of next year's apples? We cannot answer. And yet we know that they are within the living body of the tree, nowhere and everywhere.

So, within the living body of the universe, and within the living soul of man, central and omnipresent, in the fingers and lips and eyes and feet, as in the heart and bowels, and in the marshes as in the stars, lies the Presence, never to be located, yet never to be doubted, because it is *always* evident to our living soul, the Presence from which issues the first fine-shaken impulse and prompting of new being, eternal creation which is always Now. All time is central within this ever-present creative Now.

Central is the mystery of Now, the creative mystery, what we have called the Godhead. It pulses for ever, in the motion of creation, drawing all things towards itself. And the running waves, as they travel towards the perfect center of the revealed, now are buds, and infants, and children; further back, they are seed-scales and moving seed-leaves, and caterpillars; and further back, they are sun and water and the elements moving towards the center of pure Now, of perfect creative Presence. And in the outflow, the waves travel back. And the first waves are the people with hair tinged with grey, and flowers passing into fruit, and leaves passing into water and fire and mould, and the elements ebbing asunder into the great chaos, and further than the great chaos into the infinite. The reality of realities is the rose in flower, the man and woman in maturity, the bird in song, the snake in brindled color, the tiger in his stripes. In these, past and present and future are at one, the perfect Now. This is wholeness and pure creation. So there is a ripple and shimmer of the universe, ripples of futurity running towards the Now, out of the infinite, and ripples of age and the autumn, glimmering

back towards the infinite. And rocking at all times on the shimmer are the perfect lotus flowers of immanent Now, the lovely
beings of consummation.

The quick of wholeness lies in this gleaming Now. But the
whole of wholeness lies in the ebbing haste of child-faced futurity,
the consummation of presence, and the lapse of sunset-colored
old age. This is completeness, the childish haste towards the consummation, the perfect revelation, the pure Presence, when we
are fully a flower and present, the great *adsum* of our being,
and then the slow retreat of becoming old.

There is, however, the false Now, as well as the mystic Now.
Perpetual youth, or perpetual maturity, this is the false Now—
as roses that never fall are false roses. The remaining steady,
fixed, this is the false Now. And as the consummation into the
whole infinite is the antithesis of pure Presence, so is Eternity the
antithesis of the mystic Present, the great Now. For eternity is
but the sum of the whole past and the whole future, the complete *outside* or negation of being.

In Europe the desire to become infinite, one with the All, was
the adolescent desire to know everything and to be everything.
The mystic passion for infinitude is the ultimate of all our passion
for love, oneness, equality. It is all an adolescent process. It is a
process which comes to a conclusion, and out of which mankind
must issue, as the individual man issues from his period of loving
and seeking, into the assured magnificence of maturity. This
experience of infinitude, oneness with the all, is the ultimate
communion wherein the individual is merged into wholeness
with all things, through love. But it is no goal. The individual
must emerge from this bath of love, as from the baths of blood in
the old religions, initiated, fulfilled, entering on the great state of
independent maturity.

In America, however, the state of oneness was soon reached.
The Pilgrim Fathers soon killed off in their people the spontaneous impulses and appetites of the self. By a stern discipline and
a fanatic system of repression, they subdued every passion into

rigid control. And they did it quickly. England lapsed again into exuberance and self-indulgence. She produced her Congreves and Addisons and Smolletts, and Robert Burns. But America moved on in one line of inexorable repression.

Now there are two kinds of oneness among mankind. First there is that ecstatic sense, religious and mystic, of uplifting into union with all men, through love. This experience we all know, more or less. But, secondly, there is the hard, practical state of being at one with all men, through suppression and elimination of those things which make differences—passions, prides, impulses of the self which cause disparity between one being and another. Now it seems as if, in America, this negative, destructive form of oneness predominated from the first, a oneness attained by destroying all incompatible elements in each individual, leaving the pattern or standard man.

So that whilst Europe was still impulsively struggling on towards a consummation of love, expressed in Shelley or Verlaine or Swinburne or Tolstoi, a struggle for the mystic state of communion in being, America, much quicker and more decisive, was cutting down every human being towards a common standard, aiming at a homogeneous oneness through elimination of incommutable factor or elements, establishing a standardised humanity, machine-perfect.

This process of strangling off the impulses took place in Europe as in America. Spontaneous movement distinguishes one individual from another. If we remove the spontaneous or impulsive factor, and substitute deliberate purposiveness, we can have a homogeneous humanity, acting in unison. Hence the ideal Reason of the eighteenth century.

So man has a great satisfaction, at a certain period in his development, in seizing control of his own life-motion, and making himself master of his own fate. The desire is so strong it tends to become a lust. It became a lust in the French and in the American. Jean Jacques Rousseau had a fundamental lust for fingering and knowing and directing every impulse, as it was born. He intercepted every one of his feelings as it arose, caught it with his consciousness and his will, then liberated it again, so that he might watch it act within the narrow field of his own observation and permission.

All this was part of the process of oneing, the process of forming a deliberate, self-conscious, self-determined humanity which, in the acceptance of a common idea of equality and fraternity, should be quite homogeneous, unified, ultimately dispassionate, rational, utilitarian. The only difference was that whilst the European ideal remained one of mystic, exalted consciousness of oneness, the ideal in America was a practical unison for the producing of the means of life.

Rousseau analysed his feelings, got them into control in order to luxuriate in their workings. He enjoyed a mental voluptuousness in watching and following the turn of his self-permitted sensations and emotions, as one might watch a wild creature tamed and entrapped and confined in a small space. Franklin, on the other hand, had his voluptuous pleasure in subduing and reducing all his feelings and emotions and desires to the material benefit of mankind.

To seize life within his own will, and control it by precept from his own consciousness, made him as happy as it now makes us sick. With us it is a sick, helpless process. We perceive at last that if we cannot act direct and spontaneous from the center of creative mystery which is in us, we are nothing. It is no good any more giving us choice—our free will is of no use to us if we no longer have anything to choose. It only remains for us now, in the purest sense, to choose not-to-choose.

Franklin, however, proceeded with joy to seize the life-issues, to get everything into his own choice and will. His God was no longer a creative mystery—He was a reasonable Providence or Producer. And man, being made in the image of God, he too is at his highest a little Providence or Producer of the means of life. Production is the criterion of Godliness, which leads us to the plausible, self-righteous, altruistic materialism of our modern

world. The difference between production and creation is the
difference between existence and being, function and flowering,
mechanical force and life itself.

Franklin proceeded to automatise himself, to subdue life so that
it should work automatically to his will. Like Rousseau, he
makes a confession of his life. But he is purely self-congratulatory.
He tells us in detail how he worked out the process of reducing
himself to a deliberate entity. This deliberate entity, this self-
determined man, is the very Son of Man, man made by the
power of the human will, a virtuous Frankenstein monster.

Almost scientifically, Franklin broke the impulses in himself.
He drew up a list of virtues, established a set of fixed principles
—strictly machine-principles—and by these he proceeded to control his every motion. The modern virtue is machine-principle,
meaning the endless repetition of certain sanctioned motions.
The old *virtus* meant just the opposite, the very impulse itself,
the creative gesture, drifting out incalculable from human hands.

Franklin's list of virtues is as follows :

1.
TEMPERANCE
Eat not to fulness; drink not to elevation.

2.
SILENCE
Speak not but what may benefit others or yourself;
avoid trifling conversation.

3.
ORDER
Let all your things have their places; let each part
of your business have its time.

4.
RESOLUTION
Resolve to perform what you ought; perform without
fail what you resolve.

5.

FRUGALITY

Make no expense but to do good to others or yourself—
i.e., waste nothing.

6.

INDUSTRY

Lose no time, be always employed in something useful;
cut off all unnecessary action.

7.

SINCERITY

Use no hurtful deceit; think innocently and justly,
and, if you speak, speak accordingly.

8.

JUSTICE

Wrong none by doing injuries, or omitting the
benefits that are your duty.

9.

MODERATION

Avoid extremes, forbear resenting injuries so much
as you think they deserve.

10.

CLEANLINESS

Tolerate no uncleanliness in body, clothes, or
habitation.

11.

TRANQUILLITY

Be not disturbed at trifles, or at accident common or
unavoidable.

12.

CHASTITY

Rarely use venery but for health and offspring, never
to dullness, weakness, or the injury of your own
or another's peace or reputation.

13.
Humility
Imitate Jesus and Socrates.

The last clause or item, of humility, Franklin added because a Quaker friend told him he was generally considered proud. Truly he had something to be proud of.

He practised these virtues with ardour and diligence. He drew up a table, giving each of the virtues a column to itself, and having the date, like a calendar, down the side. And every day he put a mark against himself for every lapse of virtue. Unfortunately he does not give us his marked chart—we might have an even closer view of his character had he done so. He only tells us that the black column was that of "Order". In every other virtue he had considerable proficiency. Be he *could not* make himself tidy and neat in his business and in his surroundings, not even to the end of his days. So he tells us.

This is his one weakness, his Achilles heel. Had he not had this harmless failing, he would have been the very Frankenstein of virtue. There is something slightly pathetic, slightly ridiculous, and, if we look closer, a little monstrous, about the snuff-colored doctor. He worked so diligently and seriously. He was so alive, full of inquisitive interest and eager activity. He had his club for discussing philosophic questions, he made his printing business prosper, he had the streets of Philadelphia swept and lighted, he invented his electric appliances, he was such a straight-principled member of all the important Councils of Philadelphia —then of the American Colonies themselves. He defended himself with such sturdy, snuff-coloured honesty in England, and against his enemies in America, and in France. He wrestled with such indomitable integrity with the French Court, a little, indomitable, amazingly clever and astute, and at the same time amazingly disingenuous, virtuous man, winning from the fine and decadent French such respect, and such huge sums of money to help the Americans in their struggle for Independence. It is a wonderful little snuff-coloured figure, so admirable, so *clever*, a little pathetic, and, somewhere, ridiculous and detestable.

He is like a child, so serious and earnest. And he is like a little old man, even when he is young, so deliberate and reasoned. It is difficult to say which he is—a child or a little old man. But when we come to grips he is neither. In his actuality he is a dreadful automaton, a mechanism. He is a printer, and a philosopher, and an inventor, and a scientist, and a patriot, and a writer of "Poor Richard" jokes for the calendar, and he is virtuous and scrupulous and of perfect integrity. But he is never a man. It did not seem to matter at all to him that he himself was an intrinsic being. He saw himself as a little unit in the vast total of society. All he wanted was to run well, as a perfect little wheel within the whole.

The beauty of incomparable *being* was nothing to him. The inestimable splendidness of a man who is purely himself, distinct and incommutable, a thing of pure, present reality, this meant nothing to Benjamin. He liked comeliness, cleanliness, healthiness, and profusion of the means of life. He could never see that the only riches of the earth is in free, whole, incomparable beings, each man mystically himself, and distinct, mystically distinguished. To him, men were like coin to be counted up, coin interchangeable.

He was, perhaps, the most admirable little automaton the world has ever seen, the invention of the human will, working according to good principles. So far as affairs went, he was admirable. As far as life goes, he is monstrous.

If we look in the little almanacks or booklets that are printed in England, in out-of-the-way corners, even to-day, we shall find humorous, trite paragraphs, where "Poor Richard" is the speaker, and which are little object-lessons to one or another of the "virtues"—economy, or frugality, or modesty. Franklin wrote these almanacks when he was still a young man—more than a hundred and fifty years ago—and they are still printed, now as then, for the poor and vulgar to profit by. They are always trite and, in a

measure, humorous, and always shrewd, and always flagrantly
material. Franklin had his humour, but it was always of the
"don't-put-all-your-eggs-in-one-basket" sort. It always derided
the spontaneous, impulsive or extravagant element in man, and
showed the triumph of cautious, calculated, virtuous behaviour.
Whatever else man must be, he must be deliberate. He must live
entirely from his consciousness and his will. Once he lives from his
consciousness and his will, it will follow as a matter of course
that he lives according to the given precepts, because that is both
easiest and most profitable.

We do, perhaps, get a glimpse of a really wondering young
Franklin, where he has still the living faculty for beholding with
instinct the world around him—when he was a printer's work-
man, in London, for a short time. But the glimpse is soon over.
He is back in America, and is all American, a very model of a
man, as if a machine had made him.

He was so dreadfully all-of-a-piece, his attitude is always
so consistent and urbane. He has to go to the frontiers of his
State, to settle some disturbance among the Indians. And on
this occasion he writes :—

"We found they had made a great bonfire in the middle of
the square; they were all drunk, men and women quarrelling
and fighting. Their dark-coloured bodies, half naked, seen only
by the gloomy light of the bonfire, running after and beating
one another with fire-brands, accompanied by their horrid
yellings, formed a scene the most resembling our ideas of hell
that could be well imagined. There was no appeasing the tumult,
and we retired to our lodging. At midnight a number of them
came thundering at our door, demanding more rum, of which
we took no notice.

"The next day, sensible they had misbehaved in giving us that
disturbance, they sent three of their counsellors to make their
apology. The orator acknowledged the fault, but laid it upon
the rum, and then endeavoured to excuse the rum by saying:
'The Great Spirit, who made all things, made everything for

some use; and whatever he designed anything for, that use it should always be put to. Now, when he made rum, he said : "Let this be for the Indians to get drunk with." And it must be so.'

"And, indeed, if it be the design of Providence to extirpate these savages in order to make room for the cultivators of the earth, it seems not improbable that rum may be the appointed means. It has already annihilated all the tribes who formerly inhabited all the sea coast—"

This, from the good doctor, with such suave complacency, is a little disenchanting. But this is what a Providence must lead to. A Providence is a Provider for the universe, and the business of the provider is to get rid of every waster, even if this waster happen to be part of the self-same created universe. When man sets out to have all things his own way he is bound to run up against a great many men. Even to establish the ideal of equality he has to reckon with the men who do really feel the force of inequality. And then equality sharpens his axe. He becomes a greater leveller, cutting off all tall men's heads. For no man must be taller than Franklin, who is middle-sized.

Nevertheless, this process of attaining to unison by conquering and subduing all impulses, this removing of all those individual traits which make for separateness and diversity, had to be achieved and accomplished. It is not until man has utterly seized power over himself, and gained complete knowledge of himself, down to the most minute and shameful of his desires and sensations, that he can really begin to be free. Then, when man knows *all,* both shameful and good, that is in man; and when he has control over every impulse, both good and bad; then, and only then, having utterly bound and fettered himself in his own will and his own self-conscious knowledge, will he learn to make the great choice, the choice between automatic self-determining, and mystic, spontaneous freedom.

When the great Greek-Christian will-to-knowledge is fulfilled; and when the great barbaric will-to-power is also satisfied; then, perhaps, man can recognise that neither power nor knowledge is the ultimate man's attainment, but only *being;* that the pure reality lies not in any infinitude, but in the mystery of the perfect *unique* self, incommutable; not in any eternity, but in the sheer Now.

The quick and issue of our being stands previous to any control, prior to all knowledge. The centre of creative mystery is primal and central in every man, but in each man it is unique and incommutable. When we know *all things* about ourselves we shall know this, know, and enter upon our being. But first we must know all things, both bad and good. For this, the great liberating truth, is the last to be realised, the very last.

When we know that the unique, incommutable creative mystery of the Self is within us and precedes us, then we shall be able to take our full being from this mystery. We shall at last learn the pure lesson of knowing not-to-know. We shall know so perfectly that in fulness of knowledge we shall yield to the mystery, and become spontaneous in full consciousness. Our will will be so strong that we can simply, through sheer strength, defer from willing, accepting the spontaneous mystery, and saving it in its issue from the mechanical lusts of righteousness or power.

3. HECTOR ST JOHN DE CREVECOEUR

3. Hector St. John
de Crèvecoeur

This essay appeared in the English Review *for January,
1919. It is some twenty per cent longer than version 3.
Version 2, if it existed, is lost. The second half of the two
extant versions is similar. The four pages of philosophy at
the beginning of version 1 are left out in version 3. Version
1 is a serious, logical, convincing interpretation of Crèvecoeur as a divided personality, while version 3 is more
sketchy, but full of good-natured humour. Although the
essays run parallel in the second half, Lawrence arrives at
absolutely different conclusions at the end. In version 1
he doubts the truth of Crèvecoeur's assertion that
thousands of white children, captured and educated by the
Indians refused after their liberation to go back to civilization with their natural parents. But although the story of
these children is a lie, Lawrence maintains: "The truth
remains the same, as another century has proved it—it is
easier to turn white men into Indians than Indians into
white men." In version 3 Lawrence insists on the opposite,
having learnt from his experiences with the Indians at
Taos (Mabel Dodge's husband Toni Luhan was an
Indian): "I have seen some Indians whom you really
couldn't tell from white men. And I have never seen a
white man who looked really like an Indian."*

E

CREVECOEUR was born in France in the middle of the eighteenth century. As a boy he came over to England and received part of his education here. He went to Canada, served for a time there with the French in their war against the English, and later passed over into the United States, to become an exuberant American. He married a New England girl, and established himself as a farmer. In this period he wrote his *Letters from an American Farmer,* a series of delightful egoistic accounts of his own ideal existence as an American citizen. He came to France, and whilst he was there his far-off home was burnt and his wife a fugitive in the American War of Independence. Returning to America, he entered into public and commercial life. Again in France, he was known as a *littérateur,* he frequented the literary *salons,* he was acquainted with Benjamin Franklin.

The *Letters* were very popular in England among the Romanticists, such as Shelley, Coleridge, Godwin. They are quaint and effusive and affected, according to the Jean Jacques Rousseau affectation of "natural simplicity" and "pristine emotion". To us they are often tiresome and foolish, mere effusions of romantic egoism. But Crèvecoeur had in him some of the stern stuff of an artist.

Franklin was the Son of Man, as we have produced him after two thousand years of effort, from the Archetype. Crèvecoeur also is a Son of Man. That is, his whole character has been produced by the human will, through the course of Christian ages, produced according to a given idea. For two thousand years mankind was breeding the ideal type, the selfless and yet practical type. In the end we have the admirable little monster of a Franklin, produced by the Christian-ethical impulse, and we have Crèvecoeur, produced by the Christian-emotional impulse. They are the last two instances of ethical England and emotional France, and together they make the complete American.

Two thousand years of breeding to type bred us our

Shelley in England, our Rousseau in France, our Franklin and
our Crèvecoeur in America. Shelley and Rousseau, Franklin
and Crèvecoeur, these are the two halves of the one whole. The
whole duality, of body and soul, matter and spirit, is here again
exemplified. Shelley and Franklin conceive of themselves in
terms of pure abstraction, pure spirit, pure mathematical reality.
But Rousseau and Crèvecoeur exist in terms of emotion and
sensation. And surely this is the duality of spiritual and sensual
being, spirit and senses, soul and body, mind and matter.

As a matter of fact, this duality does exist, in all our living,
in all our experience. Before thought takes place, before the
brain is awake in the small infant, the body is awake and alive,
and in the body the great nerve centres are active, active both
in knowing and in asserting. This knowledge is not mental, it
is what we may call first-consciousness. Now our first consciousness is seated, not in the brain, but in the great nerve centres of
the breast and the bowels, the cardiac plexus and the solar
plexus. Here life first seethes into active impulse and consciousness, the mental understanding comes later. In the infant, life
is widely active. Yet we cannot say it is mentally so. The great
nerve centres of the upper part of the body, and the great nerve
centres of the lower part of the body, these are awake first,
these send out the first impulses and gestures, these contain the
first-knowledge, the root-knowledge. Mental consciousness is
only resultant from this. From this duality in first-consciousness,
this duality in root-knowledge, arises the subsequent oneness
and wholeness of full mental consciousness.

But all the time, and all through life, we are primarily
creatures of dual consciousness, the duality of the upper and
lower nerve centres, active in first-consciousness; and then, sub-
sequently, we are single and whole in full mental consciousness.
As long as we live our first-knowledge is dual, of the upper and
lower body. The strange consummation into oneness, of the
final understanding, which consummates the upper and the
lower knowledge into one third pure state of wholeness, whole

understanding, this only comes from a fulfilment in the duality.

We state the duality as the duality of our upper and lower body. The great nerve centre in the breast—called by the ancients the heart—this is the centre of our dynamic spiritual consciousness, our spiritual being; and the great plexus in the bowels is the centre of our dynamic sensual consciousness.

We know, if we but think for a moment of our own immediate experience, that the breast is the dynamic centre of the great, passonate, selfless spiritual love; and that in the bowels lies the dark and unfathomable vortex of our sensual passion, sensual love.

We are creatures of duality, in the first place. Our oneness is subsequent. As creatures of duality we issue from the unknown, the creative unknown which precedes us, and must for ever precede us. Beginning with the tiny infant, like a flower that opens, the breast and the eyes unfurl to the earth and the sky, to enter into a selfless communion. The breast opens day by day, and the life goes forth from it, the mysterious emanation, to be at one with the sky and the world; then the eyes also open, and the spirit goes forth through them, seeing and beholding, till the I, the self, has passed into the living universe to be at one with it, one and whole. And then this body, this breast, is but a socket or cup for the unfolded flower of the infinite cosmos.

This is the process of my upper, or spiritual, consummation. It begins in the tiny child as it lies against its mother, or waves its arms from the wonder-centre of the breast. And it culminates in us all, in every man according to his degree: in the great love of humanity, in the love of landscape, in the love of light itself.

Correspondingly, within the bowels lies the burning source of the sensual consciousness. Here the Self is positive and centripetal. Here I am I, darkly and fiercely sentient. Here I am dark-centric, all that is not me roams outside, looming, wonderful, imminent, perilous—but wonderful and unknown. And from this centre I draw all things into me, that they enter in passional communion into my self, become one with me, an increase and a magnificence in my self. This is the process of my sensual becoming, which culminates at last in the great dark glory of real almightiness, all things being added unto me for my power and perfection, wherein I am whole and infinite, that infinite which has been symbolised as a point.

The process of this sensual fulfilment begins in the tiny infant, when instinctively it carries everything to its mouth, to absorb the mysterious mouth and abdominal knowledge of the unknown thing, carry this unknown in a communion of most intimate contact, into the self; and when the child stirs mysteriously, as it hears new sounds, again receiving new impressions in the dark, sensual self, untranslatable; and when it quivers so delicately to a new touch. This is the beginning of the process of sensual fulfilment, which ends only in that strange, supreme passion, when the "I" is singly consummate and almighty, in supreme possession of the All.

This every man experiences, according to his degree, in the dark magnificence of sensual love, and in the single, rich splendour of the positive "I", the self paramount, that moves undiminished in a contributed universe. Every man, according to his degree, knows this consummation, the consummation which he lives for: for this, as well as for the other, spiritual consummation.

The third and last state is when I am fulfilled in both the great dynamic ways of consciousness, and am free, a free being. Then I need not compel myself in either of the two directions, I need not strive after either consummation, but can accept the profound impulse, as it issues from the incalculable soul, act upon it spontaneously; and can, moreover, speak and know and be, uttering myself as a tree in full flower utters itself. There is no real self-expression till there is a whole consummation.

Shelley sought for the pure spiritual consummation, that alone. It is probable the Egyptians once knew the pure sensual

consummation, that alone. Franklin, however, had reached the
point where he wished to translate what is really a passional
culmination into an established state, what is a great dynamic
condition, into a static condition. He wanted to establish the
laws of the spiritual state, as a fixed, mechanical thing. This can
only be done, at last, by destroying the impulsive being, and
a substituting of the laws of the mechanical universe. For we
must draw the great distinction between the life-mystery,
in which is the creative or God-mystery, and the mystery of
Force and Matter. The creative mystery, which is in life, is
utterly beyond control, beyond us, and before us. It is also
beyond and before the whole material universe, beyond and
before the great Forces. Life is not a Force. It is, and will ever
remain, a mystery, a limit to our presumption. All attempt to
subject life, and its inherent creative mystery, to the will of
man, and to the laws of Force, is materialism and ultimate
death.

Crèvecoeur and Franklin, however, both asserted the triumph
of this materialism, the triumph of the will of man and of the
laws of the mechanical universe, over the creative mystery itself.
But whereas Franklin's satisfaction was in selfless working for
the good of mankind, Crèvecoeur had his satisfaction in his
own emotional triumph in concord and production. Franklin
lived in the breast, in so far as he had an impulsive or passionate life, Crèvecoeur in the bowels. Both were under the control
of the same idea, the same mental prescription. But Crèvecoeur
had his dynamic being in the sensual consciousness, whilst
Franklin's dynamic being—such as it was—was in the spiritual
consciousness. Crèvecoeur was an emotional idealist, the idea
or ideal being the same as Franklin's.

Thus the *Letters from an American Farmer,* affecting a
naïve simplicity, are in reality most sophisticated. They tell of
Crèvecoeur's struggles to establish his farm in the wilderness,
of the beneficient help of his "amiable spouse", the joy of seat-
ing his infant son on the shafts of the plough, the happiness

of helping a neighbor build a barn, the supreme satisfaction of finding himself a worthy and innocent member of a free community. But none of it is spontaneous emotion. It is all dictated from the head. "Now," says Crèvecoeur to himself, "I am a pure child of Nature, Nature sweet and pure." So he proceeds to luxuriate in his *rôle,* to find everything sweet and pure. "That is my spouse," he says, "amiable, sweet, and pure, a deep-breasted daughter of Nature, fountain of life." Thus she is a kind of living image of Crèvecoeur's own intention. That she was a woman, an individual, a being by herself could never occur to the American Farmer. She was an "amiable spouse", just as an oaken cupboard is an oaken cupboard. Likewise a little boy is a healthy offspring, and when this same healthy offspring is seated on his father's plough, the whole picture represents the children of Nature—sweet and pure—toiling in innocence and joy.

All this, as we see, is exactly according to prescription, it is life according to Man, not man according to Life. French romantic idealists prescribe this life, and American farmers proceed to exemplify it—not only American farmers, but Châteaubriand and Bernardin de St. Pierre and the most ridiculous François le Vaillant and even the Queen Marie Antoinette herself, playing dairymaid. The prescription still holds good : we still have Arcadians, simple life, and garden suburbs. It is all a most artificial business of living according to prescription, keeping every impulse strangled, and ending where it begins, in materialism pure and simple. For this subjecting life to a prescription, according to the will of man, is materialism itself. It is a subjecting of the creative or life-mystery to the material or mechanical, psychic-mechanical law.

Crèvecoeur, however, is an artist as well as an emotional idealist. And an artist is never, in being an artist, an idealist. The artist lives and sees and knows direct from the life-mystery itself. He sees the creative unencompassable mystery in all its nakedness of impulse and gesture. And living, as he does, from the ego-centric centres, as an idealist, Crèvecoeur as an artist lives from the great sensual centres, his art is in terms of the great sensual understanding, dark and rich and of that reserved, pagan tenderness to which we have lost the key.

In the sensual vision there is always the pause of fear, dark wonder, and glamour. The creature beheld is seen in its quality of *otherness,* a term of the vivid, imminent unknown. And the new knowledge enters in rich, dark thrills into the soul. In the thrill and pulse within the bowels I gather the new creature into myself, into blood knowledge, I encompass the unknown within the dominion of myself.

Thus all wild creatures are shy—even the fiercest. They are reluctant to let themselves be seen. This is not fear of physical hurt, but fear of being *known.* No free thing can bear to be encompassed by the psyche of another being, save, perhaps, in sheer fright or in sensual love. Thus Dmitri Karamazov, when he is exposed naked, is virtually killed. It is the encompassing and overthrow of the immune sensual being which he is. Thus it is hard to catch weasels, or any wild creatures, at play. No free creature willingly yields itself to the *touch* of another being. It cannot bear to be sensually encompassed. The true self is like a star which must preserve the circumambient darkness which gives to it its distinction and uniqueness. It must keep the splendid, vivid loneliness. Dawn only removes the gulf from between the stars, and makes them as nothing in the great one web of light, the universal sun-consciousness, the selfless spiritual being.

None the less, in the sensual mystery there is that impulse to trust or love which leads to worship and empire. There is the impulse of the lesser sensual psyche to yield itself, where it trusts and believes, to the greater psyche, yielding in the great culminating process which unifies all life in one gesture of magnificence. In this way we have acquired the domestic animals, which have yielded their psyche to us implicitly. In the same way the Egyptian pyramids were built, symbolic of the culminating process, the lesser life yielding and culminating, step by

step, towards the apex of the God-King. In this same spirit
of yielding and culminating through dark faith, or trust, our
mediaeval cathedrals were erected : otherwise they never would
have been erected. In the same way Napoleon, the last great
leader, attained his brief ascendancy. It is necessary, before
men can unite in one great living gesture, that this impulse
towards the mystic sensual yielding and culminating shall find
expression. In the modern spirit of equality, we can get tremendous concerted action, really machine action, but no culminating living oneness, no great gesture of a creative people. Hence
we have no architecture : we have only machines.

Crèvecoeur the artist, however, glimpsed some of the passional dark mystery which Crèvecoeur the idealist completely
ignores. The artist is no longer European. Some little salt of
the aboriginal America has entered into his blood. And this
aboriginal Crèvecoeur sees as the savage see, knows as they
know, in the dark mystery of division, difference, culmination,
and contest. It is true his vision is rudimentary. He can only see
insects, birds, and snakes in their own pristine being. Above this
level, all life should be innocent and pure and loving, merging
in oneness. But so far as insects, birds, and serpents are concerned, he sees the pride, the recoil, the jewel-like isolation of
the vivid self, the pure, tender trust which leads to culmination,
and the frantic struggles for the enforcing of this culmination.
If he had been an Aztec, confirmed in blood-sacrifice and wear-
ing the dark-lustrous mantle of the feathers of birds, he would
have had the same way of knowledge.

"I am astonished to see," he writes quite early in the
Letters, "that nothing exists but what has its enemy, one species
pursue and live upon another : unfortunately our kingbirds are
the destroyers of those industrious insects (the bees); but on
the other hand, these birds preserve our fields from the depre-
dations of the crows, which they pursue on the wing with great
vigilance and astonishing dexterity."

This is a strange admission from the Child of Nature,

sweet and pure, a sad blow in the midst of romantic, pastoral, idyllic idealism. But the glimpsing of the king-birds is still more striking, the strength of Crèvecoeur's vision in winged hostility and pride, the swinging of the dark wings of the sensual ascendancy. We begin to look round for the "One Being Who made all things and governs the world by His providence."

He saves himself, however, when he proceeds further in the animal kingdom. The horse is the friend of man, man is the friend of the horse : and as for men, why, by Nature they all love one another innocently, but sometimes they lapse into atrocities, by some miscarriage in the womb of the events.

Some great hornets have fixed their nest on the ceiling of the living-room of the American Farmer, and these big, fierce, tiger-striped insects fly above the pastoral family, healthy offspring, and amiable spouse, apparently doing them no harm, though we are sure the amiable spouse had no say in the matter. The Farmer himself loved the creatures. There must have existed between him and the little winged tigers that mysterious *rapport*, the sensual sympathy and confidence that balanced man and wasps, and enriched both. This magic immediacy between Crèvecoeur and other life is the real beauty of the *Letters*. Again, on the useful plane, the hornets kept the house free of flies, we are told.

There is also an anecdote of wrens and swallows, that built in the verandah of the house. The wrens took a fancy to the nest of the swallows, and determined to occupy it. They pugnaciously attacked the larger, swift birds, attacked them and drove them from the nest. The swallows returned upon opportunity. But the wrens, coming home, violently drove them forth again. Which continued until the swallows patiently set about to build another nest, whilst the wrens installed themselves in triumph.

This event Crèvecoeur watches with full delight. He takes no sides and feels no pangs. We can imagine Franklin, in a similar case, applying justice. But Crèvecoeur only delights in the little living drama, watching the mysterious nature of birds asserting itself in arrogance and pugnacity.

Again, he has some doubtful stories. One is, that he shot a king-bird which had been devouring his bees. He opened its craw, and took out a vast number of bees, which little creatures, after they had lain a minute or two in the sun, roused, revived, preened themselves, walked off debonair, as Jonah up the sea-shore when the whale had spewed him out.

This story is considered improbable. It may be true. And even if not, it has a kind of mythical or legendary quality which attracts us. It is like Herodotus. Herodotus sees with the dark sensual eyes, in the reality of division of otherness. But his haste in asserting his own self dominant and cognisant over the being of the strangers makes him invent or repeat fables. He assumes a victory in sensual cognition which he has not actually won. So with Crèvecoeur. He too easily leaps at authority, and invents from his own ego, instead of comprehending.

Again he describes the humming bird:

"Its bill is as long and as sharp as a coarse sewing needle; like the bee, Nature has taught it to find out in the calyx of flowers and blossoms those mellifluous particles that serve it for sufficient food; and yet it seems to leave them untouched undeprived of anything that the eye can possibly distinguish. When it feeds, it appears as if immovable, though continually on the wing; and sometimes, from what motives I know not, it will tear and lacerate flowers into a hundred pieces; for strange to tell, they are the most irascible of the feathered tribe. Where do passions find room in so diminutive a body? They often fight with the fury of lions, until one of the combatants falls a sacrifice and dies. When fatigued, it has often perched within a few feet of me, and on such favourable opportunities I have surveyed it with the most minute attention. Its little eyes appear like dia-monds, reflecting light on every side; most elegantly finished in all parts, it is a miniature work of our Great Parent, who seems to have formed it the smallest, and at the same time the most beautiful, of the winged species."

He might have remembered, in his peroration, "the most irascible." We have read various descriptions of humming birds. W. H. Hudson has a good one. But this one gives a curiously sharp, hard bit of realisation, something surely intrinsic, a jewel-sharpness and refraction inherent in the little soul of the creature.

Indeed, Crèvecoeur sees birds, not in their "little singing angel" aspect of modern sentiment. He has the more ancient vision. He sees their dark, primitive, weapon-like souls. He sees how they start and flash their wings darkly, in the spontaneous wonder of the retraction into isolation, or in a kind of vindictive self-arrogance. But he sees, also, that they come in the breath of the first creation, the breath of love. They issue on the spirit of tender confidence, the mute, shy, reserved love of the wild creature.

He is very beautiful about the quails. "Often," he writes, in a paragraph about quails in winter, "in the angles of the fences, when the motion of the wind prevents the snow from settling, I carry them both chaff and grain; the one to feed them, the other to prevent their tender feet from freezing fast to the earth, as I have frequently observed them to do."

The pure beauty of the sentiment here lies, not in a selfless or self-abandoning or spiritual love, but in the deep, tender recognition of the life-reality of the *other,* the other creature which exists not in union with the immediate self, but in dark juxtaposition. It is the tenderness of blood-knowledge, knowledge in separation. Crèvecoeur knows the touch of the birds' feet, as if they had stood, with their vibrating, sharp, cold cleaving balance, naked-footed on his naked hand. He knows there is no selfless oneing. They are they and he is he. And over the mysterious, dark gulf reaches his tenderness and the wild confidence of the quails, leaving their two natures uncommingled, yet strangely in contact. This is the barbaric tenderness and love.

Crèvecoeur makes no attempt to identify himself with the

birds. To him they are no "little sisters of the air." He knows
them as strange, hot-blooded concentrations of dark presence.
He could never have preached to them, as St. Francis preached.
For to him they existed in the unutterable retraction of otherness,
as all creatures exist to the barbarian. And he felt the blood-
sympathy which allows and accepts this otherness as an enrich-
ing, a joy. Accepting the quails into the spell of himself, he is
enriched with the glamour of their contact, filled with passionate
tender joy.

This is the glamour and richness of the sensual, barbarian
way. For if we reduce all things to terms of spirit and oneness,
we impoverish life at last beyond bearing.

The "Letter" about snakes and humming-birds is a marvellous
essay, in its primal, dark veracity. The description of the fight
between two snakes, a great water-snake and a large black serpent, follows the description of the humming-bird: "Strange was
this to behold; two great snakes strongly adhering to the ground,
mutually fastened together by means of the writhings which
lashed them to each other, and stretched at their full length,
they pulled but pulled in vain; and in the moments of greatest
exertions that part of their bodies which was entwined seemed
extremely small, while the rest appeared inflated, and now and
then convulsed with strong undulations, rapidly following each
other. Their eyes seemed on fire, and ready to start out of their
heads; at one time the conflict seemed decided; the water-snake
bent itself into two great folds, and by that operation rendered
the other more than commonly outstretched. The next minute
the new struggles of the black one gained an unexpected superiority; it acquired two great folds likewise, which necessarily extended the body of its adversary in proportion as it had con-
tracted its own."

This fight, which Crèvecoeur describes to a finish, he calls
a sight "uncommon and beautiful." He forgets the benevolence
of nature, and is for the time a sheer ophiolater, and his chapter

is as handsome a piece of ophiolatry, perhaps, as that coiled Aztec rattlesnake carved in stone.

And yet the real Crèvecoeur is, in the issue, neither farmer, nor child of nature, nor ophiolater. He goes back to France, and figures in the literary salons, and is a friend of Rousseau's Madame d'Houdetot. Also he is a good business man, and arranges a line of shipping between France and America. It all ends in materialism, really. But the *Letters* tell us nothing about this.

We are left to imagine him retiring in grief to dwell with his Red Brothers under the wigwams. For the War of Independence has broken out, and the Indians are armed by the adversaries; they do dreadful work on the frontiers. While Crèvecoeur is away in France his farm is destroyed, his family rendered homeless. So that the last letter laments bitterly over the war, and man's folly and inhumanity to man.

But Crèvecoeur ends his lament on a note of resolution. With his amiable spouse, and his healthy offspring, now rising in stature, he will leave the civilised coasts, where man is sophisticated, and, therefore, inclined to be vile, and he will go to live with the Children of Nature, the Red Man, under the wigwam. No doubt, in actual life, Crèvecoeur made some distinction between the Indian, who drank rum *à la* Franklin, and who burnt homesteads and massacred families, and those Indians, the noble Children of Nature, who peopled his own pre-determined fancy. Whatever he did in actual life, in his innermost self he would not give up this self-made world, where the natural man was an object of undefiled brotherliness. Touchingly and vividly he describes his tented home near the Indian village, how he breaks the aboriginal earth to produce a little maize, while his wife weaves within the wigwam. And his imaginary efforts to save his tender offspring from the brutishness of unchristian darkness are touching and puzzling, for how can Nature, so sweet and pure under the greenwood tree, how can it have any contaminating effect?

But it is all a swindle. Crèvecoeur was off to France in high-heeled shoes and embroidered waistcoat, to pose as a literary man, and to prosper in the world. We, however, must perforce follow him into the backwoods, where the simple natural life shall be perfected, near the tented village of the Red Man.

He wanted, of course, to know the dark, savage way of life, within the unlimited sensual impulse. He wanted to know as the Indians and savages know, darkly, and in terms of otherness. But this desire in him was very strictly kept down by a fixed will. For he was absolutely determined that Nature is sweet and pure, that all men are brothers, and equal, and that they love one another like so many cooing doves. He was determined to have life according to his own prescription. Therefore, he wisely kept away from any too close contact with Nature, and took refuge in commerce and the material world.

For the animals and savages are isolate each one in its own pristine self. The animal lifts its head, sniffs, and knows within the dark, passionate belly. It knows at once, in dark mindless-ness. And at once it flees in immediate recoil; or it crouches predatory, in the mysterious storm of exultant anticipation of seizing a victim; or it lowers its head in blank indifference again; or it advances in the insatiable wild curiosity, insatiable passion to approach that which is unspeakably strange and incalculable; or it draws near in the slow trust of wild, sensual love.

Crèvecoeur wanted this kind of knowledge. But to have it he must forfeit all his fraternity and equality, his belief in a world of pure, sweet goodness, in the oneness of all things, and, above all, he must forfeit his own *will*, which insists that the world shall be so, because it is easiest so. And he will die rather than forfeit his fixed will and his fixed intention. He *will* have life according to his own prescription, come what may. And life actually is *not* according to his prescription. So he eschews life, and goes off into sentimental, idyllic fancy, and into practical commerce, both of which he *can* have as he likes it. For though he has a hankering after the wild, sensual life, he so hates the true, sensual mystery

of otherness, and of proud culmination, that he will do anything
to deny this mystery, and to down it. So he is divided against
himself, which makes for madness.

It is amusing to see him calculating the dangers of the step
which he takes so luxuriously, in his fancy alone. He tickles his
palate with a taste of true wildness, as men are so fond nowadays
of tickling their palates with a taste of imaginary wickedness—
just a taste.

"I must tell you," he says, "that there is something in the
proximity of the woods which is very singular. It is with men
as it is with the plants and animals that live in the forests; they
are entirely different from those that live in the plains. I will
candidly tell you all my thoughts, but you are not to expect that
I shall advance any reasons. By living in or near the woods, their
actions are regulated by the wildness of the neighbourhood. The
deer often come to eat their grain, the wolves destroy their sheep,
the bears kill their hogs, the foxes catch their poultry. This surrounding hostility immediately puts the gun into their hands;
they watch these animals, they kill some; and thus by defending
their property they soon become professed hunters; this is the
progress; once hunters, farewell to the plough. The chase renders
them ferocious, gloomy, unsociable; a hunter wants no neigh-
bours; he rather hates them, because he dreads the competition
. . . . Eating of wild meat, whatever you may think, tends to
alter their temper . . . . "

Crèvecoeur, of course, had never intended to return as a
hunter to the bosom of nature, only as a husbandman. The
hunter, like the soldier, is engaged in the effort to win the fatal
ascendancy, the last, over the enemy or the prey. This is the
sensual passion in its overweening, destructive activity, the terrible consummation in death. The husbandman, on the other
hand, brings about the sensual birth and increase. But even the
husbandman strains in dark mastery over the unwilling earth and
beast; he struggles to win forth substance, he must master the
soil and the strong cattle, he must have the strange blood-

knowledge, and the slow, but deep, mastery. There is no equality
or selfless humility, no ecstasy of selfless communing in oneness.
It is the dark reality of blood-mastery and blood-sympathy.

Again, Crèvecoeur dwells on "the apprehension lest my younger children should be caught by that singular charm, so
dangerous to their tender years"—meaning the charm of savage
life. So he goes on: "By what power does it come to pass that
children who have been adopted when young among these
people (the Indians) can never be prevailed upon to readopt
European manners? Many an anxious parent have I seen last
war who, at the return of peace, went to the Indian villages
where they knew their children to have been carried in captivity,
when to their inexpressible sorrow they found them so perfectly
Indianised that many knew them no longer, and those whose
more advanced ages permitted them to recollect their fathers and
mothers, absolutely refused to follow them, and ran to their
adopted parents to protect them against the effusions of love
their unhappy real parents lavished on them! Incredible as this
may appear, I have heard it asserted in a thousand instances,
among persons of credit.

"There must be something in their (the Indians) social bond
singularly captivating, and far superior to anything to be boasted
of among us; for thousands of Europeans are Indians, and we
have no examples of even one of those aborigines having from
choice become Europeans . . . . "

Crèvecoeur's thousands of instances against not even one instance remind us of our cat and another. Some children may
have refused to return to their European parents—but the
thought of thousands of these obdurate offspring, with faces
averted from their natural father and mother, is too good a
picture to be true. Also we know that some Indian brides of
white men became very good civilised matrons.

The truth remains the same, as another century has proved
it—it is easier to turn white men into Indians than Indians into
white men. Crèvecoeur exulted in the thought. He disliked

F

civilisation even whilst he continued one of the most civilised of
all beings. He knew the awful barrenness even of emotional self-
gratification. He knew the dreariness of living from the pre-
determined will, admitting no otherness, only the mechanical
oneness, as of two buttons from the same machine. He wanted
equality and fraternity, and he would allow nothing else. At the
same time he wanted to know the mystery of the sensual being.
He wanted to know the thing which he determinedly excluded
from knowledge. Which cannot be done. He wanted to have his
cake and eat it—the very nice cake of the human free-will, and
the human ego self-determined; the creed of the ultimate oneness
of all things, in a union of love. He had his cake—kept it whole.
Only he nibbled the corners. He opened the dark eyes of his
blood to the presence of bees, birds, and serpents. He saw them
in their magnificent struggling division, and their wonderful co-
existence in luminous strangeness.

4. FENIMORE COOPER'S ANGLO-AMERICAN NOVELS

4. Fenimore Cooper's Anglo-American Novels

This essay on Cooper's novels Homeward Bound *and* Home as Found *(In England the title of the second novel is* Eve Effingham*) appeared in the* English Review *for February, 1919. Version 2, if it existed, is lost. In the book of 1923, Lawrence changed the title to "Fenimore Cooper's White Novels". The two extant versions are equal in length. The first half of version 1 consists of "philosophy." This is left out in version 2 which is an enlarged revision of the second half of version 1. Version 3 is full of humorous digressions and more detailed.*

Both versions are more concerned with Lawrence than with Cooper. In version 1 Lawrence is thinking of his own mother when he says: "What is the use of a mother's sacrificing herself for her children if after death her unappeased soul shall perforce return upon the child and exact from it all the fulfilment that should have been attained in the living flesh, and was not?" In version 3 Lawrence states again that a "reconciliation, in the flesh" between white and red men is impossible, and he analyses the disaster resulting from a marriage of an Indian with a white woman, an analysis exactly adapted to the marriage of Mabel Dodge with Toni Luhan.

Both versions arrive at the same conclusion as the essay on Whitman : the absurdity of democracy is compared with a natural aristocracy of the soul. Version 3 is written in a lighter, more humorous style, but it does not bring in anything which has not already been said in version 1.

W E HAVE seen that, when we try to trace our consciousness to its source and fountain-head, we must approach the great nerve-centres of the sympathetic and voluntary system. We have seen further that the moment we enter this field of primal or pre-cerebral consciousness we enter the field of duality. Science has of late asserted the universal law of polarity —a law of dual poles. This law applies as much to the human psyche as to the cosmic forces.

From the sympathetic centres in the abdomen rush out the vital vibrations of our first-being, our first-consciousness. In the solar plexus, and the other centres of the lower body, we have the inscrutable well-heads whence the living self bubbles up and enters into creation. What lies before is a mystery, and must ever remain a mystery. When we follow the mystery to its gates we find it entering by the great sympathetic plexuses of the body, entering and appearing in spontaneous motion and spontaneous consciousness. And we find that at its very entry this motion, this being, this consciousness, is dual. What we know as sensual consciousness has its fountain-head in the plexus of the abdomen; what we know as spiritual consciousness has its issue in the cardiac plexus, the great sympathetic centre within the thorax. Our mental consciousness is a third thing, resultant from this duality in pre-cerebral cognition. But connected with the lower or sensual system we have the mouth, which tastes and embraces, the nostrils which smell, and the ears which hear. Connected with the spiritual system of the upper body we have the eyes which see, and the hands which touch.

This knowledge, which is the very beginning of psychology—the psyche comprising our whole consciousness, physical, sensual, spiritual, pre-cerebral as well as cerebral—seems to have been familiar to the pagan priesthoods and to the esoteric mystics of the past. We can only begin to understand the initiation into the religious mysteries, such as the Eleusinian mysteries, when we can grasp the rise of pre-cerebral consciousness in the great plexuses, and the movement of passional or dynamic cognition from one centre to another, towards culmination or consummation in what we may call whole-experience, or whole-consciousness.

It is quite certain that the pre-Christian priesthoods understood the processes of *dynamic* consciousness, which is pre-cerebral consciousness. It is certain that St. John gives us in the Apocalypse a cypher-account of the process of the conquest of the lower or sensual dynamic centres by the upper or spiritual dynamic consciousness, a conquest affected centre by centre, towards a culmination in the *actual* experience of spiritual infinitude. This account is of scientific exactitude. But the cypher of symbols and number-valuation is exceedingly complicated. None the less it can be solved. And then we realise that the old, immense religions were established upon a scientific knowledge so immediate and profound that we cannot grasp it. They understood—at least, those initiated understood—the rise and movement of the dynamic consciousness in the individual, that which we might call our unconsciousness or sub-consciousness, but which is more than these, and which, though in very fact the bulk of our being and knowing, is regarded from our mental standpoint as *nothing*, or nothingness. That which we regard as nothing, that which is our pre-cerebral cognition, this the priests understood as the great dynamic human consciousness, the mind being no more than an abstract from it. And this profound priestly understanding was scientific in its exactitude. It was of necessity symbolic in its expression—as when, in the Eleusinian mysteries, a golden snake was crowded into the bosom of the postulant, and drawn forth from the lowest part of the body— because there are perhaps no mental terms to express, at least dynamically, that which takes place. But in fact of *process* the initiation was a piece of most profound scientific exposition, perfectly expressing the secret and vital movement of the psyche in its pre-cerebral activities.

This priestly knowledge, however, was inevitably sensual. The sensual understanding was the living field of the ancient world. The one-sidedness of exclusively sensual understanding caused the downfall of the old systems. The Greeks seem to have discovered the process of the conquest of the sensual centres by the spiritual consciousness. They worked this into an esoteric system, quite scientific, and much more profound, nearer the quick, than anything we have since known in psychology. But their knowledge still was based upon the sensual activities, even though it were but the knowledge of the process of conquest of these activities. And if we were ever to escape into spiritual freedom, into pure spiritual or upper understanding, what we have called freedom itself, then all idea of duality would have to be wiped out, the sensual understanding would have to be blanked out, as if it did not exist.

Which is what the early Christian world proceeded to do, by amazing instinct. The Gnostics, the Manicheans, all those strange and obscure sects which really derived their understanding from the Greek esotericism, or from the Persian, were destroyed by the new rising instinct, the instinctive passionate longing to be freed from the sensual self altogether, and from the whole body of ancient understanding. For the sensual consciousness, hopelessly dominant, had become destructive and tyrannical in the human psyche. Hence the strange wild rage of Byzantine—or Greek—Christianity, the frenzy of destruction that possessed it. Hence a world gone mad over the intricacies, to us nonsensical, of the Homoousion. Slaves were as mad as priests over these mystical absurdities. But it was not absurd. It was a subtle, amazing process of displacing utterly, even destroying, one body of knowledge, one way of dynamic cognition, and giving all the scope to the other body. The curious decisions of the early Councils, the Council of Nice, and the General Councils, only show us how perfect the instinct was which rejected every trace of the old true science—every trace save, perhaps, the unreadable riddle of the Apocalypse.

Now, after two thousand years of effort, we have so subjected the centres of sensual cognition that they depend automatically on the upper centres. Now, after two thousand years, having established our knowledge and even our experience all in one sort, a halfness, we find ourselves in a prison. We reach the condition when we are so imprisoned in the cul de sac of our mutilated psyche that we are in the first stages of that madness and self-destruction into which the ancients fell when they were imprisoned and driven mad within the cul de sac of the sensual body. *Quos vult perdere Jupiter, dementat prius.*

What lies before us is either escape or death. We choose death. But is that any escape? We are always faced with the problem of the immortality of the soul. We elude it by imagining that souls can dissolve into an infinite, evaporate away as liquids can evaporate into space. But since the very definition of a soul is that it is a unique entity, how can that which is a unique entity remain itself by merging into the infinite? It can only lose itself by so doing. And the soul does not lose itself in death.

We can no longer believe in angels, though we try. And all our efforts will not win from our souls a belief in disembodied spirits which cluster innumerable in the invisible ether. What we believe without knowing it, first of all. In the first place, my belief lies in my active breast and in my active belly, potent there. I have to find the mental idea which will correspond.

The only thing to do is for each man to remember his own dead. Do we imagine our dead lying in some distant grave?— our own dead? We do not. Do we imagine them merged into some infinite? For my part, I find this impossible. When I hush

my soul perfectly, to attend, as it were, to the dead I have loved
and love, then I find that it is nonsense to try to project my
attention in any outward direction, either upward or downward,
or into universal space. My dead is neither above nor below, nor
everywhere. My own dead, whom I have loved and love, is with
me, within me, here, now, at one with me, and not elsewhere.

Those that die return to the most beloved, enter in, and at
last live in peace, gladly, at one with the most beloved. So that
the living are always living. The present is one and unbreakable.
The present is not a fleeting moment. Moments may flee, but I
am here. And with me is one who is dead and who yet lives in
me. So that all life is always living, and the Present is one and
unbroken. The Present is always present, as the sun is always
present. It is eternity that is an abstraction, an inference reached
by negation of the present. My immortality lies in being present
in life. And the dead have presence in the living. So that the
dead are always present in life, here, in the flesh, always. It is
inexplicable *how* they are present in us, but it is a physical fact
that they are. So are the unborn which issue from us. Here, in
our tissue, we know it, lie the unborn. And as surely, here, in
our tissue, live the dead, present, and always present.

The great problem of the survival of the soul is not the same,
however, as that of the survival of the will after death. The
human self is not the same as the individual will. The self is the
inexplicable, the mystery. The will is the dynamic force which
belongs to the self, but which is subject to the consciousness,
the mental consciousness. So that the mental ego can fix the will
and use it in contravention to the primal spontaneous self. Which
very often happens.

When, through the fixing of the will, a deadlock ensues in the
soul, our living becomes an automatic process. And then the
soul is frustrated, coiled, angry. Will death release this deadlock,
save the soul from frustration? It will not. Only living will fulfil
a frustrated soul.

Now, many of our dead have died in the misery of this frus-

tration; automatised and unable to live, they have even sought
death as an escape, only to find it no escape. Souls frustrated in
life are not fulfilled by death, save they die in a passionate consummation. Souls that find in death itself a passionate consummation return to us appeased, and add the beauty and richness
of their presence to us. But what of the souls that are caught out
of life unliberated and unappeased? They return to us unfree
and girning, terrible ghosts. They enter into us angrily and fill
us with their destructive presence. There is no peace in death to
those who die in the terrible deadlock of frustration. And if
there is no peace for them, there is none for us. They return
home to us. They are the angry, unappeased shades that come
darkly home to us, thronging home to us from over the seas,
entering our souls and filling us with madness, ever more and
more madness, unless we, by our active living, shall give them
the life that they demand, the living motions that were frustrated
in them now liberated and made free.

This explains the futility of sacrifice. What use is it to me if
a man sacrifice and murder his living desires for me, only to
return in death and demand this sacrifice again of me, tenfold?
What is the use of a mother's sacrificing herself for her children
if after death her unappeased soul shall perforce return upon the
child and exact from it all the fulfilment that should have been
attained in the living flesh, and was not? We cannot help this
returning of our soul back into the living. What we can help is
its returning unappeased and destructive. We have now the hosts
of weary, clamorous, unsatisfied dead to appease by our living.
If we cannot appease them we shall go on dying until somewhere, in some unknown people, life can start afresh.

Which brings us to Fenimore Cooper and the Red Indians.
Franklin had an equation in providential mathematics: —

$$\text{Rum} + \text{Savage} = 0.$$

It is a specious little equation. Proceeding like that we might add
up the universe to nought.

Rum plus Savage may equal a dead savage. But is a dead

savage nought? Bullet plus Yankee may equal a dead Yankee.
But is a dead Yankee nought, either?

The Aztec is gone, the Red Indian, the Esquimo, the Incas, the
Patagonian—and whither? *Où sont les neiges d'antan?* They
are not far to seek. They are no further off than the coming
snows.

Do we imagine that the Aztecs are installed within the souls
of the present Mexicans? And are the Red Men at home within
the breasts of the Yankees of to-day? Assuredly the dead Indians
have their place in the souls of present-day Americans, but
whether they are at peace there is another question. It is said
that Americans begin to show obvious Red Indian qualities. But
they show no signs of peace in themselves.

It is plain that the American is not at one with the Red Man
whom he has perforce lodged into his own soul. It is a dangerous thing to destroy any vital existence out of life. For then the
destroyer becomes responsible, in his own living body, for the
destroyed. Upon the destroyer devolves the necessity of continuing the nature and being of the destroyed. This is an axiom. It
follows from the law of polarity. If we destroy one pole, the other
collapses, or becomes doubly responsible. The tiger destroys deer.
If all deer are destroyed, the tiger collapses. Similarly, if all
tigers are destroyed, deer will collapse, for then there is no equipoise to keep them vivid in their being. Between the beast
predative and the beast ruminative is a balance in polarity, and
the destruction of either pole is a destruction of both in the long
run.

With humanity it is not quite so simple. When the White
American destroys the Red Indian, he either ultimately brings
about his own destruction or he takes upon himself the responsibility for the continuing and perfecting of the passional soul
of the destroyed. This is true of any creatures, balanced either in
a true polarity of love or of enmity. The Aztec lives unappeased
and destructive within the Mexican, the Red Indian lives unappeased and inwardly destructive in the American.

It is presumable, however, that at length the soul of the dead red man will be at one with the soul of the living white man. And then we shall have a new race. Meanwhile, the will is fixed in the white man; he works his automatic conclusions. How different is the deep, unexpressed passion in the American, from the automatic spiritual ego which he demonstrates to the world, this is a matter for the world to discover later on.

Fenimore Cooper very beautifully gives the myth of the atonement, the communion between the soul of the white man and the soul of the Indian. He also gives the frenzied, weary running-on of the self-determined ego, the mechanical spiritual being of America. Here are two classes of books—the famous Leatherstocking Series, and what we will call the Anglo-American Series, such as *Homeward Bound, Eve Effingham, The Spy, The Pilot,* and others, stories concerning white Americans only. These last are now almost forgotten. They are thin and bloodless. But they are not by any means without point, for Cooper was a profound and clever man.

Cooper himself was rich and of good family. His father founded Cooperstown, in the Eastern States. Fenimore was a gentleman of culture. He shows in *Homeward Bound* how bound he was, hand and foot, to the European culture-tradition.

It should not be forgotten how intensely cultured these Americans of the early nineteenth century were. It is only necessary to read their familiar literature, the light verse, to know that they were much more *raffiné* than Englishmen have ever been. In this matter of refined material culture, external and dis-illusioned, the Americans were ahead even of the French. Cooper quotes a Frenchman, who says, *"L'Amérique est pourrie avant d'être mûre."* And there is a great deal in it. America was not taught by France—by Baudelaire, for example. Baudelaire learned his lesson from America.

The Effinghams are three extremely refined, genteel Americans who are homeward bound from England to the States. Their party consists of father, daughter, and uncle, and faithful nurse. The daughter has just finished her education in Europe. She has, indeed, skimmed the cream off Europe. England, France, Italy, and Germany have nothing more to teach her. She is a bright and charming, admirable creature; a real modern heroine; intrepid, calm, and self-collected, yet admirably impulsive, always in perfectly good taste; clever and assured in her speech, like a man, but withal charmingly deferential and modest before the stronger sex. It is the perfection of the public female, —a dreadful, self-determined thing, cold and mechanical and factitious.

On board is the other type of American, the parvenu, the demagogue, who has *done* Europe and put it in his breeches pocket, in a month. No European writer has ever given us such a completely detestable picture of an American as did the American Cooper. Septimus Dodge is the object of loathing and contempt to the Effinghams. Yet they cannot get away from him —neither on ship-board nor even when they reach their own estates. He is the bugbear of their lives—but he is the inevitable negative pole of their Americanism.

Mr. Dodge, the democrat, of Dodgetown, alternately fawns and intrudes, cringes and bullies. For the Effinghams are most terribly "superior" in a land of equality. No foreign count was ever as icily superior to his lowest peasant as are the Effinghams to their successful, democratic compatriot, Septimus. Mr. Dodge cringes like the inferior he really is. But he is an American, and by asserting his democratic equality he gets the haughty Effinghams on the hip. They writhe—but Septimus has them fast. They will not escape. What tortures await them in the free land of America, at the hands of the persecuting Dodge! There, all their superiority writhes transfixed on the horns of the Dodge dilemma, the acute dilemma of democratic equality.

Through these American-social books of Fenimore Cooper— at least, through the most significant—runs this same helpless struggle with a false position. People are not free to be people. They are all of them all the while impaled on a false social

assumption, and all their passion and movement works back to
this social assumption. They are never full, spontaneous human
beings. All the while they are mere social units, social conscious,
never passionately individual. For this reason the books are
empty of life, while they are full of sharp social observation.

Miss Effingham never confronts Mr. Dodge as a real individual confronts another. She is a social unit confronting another social unit. She is a democrat—or at least a republican—
confronting her fellow-democrat. And no matter how she despises
and detests Mr. Dodge, the individual, she has in some degree
to accept an equality with him as an American citizen. All her
patrician nature rebels. But it is mercilessly impaled. She pushes
a pin through her haughty, winged soul, and pins it down on
the *Contrat Social*. There it writhes and flaps ignominious. All
her loves and adventures move us not at all. How can they?
What do pursuits at sea, fleeing scoundrels, lords in disguise,
shipwrecks, ferocious savages of the Sahara—what do these
amount to to a soul which is pinned down on the *Contrat Social*?
Nothing at all. Nothing matters, save the pin which holds down
Eve Effingham on the same card with Septimus Dodge.

Yet Eve Effingham will die rather than pull out the pin. She
will die rather than simply dismiss Septimus as a hopeless inferior—a natural inferior. He is the thorn in the proud Effingham
flesh. But the Effinghams love their thorn. They believe in the
equality of men and in the Rights of Man. They believe tremen-
dously in social freedom. This is why they have impaled their
souls. First, they are republican, American citizens. And then, a
long way behind, they are living individuals.

Which is nonsense. A man is, and can be, no more than himself: his own single, starry self, which has its place inscrutably
in the firmament of existence. But if a man is to be himself he
must be free. That is, by general consent all men must be free
to be themselves. Nothing could be more just or wise.

But to go on from this, and declare that all men are equal,
and even, ultimately, identical, is nonsense. When men are most

truly themselves, then the difference is most real, and most evident. And it is not only a difference in kind, it is a difference in degree. Eve Effingham is not only a finer being than Septimus Dodge, she is by nature a superior being. Septimus should yield her the reverence and respect due to a higher type from a lower. And she should implicitly command that reverence and respect.

Instead of which, Septimus, having money in his pocket, presumes that the difference between him and the Effinghams is a mere impertinence on their part, which ought to be done away with. And they feel a little guilty and confused by their own instinctive superiority. If this is not the ruin of all high things, and the triumph of all base things, what is? It is like the Buddhists who bless the lice that eat them, because all life is sacred.

Democracy as we have it is mere falsity. It is true that the aristocratic system of the past is arbitrary and false. But it is not so arbitrary and false as our present democratic system. Every man knows that intrinsically men are not equal. Intrinsically, in his true self which issues from the mystery and is a term of the Godhead, one man is either greater or less than another man, or perhaps approximately equal. But the deepest social truth about men is that some are higher, some lower, some greater, some less, some highest, and some lowest, even in the sight of the everlasting God. To pretend anything else is mere sophistry. Some men are born from the mystery of creation, to know, to lead, and to command. And some are born to listen, to follow, to obey. Each man has his beauty and his wholeness in fulfilling his own true nature, whether it be the fulfilment of command or of service. And all that democracy needs to do is to arrange the material world so that each man can be intrinsically himself, yielding service where he must instinctively yield respect or reverence, and taking command where instinctively he feels his own authority.

The old aristocratic system at least recognised this prime reality of the intrinsic and holy disquality between men. It was wrong in establishing an artificial distinction of mere birth. If

we are to recognise true beauty and superiority it must be from
the inmost sincere soul; we cannot proceed on accidents of here-
dity. But the aristocratic system was not so wrong as the democratic, which refuses, theoretically, to recognise any intrinsic
difference at all, and asserts that, since no man is higher than
another, since we are all leaves of grass, no man shall presume to
put the grass in the shade. No man is any higher than another
man; no soul has any intrinsic right to command another soul. So
says democracy. And if this is not far more arbitrary, far more
sweeping, and far more deadly than any arbitrary aristocratic
system, then there is no reality in living whatsoever. All men
must be mown level with the grass, because most men, the aver-
age, are leaves of grass, and therefore it would be impertinent
and arrogant to rise above the grass. So we mow life down.

Worse still. Though no man is higher than any other man,
intrinsically, still, some men are superior mechanically. Some
men are more productive materially than others. They know how
to combine the mechanical forces of the universe to bring forth
material produce. Those that can most successfully subject living
and being to the mechanical forces, destroy the intrinsic self and
substitute the machine unit, thereby increasing material production, let them be lords of material production. Let money rule.

Which is the inevitable outcome of democracy—Liberty,
Equality, and Fraternity. And as long as we believe in Equality,
so long shall we grind mechanically till, like most Jews, we have
no living soul, no living self, but only a supermachine faculty
which will coin money. Then no doubt we shall all be satisfied,
negative, anti-life.

How dreary we are, putting up the social and political self as
a first reality, dwindling the true self into a nothingness. So we
all turn ourselves into ridiculous little political gramophones, all
wound up and braying together, without a notion of the foolish
and despicable sight we offer to the gods above. A man is either
himself, or he is nothing. A braying little political gramophone

G

is worse than nothing. We should teach our children a new prayer : "Dear God, let me not be wound up."

Let every man get back to himself, and let the world at large sink down to its true perspective as the world at little, which it really is. Let every man learn to be himself, and in so being to give reverence and obedience where such is due, and to take command and authority where these are due. Let this be done spontaneously, from the living, real self. Otherwise we shall wind ourselves up till the spring breaks.

And let us recognise secondarily, that truth of duality or polarity which is within us and without us, and which makes of equality a mechanical round-about at the very outset. St. Francis falling down before the embarrassed and astonished peasant, what was he doing? He was doing the same as Father Zosimus, who falls down prostrate before Dmitri Karamazov. He, the spiritual saint, a creature of the one half, fell in recognition before the pure sensual being, the creature of the other half of life. Already, where is equality between beings established in such opposite mysteries, so utterly different both of them, but so utterly real?

But the duality is within us, as well as outside us. It is the duality of life itself, the polarity of the living. The social units such as Miss Effingham, impaled, whirl round on their pivot of negation like little machines, depolarised. When we depolarise ourselves we cease to live, as even St. Francis shows us. We must return to the great polarity of the life motion.

The tiger was a terrible problem to Shelley, who wanted life in terms of the lamb. I should think the lamb must have been a puzzler, say, to Sennacherib, who wanted life all in terms of the winged and burning lion. We must admit life in its duality.

We must admit that only the juxtaposition of the tiger keeps the lamb a quivering, vivid, beautiful fleet thing. Take away the tiger and we get the sheep of our pasture, just clods of meat. If there were no hawks in the sky the larks would lose their song. It is the fanning of fear which makes the song flicker up, as well as the expansion of love. The soft, rolling sound of the dove among the leaves, her silken iridescence, depends on the hawk that hangs on sultry wings like a storm in bird-life. The one concentrates the other. From the soft, loving principle there is a tendency to expand into disintegrate formlessness. The sharp compulsion of the fierce sensual principle drives back the soul from its looseness, concentrates it into the jewel-isolation of a perfected self. Fear and suffering are great formative principles.

The full eye of the deer or the rabbit or the horse would stagnate and lose its lustre, save for the keen, strange eye of the wolf and the weasel, and of man. The electric, almost magical, flash of a rabbit's mysterious passion depends entirely on the existence of the stoat. Destroy the mysterious circuit, teach the stoat to eat dandelion leaves, and life crumbles into dross and nullity. We must live in a world of perilous, pure freedom, having always the tincture of fear, danger, and exultance. Nothing else will keep us living. As jewels are crushed between the valves of the earth, and driven, through unutterable resistance, into their own clear perfection, leaving the matrix exempt; so must the human soul be purified in unspeakable resistance to the mass. We wear the ruby and the sapphire as symbols of our splendid pride in singleness, our jewel-like self.

5. FENIMORE COOPER'S LEATHERSTOCKING NOVELS

5. Fenimore Cooper's Leatherstocking Novels

This essay appeared in the English Review *for March, 1919. Version 2, if it existed, is lost. Version 3, published in the book of 1923, is of equal length, but otherwise quite different. Cooper meant much to Lawrence. He had probably read the Leatherstocking Novels in his youth (see the essay "Indians and an Englishman",* Dial, *February, 1923, reprinted in* Phoenix, *1936). Later, in a letter to Catherine Carswell, written on November 27, 1916, he says: "I read* Deerslayer *just before the Turgenev. And I can tell you what a come-down it was, from the pure and exquisite art of Fennimore [sic] Cooper—whom we count nobody—to the journalistic bludgeonings of Turgenev. They are all—Turgenev, Tolstoi, Dostoevsky, Maupassant, Flaubert—so very obvious and coarse, beside the lovely, mature and sensitive art of Fennimore Cooper or Hardy" (H. T. Moore:* The Intelligent Heart, *p. 219). T. S. Eliot, usually quite hostile towards Lawrence, said in a talk at the University of Washington on July 9, 1953: "Cooper has suffered, like Walter Scott, from being read in early youth, and by many people never read again: it remained for D. H. Lawrence, who discovered Cooper later in life, to write probably the most brilliant of critical essays on him."*

Version 1 *is less critical of Cooper than version* 3. *In version* 1 *Lawrence mentions biographical details about Cooper's life in Paris as a man of society. Most of the essay is concerned with the five Leatherstocking Novels. In version* 3 *Lawrence fills the first half of the essay with thoughts and jokes about democracy and other subjects, while the other half repeats the whole of version* 1 *in a more concentrated form.*

In both versions Lawrence quotes the passage from Mrs. Cooper appearing in the foreword to the Everyman's Library edition of The Prairie, *which Lawrence had used :* "*It was a matter of course that he* [Cooper] *should dwell on the better traits of the picture rather than on the coarser and more revolting, though more common points. Like West, he could see Apollo in the young Mohawk.*" *The conclusions which Lawrence drew from this quotation are amusingly different : in version* 1 *he says :* "*This tiny speech shows us Mrs. Cooper's attitude. She was impatient of her husband's Indian passion.*" *In version* 3 *he says :* "*You see now why he depended so absolutely on* MY WIFE. *She had to look things in the face for him. The coarser and more revolting, and certainly more common points, she had to see.*"

The fundamental ideas in both versions are the same. Lawrence is not in one of his best moods in version 3, *rather he is derisive, disrespectful, somehow affected. The* "*curious, amusing 'Hall' of the village*" *of version* 1 *becomes a* "*ridiculous, commodious 'hall' *" *in version* 3. *Again and again he restricts his admiration for Cooper which he had shown in version* 1 : "*Perhaps my taste is childish, but these scenes in* Pioneers *seem to me marvellously beautiful.*" Deerslayer *is the book which Lawrence appreciates most.* "Deerslayer *is, indeed, one of the most beautiful and most perfect books in the world : flawless as a jewel and of gem-like concentration. From the first words we pass straight into the world of sheer creation, with so perfect a transit that we are unconscious*

of our translation." This becomes in version 3 : "It is a gem
of a book. Or a bit of perfect paste. And myself, I like a bit
of perfect paste in a perfect setting, so long as I am not
fooled by pretence of reality."

   There is no philosophy in version 1 this time : Lawrence
does not lose the track of his theme, while the first fifty per
cent of version 3 has no direct connection with the Leather-
stocking Novels. In version 3 the summaries of the novels
at the beginning are superfluous because, later on, they are
summed up a second time. Four pages of version 3 are con-
cerned with the Pilgrim Fathers who have already been
discussed in the essay "The Spirit of Place." The only posi-
tive gain of version 3 are the humorous lists which sum up
Cooper's life and Cooper's character.

I N COOPER's Leatherstocking series we broach another world
of reality. Here there are mystery and passion and the further
progress into the unknown. We are not involved in the
mechanical workings of the will, as it works itself into automatic
self-determination.

   It is the search for his own consummation, for the mystical
"next step," which Cooper records in the Leatherstocking books.
In the Anglo-American novels, the so-called love theme is the
predominant interest. But it is not interesting. One does not care
who marries Eve Effingham, because there is no vital marriage
possible. There are only the intricacies of the self-determined
psyche to record.

   Cooper symbolises his own actual, mechanical, self-determined
life in the Effinghams. But in Leatherstocking he symbolises his
own last being, strange and wrought to a conclusion, seeking its

consummation in the American woods and the Indian race, his pure complement in the Chief Chingachgook. As an American citizen he lived correct, impeccable—a clock-work man. Yet his living soul moved on in passional progress.

It is amazing the subjection a human being can suffer. A fakir can live buried up to the chin in earth, asserting the mechanical will and annulling the creative substantial bonds. And Cooper lived buried even over the head in the old concept—the European convention.

And still he had his vital reaction, his progressive mystery. He had still a last communion to make, a last consummation to effect. He describes this in his Indian novels.

He tells one of the last tales of the Odyssey of the white soul, as it vanishes into the unknown. The Odyssey of Homer is the story of the unfolding of the pristine soul of a race, in the potency and wonder of the surrounding unknown, until it consummates and perfects itself like a flower in spring. The novels of Leatherstocking give us the opposite story, of the passing of the final race-soul into the unknown, towards a surpassing of the old race being. This is the strange autumn-flowering, as pallid crocuses flower in autumn, the last flame on the brink of darkness. It is a consummation on the brink of oblivion, seeding in oblivion. It is the mystery of conjunction in finality, when at last the soul in the conqueror embraces and is at one with the ghost of the conquered. It is the passing of Orpheus into hell, whence he has not yet returned. The new birth is the birth of a new race, risen from the inscrutable consummation of two past races.

Crèvecoeur imagines himself under the wigwam. Cooper goes much further. He spends a whole life-time, imaginatively, in the backwoods. He has a passion for the aboriginal life, the aboriginal scene, and the native savage. His innermost desire is polarised all the time by the primitive America of the Red Man and the Red Man's way of life. His whole soul embraces the dark aboriginal soul with unceasing, fertile love.

It is singular that the refined, cultured, nervous, snobbish Fenimore Cooper should choose as his real hero, the symbol of his own innermost man, Natty Bumppo, or Leatherstocking, Pathfinder, Deerslayer, as he is severally called. We have Cooper, living in a Louis Quatorze *hôtel* in Paris, lying looking up at the painted ceiling, dreaming passionately of the naked savages, yearning for them; or Cooper walking down the long *salon,* a gentleman in every thread, a finished social product, with his soul courting the bloodthirsty Indian of his own American backwoods.

Natty is an unaesthetic figure, especially as we see him first, when he is an old man, uncouth, ungainly, even ugly, with his wide mouth and unlovely manner of speech, and with gaps in his old teeth. Yet he is the innermost man of this Parisian-American. He is uneducated, and, in the cultured sense, stupid, offensive. Yet he is Cooper's very self of selves, the quick of his being. He is the twin, the "little man" of the American's soul, the passional, so-called phallic dual or Doppelgänger which figures so often in the myths. In social reality, Cooper is an Effingham. In *passional* reality he is Natty Bumppo. And this is symbolic of the American, who is at once so over-cultured and so crude or naïve or child-like.

"It was a matter of course," says Mrs. Cooper, speaking of her husband, "that he should dwell on the better traits of the picture rather than on the coarser and more revolting, though more common points. Like West, he could see Apollo in the young Mohawk."

This tiny speech shows us Mrs. Cooper's attitude. She was impatient of her husband's Indian passion. To her the coarse and revolting traits of the savage were most in evidence—as they were to Franklin. She was an Eve Effingham, fixed in the will of the old idea. Natty Bumppo to her would be just a vulgar nonentity, almost a renegade of the great white civilisation, and Chingachgook a disgusting old drunkard. In face of the great demon of the aboriginal Spirit of Place, she became only more cultured, more Parisian, and more self-determined.

Her husband and herself were associated in the old culture and the old will. It was a strong, though external association. In passionate reality they were mutually exclusive of one another. In passional being they were alien, even opposed.

To Fenimore Cooper himself there was one beloved, whom he loved ceaselessly. It was the aboriginal American, beloved in the same way by Longfellow and Prescott, though not so passionately. The great demon, the vast Spirit of Place in the New World, drew him, polarised the whole of his living psyche. Europe was the fixed pole of his cultured ego, his finished self. But she was the extreme negative pole of repulsion to his vital, innermost being. He yearned mystically to the soul of his Red brother; he brooded over him and asked for him with superlative desire.

And he dreamed his true marriage with the aboriginal psyche. All futurity for him lay latent, not in the white woman, but in the dark, magnificent presence of American warriors, with whom he would be at one in the ultimate atonement between races.

In *Pioneers,* the first of the Indian series, Leatherstocking is old and paltry-looking, as Odysseus in the eyes of Ithacans on his return. This is no doubt something of a picture from Cooper's own life. Without doubt he draws the scene of his childhood and the actual people of his knowledge. For *Pioneers* is half-way between Europe and aboriginal America. It is a story of the early settlement of Cooperstown, as Cooper knew it, no doubt, when a boy, at the close of the eighteenth century. It is the story of the return of Leatherstocking to the European shores, the outposts of the white settlement of America.

There is a mixture of the Anglo-American novel and the Leatherstocking novel in *Pioneers.* We have a set of white people, social units, performing their necessary evolutions in the form of a plot; a Judge Temple and a favourite and only fair daughter of the admirable type, just home from school, from the finishing of her education in the eastern cities; also a mysterious Major Effingham and a young Edward Effingham in disguise. Half in contrast to these, half in the same world, are Leatherstocking, an uncouth old hunter, and Chingachgook, Christianised and christened John, a degenerate chief of the Delawares; also various frontier types, the prototypes of Hurry Harry and Hetty Hutter and other later-developed characters. There is a wrong done by Judge Temple to old Major Effingham, to be put right by the inevitable but somewhat complicated love-match of Miss Temple with the young Effingham—just a favourite bit of old social machinery—a satisfactory restitution of property through a love-match.

The book exists, really, as a wonderful and beautiful picture of an outpost village. It is England—but England lost on the edge of the unknown; England more English and characteristic than England ever was, asserting itself in the toils of the great dark spirit of the continent.

There is the actual village itself—the long, raw street of wooden houses, with wood-fires blinking and flashing through the un-curtained windows, in the winter nights. There is the curious, amusing "Hall" of the village, Judge Temple's somewhat fantastic replica of a squire's residence. The inn, with the drunken Indian; the church, with the snowy congregation crowding to the fire; the astounding Christmas abundance of the tables, that groaned as English tables never groaned, with weight of good things, splendid things to eat; the turkey-shooting, on the snow; the sports of the rough people; then summer coming, with heavy clouds of pigeons, myriads of pigeons, destroyed in heaps; the night fishing on the teeming, virgin lake; the deer-hunting, the forests all green, the maple sugar taken from the trees—all this is given with a beauty and a magnificence unsurpassable. It is rich with that pristine magic of futurity, like the Odyssey. There is a glamour and an extravagance about the white men as they move, so very English, on this strange landscape; a mystery of

the Red life as they pass in shadow against the glow of the burning night-fires.

No man could sufficiently praise the beauty and glamorous
magnificence of Cooper's presentation of the aboriginal American
landscape, the New World. We cannot think of the opening of
Pioneers, as the sledge drives over the snow, the negro guiding
the horses through the wild, precipitous forest roads, the Judge
and his daughter folding themselves in furs as the twilight
advances over the pine-dusky winter, without experiencing that
strange, almost unbearable leap of enchantment such as we get
only from the Odyssey. It is the magnificence of futurity flooding
the heart.

Then there is the story of pain. The old, lean, uncouth hunts-
man, Natty Bumppo, a figure rather pathetic than attractive,
lives in a hut on the verge of civilisation with his grey-haired
friend, the Delaware chief, christened John since he is converted
to Christianity. The Great Serpent, the splendid Chingachgook
of the later novels, is here a mere degraded John, who humiliates
his grey hairs in drunkenness, and dies, thankful to be dead, in
a forest fire, passing back into fire, whence he derived.

Meanwhile Natty also is humiliated. The game laws have just
been passed, partly owing to Judge Temple's wise provision. But
Natty has shot through all the wild woods since he was a child
and cannot understand that he is poaching on the Judge's land.
He has lived all his life by his gun; so how can he hold back his
bullet in the close season? He must shoot to live.

Judge Temple is kind; but the laws must be enforced to
prevent the wasting of all the natural supplies. Natty is convicted
of shooting a deer in the close season. He is shut up in the village
prison for a short term. He is an old man of seventy, simple
almost as a wild animal, gentle and natural. Yet, in the interest
of humanity, he must be put in stocks and in prison.

This drives him off. The Indian chief is broken by shame in
drink. He perishes. Natty goes west. He leaves the woods and
waters where he has hunted all his life with the Red Man, and

goes west, in his lonely age, departing before the advance of civilisation. A strange, lonely, aged man, he advances into the void of the prairie.

It is the same bitter tale of the horrid advance of civilisation that subjects all life to its mechanisation of laws and penalties and benevolent Providence. Over the whole world we hear the great wail of natural life under the triumph of civilisation. But the violated Spirits of Place will avenge themselves. How long will such a civilisation sterilise the creative world? Not long. The Spirits of Place take a slow, implacable revenge.

Chronologically, *The Last of the Mohicans* follows *Pioneers* in the list of books. But, according to internal chronology, *The Prairie* is second. Here we follow the old hunter to his last place, to his last outlook on the hills of the Far West, and to his grave out there.

The Prairie is different from the other books of the series. It is the story of the recoil and death of the white element in the force of the native daimon. It is strange, and almost mythical, with a sense of vast, inordinate doom. Great wings of vengeful doom seem spread over the western prairie, vengeful against the white men. We find them there still in the late book of Frank Norris, the novel about the wheat. There is a shadow of violence and dark cruelty flickering in the air. It is the last stronghold of the aboriginal Daimon.

Upon this scene enters the huge figure of Ishmael. The ponderous, pariah-like Ishmael and his huge sons and his great werewolf of a wife roll lonely and inevitably forward from the frontiers of Kentucky into the vast, void prairie. They are primitive as the Cyclops themselves, and shadowed with a sense and a reality of crime. Huge, violent, barbarous figures, they roll impassively on, with their few wagons, surrounded by the immensity of land space. Day after day they pass west into the vast oblivion. But their force of penetration ebbs. They are brought to a stop. They recoil in the throes of murder and entrench themselves in isolation on a hillock in the midst of the prairie. There they hold out like rude demi-gods against the elements and the subtle Indian.

The plot is nothing—a mere excuse for the presentation. The presentation itself is marvellous, huge, vast, mythical, almost super-human in its import, like the story of the Sons of Anak.

The old hunter and the suave, dark, horse-riding western Indians seem almost like shadows temporarily passing across the landscape. They do not inhabit the place; they are seen in a state of evanescent transit, and their settled habitations seem more like camps of invaders than homes of an established people. There is a difference between the Indians of the west and of the east. The brutal spirit of the prairie, the brutal recoil of Ishmael, these are the place-reality. But as the hills rise softly west we come to a region of suspended abstraction, a borderland that has no force of its own, only an outlook.

The Indians of these hills have some sensuous, soft, Asiatic or Polynesian quality, according to Cooper's vision. They have a suave, swift beauty, physical and sensuous, and utterly dependent on horses. They seem to lie under the last spell of the Pacific influence; they have the grace and physical voluptuousness, as well as the subtlety and sudden ferocity of the lands of the great Ocean. It is quite a different Indian from the stern, hard warrior of the east, whose sensual activity is all in death. And it is in these western Sioux, the despised nations, that one sees, if anywhere, the touch of Apollo in the young Indian. They have beautiful limbs, that cleave close to their horses, almost in one flesh. They are not abstracted, as the great nations of the east, in sensual intensity.

Among these men the old hunter dies, gently, in physical peace and soft affection, there west, in his chair on the western hills, under the heavens that are the limits of the world, looking far eastward, where his soul's land lies, among the forests and darkness of the trees and the great sweet waters. He had gone beyond himself, there in the west, in the village of his last days.

The Last of the Mohicans brings us back to the trees and the

lakes, the Delawares, and the white men. But in this book Cooper
again seeks a pretext for his plot. He must describe actual historical events, and, hanging on to the skirts of history, hamper
and spoil his natural movement. Perhaps *The Last of the
Mohicans* is the most imperfect of all the Leatherstocking books,
the most broken, hesitating as it does between historical narrative, desire for verity, and the true impulse of pure imaginative,
creative revelation. It is not till the book passes away from contact with history and white man's settlement and enters the confines of the Red Man that it expands into sheer significance.

Natty is now Leatherstocking, a man in the prime of life. So
we move backwards, from the old age of the *Pioneers,* and the
death in the *Prairie,* successively backwards, to the lovely pristine youth of Deerslayer. It is the reverse of the ordinary course
of biography. But this is not historical biography, record of the
past as it approaches towards the present. This is biography in
futurity, record of the race-individual as he moves from the
present old age of the race into re-birth and the new youth which
lies ahead. It is the story of the return of the aged Ithacus and
of his rejuvenation.

As far as the narrative concerns the actual struggle of the Red
race with the White race, it is not the object of our present
interest. The real story lies in the flight and adventure of the two
sisters, daughters of the British officer, with their young guard,
Major Heyward, all under the care of Leatherstocking, with
whom is associated the Indian chief, Chingachgook, and the
chief's beautiful young son—a young Dionysos rather than an
Apollo of the West—Uncas, the last of the Mohicans.

For the first time, in the two sisters—the dark, handsome Cora
and the fair, frail creature, the White Lily—Cooper gives us the
vital presence of women. Cora is the passionate, fierce nature,
child of some mysterious union between the British officer and
a Creole of the West Indies. She is the scarlet flower of woman-
hood; and she loves, and is loved by, the young Uncas. Magua

H

also, the subtle and wicked Indian who causes the destruction of
the young pair, loves her violently.

Magua, Uncas, and Cora all die a violent death. There is to
be no marriage between the last fiery slips of the Red and the
White race—no marriage in the flesh. So we read the art-
symbology. In the passionate physical reality both races die.
Even the vivid and wicked Magua is shot in mid-air, and his
beautiful if destructive body falls extinct like a meteorite. It is
strange and appalling in this book that twice the hostile Indians
are shot from overhead, and plunge down almost as from the
skies into death, struck by the bullet of the inevitable white-
hunter. They are the destroyed sun-children. Natty, in his fearful
and unerring aim, is the mystic destroyer of the Red Man out
of life.

The gentle sister of Cora, however, the timorous, will-less
White Lily, she so frail and fainting, lives through all peril, beloved of the sturdy and straightforward young Major. Later, we
know, she marries and brings up her family of children. She is
the woman of the white race, as she fades out of positive being
and becomes just the medium of the man. She lives in the old
idea, the old will. The governing principle of the young Major
is the same as the governing principle of Franklin. Duty is his
first call. He is the brave and manly social unit; he has no single,
separate existence. In the woods and in danger he shows a manly, if unsubtle, slightly uninteresting figure. In civilised life he
would be an open-handed, but unoriginal, citizen and officer. To
Cora, however she might esteem him, he would appear, we imagine, another of the innumerable meaningless figures of social life.
The White Lily is his counterpart. She is unutterably passive and
subject to the will of the man. She is the passive instrument of
the will of the man, as he seeks his ideal self-ratification. And of
her the children of the next generation are born.

And over and above all this turmoil of loving and fighting
and killing and dying we have the two impressive figures of the
middle-aged men, Natty and Chingachgook. They are the dual

centre of all the whirl of life. All the tides of death and marriage and birth seem to turn about their stable polarity. Two mature, silent, expressionless men, they stand on opposite shores of being, and their love, the inexpressible conjunction between them, is the bridge over the chasm.

Each of them is alone, and, since the death of Uncas, conclusive, concluded in himself. They are isolated, final instances of their race: two strangers, from opposite ends of the earth, meeting now, beholding each other, and balanced in unspeakable conjunction—a love so profound, or so abstract, that it is unexpressed; it has no word or gesture of intercommunion. It is communicated by pure presence alone, without contact of word or touch. This perfect relationship, this last abstract love, exists between the two isolated instances of opposite race.

And this is the inception of a new race. Beyond all expression, save the pure communion of *presence,* the abstract love of these two beings consummates itself in an unimaginable coalescence, the inception of a new psyche, a new race-soul that rises out of the last and first unknowable intercommunion of two untranslatable souls. That which Chingachgook was, Natty was not; nor could he ever know. In the same way, Natty himself was the untranslatable unknown to Chingachgook. Yet across this unsuperable gulf in being there passed some strange communion between the two instances, invisible, intangible, unknowable—a quality of pure unknowable embrace. And out of this embrace arises the strange wing-covered seraph of new race-being. From this communion is procreated a new race-soul, which henceforth gestates within the living humanity of the West.

The birth in flesh continues *almost* automatically. Physical population goes on in the intervals of being, like a mechanical marking-time of the creative presence. Until, from some perfect communion between living souls or some perfect passing of a soul through the extremes of spiritual and sensual experience, both, there arises a new soul-unit, a first term of creation, a

potential anima, which henceforth informs the fit souls of the
children of men. So all new being comes into existence : first, in
the consummation within the perfected soul of a mature creature;
then in the translation of this consummated *new term* of creation
into the fresh soil of the succeeding life. It is the flower that
generates the seed in the first instance, not the seed the flower.
This is the process of creation : the rose itself appears in triumph
out of chaos, and leaves behind it the seed of its own perpetuity.
It is not in children that the new takes place : it is in the mature,
consummated men and women.

The book that follows *The Last of the Mohicans* is *Pathfinder*.
This is a beautiful and finished work, but it has not the passional
profundity of its predecessors. What it gains in finish and harmony and unified beauty it loses, perhaps, in depth of
significance. We are given Natty's abortive love story. But the
splendour lies in the revelation of the spirit of place, the pristine
beauty of the Great Lakes, the insuperable glamour of sailing
the sweet-water seas in the early days when the continent was
still virgin to white man, the lakes ringed round with forest and
Indians.

Natty is now called Pathfinder. He is a man of thirty-four
or thirty-five, a scout attached to a British outpost garrison on
one of the Great Lakes. At the beginning of the story he is found
in the woods with Chingachgook, escorting Sergeant Dunham
and the sergeant's handsome and admirable daughter, Mabel
Dunham, to the garrison on the lake. The life at the outpost is
well given, almost in the same spirit as *Pioneers*. The action and
climax of the story are removed far down the waters to an island
in the narrows. The sense of wide, glimmering expanses of shiny
water; the ship with her sails all spread, inland, footing the new,
sweet waves; the tiny and furtive Indian canoe, venturing so
fearlessly into space; the steep hills, the wild, high, virgin shores;
then the lonely log-house on the island, hidden with trees in the
narrow passage, garrisoned with outpost souls, uneasy and adven-
turous—all this makes up a magnificent American epic.

But the love of Pathfinder for Mabel Dunham leaves us cold. It is a love which proceeds from the head and the will of the hunter. He finds himself perilously departing from the season of youth into the rigidity of age. And he experiences the inevitable misgiving. He is alone, without kith or kin or place of abode. He trembles on the edge of space. And the inevitable fear seizes him —the necessity for some fixed place, some fixed condition, something which shall *determine* his existence, give him a sense of stability, even of perpetuity. He must have a sheet-anchor somewhere. And the orthodox sheet-anchor is marriage and children. Most men would rather have a home which is misery and torment than suffer from the sense of exposure to the winds of fate. They must have children to give them the sense of perpetuity. It is one of the deepest characteristics of the human nature, this craving for a sense of external support, of fixity, even if the fixity be but a chain and an imprisonment.

Pathfinder falls, as all men are inclined to fall. His love for the admirable Mabel is dictated from ulterior purpose; he has, perhaps, unknown to himself, an ulterior motive. It is not the love of a man for a woman, in sheer impulse. It is the uneasy ego providing for itself. It is a shrinking from the sheer communion in isolation, which lies ahead, the mystic consummating of the White soul with the Red. It is the inevitable denial of the extreme mystic impulse. When he is refused, Pathfinder has one horrible struggle with his *amour propre,* then he has recovered. He has got back to the right track. The passion for the young woman, which in him has been somewhat ugly—a quality of roused function and of *fear* rather than of deep desire—is gone in one breath as soon as his *amour propre* is really struck by her rejection of him. We see him writhe in humiliation of a man who has been foiled in making a bargain advantageous to himself—then we draw a free breath. It is all over.

Mabel Dunham is another Eve Effingham, or a Miss Tempest from *Pioneers,* or the Ellen of the *Prairie,* or the admirable young female of *Oak Openings.* She rejects Pathfinder quite decently, for she loves the young Jasper, the half-French master-mariner of the inland waters. He is an admirable character, who will die at his duty like Major Heyward, and who will never do anything that he should not do. Their love is just the continuing of the ordinary colonial population and purpose, without profound significance.

Cooper's last book of the Leatherstocking series, *Deerslayer,* is the loveliest and best. It has the purity of achievement of *Pathfinder* and the passional depth of the earlier works. *Deerslayer* is, indeed, one of the most beautiful and most perfect books in the world: flawless as a jewel and of gem-like concentration. From the first words we pass straight into the world of sheer creation, with so perfect a transit that we are unconscious of our translation.

The world—the pristine world of Glimmerglass—is, perhaps, lovelier than any place created in language: lovelier than Hardy or Turgenev, lovelier than the lands in ancient poetry or in Irish verse. And the spell must lie in the luminous futurity which glimmers as a plasm in all the landscape.

Deerslayer is now a young man—little more than a youth. He is illiterate, and yet by nature thoughtful, of philosophic temperament. Having been brought up all his life among the Indians and in the backwoods, he has a quality of virginity, and at the same time he has the terrible oldness, the old man's deliberateness, of his race. He is race-old; racially, he is an old man. Sensually, he is an infant. And then there is a new, suspended quality in him: the strange blankness that precedes a dawn. He is found in the woods with a great, blonde-bearded, handsome backwoodsman, called Hurry Harry. The two young men direct their steps to the smallish lake, Glimmerglass.

On this water the Hutter family is established. It is suggested that the coarse old man, Hutter, has been a buccaneer, and that he has retired beyond the reach of the law. He has been married to a woman of superior station, who had fallen into shame, and was given to this coarse scoundrel to cover her fall.

This is the element of sin which has a fascination for Cooper, and which he must introduce to justify any dark, sensual type —such as Cora in *The Last of the Mohicans*. The flower of sin is Judith Hutter, daughter of the buccaneer—dark, handsome, fearless, and passionate, a scarlet-and-black blossom. She is juxtaposed by the fair Hetty Hutter, her sister, another White Lily, of almost angelic innocence, but, alas! touched with idiocy. She is weak in her mind.

Hutter, the brutal old scoundrel, is none the less an ingenious character and a good father to the two girls—or young women, as they are now. On the remote Glimmerglass, away from all white men, he has constructed his castle and his ark, and has made a fair living by trapping the furred animals. His castle is a heavy log-house, built away in the water on piles driven deep into the bed of the lake. It is surrounded by a palisade, and is thus almost impregnable : inaccessible save to the canoes of the Indians, and secure against these when the heavy watergate is fast. His ark is a clumsy kind of boat-house, a square cabin built on a sort of raft. This can be slowly rowed from place to place, and the family transported to whatever spot is most favourable to the old trapper's business. Meanwhile the castle is locked up.

So the two young hunters find it when they arrive on Glimmerglass. The ark is moored and hidden at the mouth of a stream which enters the lake. But war has broken out, and, unrevealed, the Indians are on the shores of the lake, hostile. The story of peril and conflict begins at once in the midst of the marvellous peace and beauty of the wooded lake.

Cooper, like Hardy, has an inevitable break between fair and dark. He has only three types : the dark and sensual, the blonde and spiritual, and the mechanical, material, conventional type. In Cooper it is Cora and the White Lily and Miss Tempest. In Hardy, the division is obvious.

This division into duality, and the conflict in dualism in the self, and the inevitable ensuing tragedy, is Hardy's theme as

well as Cooper's. Hardy had no way out. He throws his appro-
bation in the spiritual scale, his passion in the sensual scale, and
the balance is so equal and opposite that the scales themselves,
the human life, can only break into death. Cooper has the same
division, the same tragedy. But he has two ways out: either
the material-social successfulness into which his admirable
Mabels betake themselves, or the strange, blank reality of Deerslayer.

Hurry Harry, the big, blustering backwoodsman, has come
to woo Judith Hutter. His deepest quality is a cowardice in the
soul: not physical cowardice, but soul cowardice. He loves
Judith, not with any intensity or real discrimination, but with
prostituting appetite. Judith is the sensual flower of woman-
hood, a dark blossom, yet a pure blossom: whereas Hurry
Harry can conceive of no blossoming. He is in the vulgar sense
a sensualist, greedy, full of appetite, but without true passion:
a bully, established on an innate sense of his own insufficiency
and weakness, giant as he is. There is a cringing, craven defi-
ciency in his soul, so he becomes an outward blusterer. All of
him is handsome except the very core, the middle of the pupil
of his eye, where there is a mongrel fear.

Judith rejects him with scorn. She is a flower of sin; for in
her race the sensual mystery is the sin mystery. But she has a
real magnificence and pathos. She loves Deerslayer, loves him
profoundly; for he is as pure a spiritual type as she is a sensual
type. If she could possess him, sensually, she would yield to him
utterly, in the rest of life.

But Deerslayer will not be sensually possessed by any woman.
He is the spiritual type. He would melt like wax in the hot,
possessive passion of Judith; she would absorb him, envelop
him utterly. He would become an inclusive part of herself,
flowing into her down the vivid current of his negative sensuality, like some sheer fire she had drunk. She would be fulfilled
and suffused with him, and he would be gone, merged, consumed into the woman, having no being of his own apart from

her. And she, possessing him utterly, as if he were enveloped in her own womb, would worship him.

This Deerslayer will never have. He sticks to his own single-ness. A race falls when men begin to worship the Great Mother, when they are envoloped within the woman, as a child in the womb. And Deerslayer represents the heroic spirit of his race passing in singleness and perfection beyond his own race, into the pure unknown of the future. For him there is no slipping back into the womb. He is young, perhaps a little priggish, but candid, even candescent: a delicate hero, frail like an autumn crocus, and as deathly, but perfect.

Hetty Hutter, the fair child of God, falls in love with Hurry Harry. This is the horror of her imbecility, which, like a scotched snake, turns back and bites itself, envenoms itself with its own poison. Wandering with her Bible into the hostile and dangerous camp of the Red men, she lisps to them, in her child-ish innocence, of the God of immaculate love, the beauty of holiness and humility. The chiefs listen and slowly, sadly smile. They see she is imbecile; and they see the fatality of her message. She is one of God's fools, the White Lily already festering at the quick.

For she falls violently and helplessly in love with Hurry Harry. This is the malignant mockery of imbecility. She herself longs to defile that which she most purely is. The child of immaculate love, she longs to prostitute herself to the mongrel embrace of Hurry Harry. This is the cunning of imbecility, which malignantly betrays that which it most purely worships. This fatal and hideous division of the self against the self, help-less, malignant, is the horror of imbecility.

The book ends sadly. Judith goes her way, to shame, as it seems. There has been killing and violence. Hetty is dead; so is old Hutter. The castle, the ark, the wonderful lake, are abandoned. Deerslayer goes his way into the woods with the young Indians.

And even he is really a slayer, as his name says. He, the last exponent of the Christian race in the West, whose God is symbolised as the Lamb, has the name of Deerslayer—Slayer of the Lamb. This is the paradox, almost as paradoxical as imbecility itself. Deerslayer remains true to the Christian tenet of humility, mercy, selflessness. A great deal of the Sermon on the Mount would apply to him. He lives for others.

And yet he can only live in presence of danger and death. He is the most perfect shot in the backwoods. He brings the highest bird dead from mid-heaven. He loves poignantly to see the deer stoop and drink at the edge of the lake. And perhaps he has an even more poignant thrill of pleasure as he sends a bullet clean to the heart of that deer—but only, of course, if it be necessary for food. He has a passion for the experiences of danger and death. No woman could give him the sheer flame of sensation he feels when the hand of a hostile Indian is laid on him as he lies in his canoe believing himself to be far out on the water.

But Deerslayer is at the end of his race-journey. In him there is no succumbing to the woman, the Magna Mater of his shame. Nor is there any break into imbecility. He has come to the end of his journey, and before him lies the leap into space, into oblivion, into death. And he will take it.

But now, at the end, he sees beyond him, in face of him, that which he has been journeying away from. Beyond him and in front of him he sees the Red Man, the sensual being which for ages he has been destroying or fleeing from. And that which he has most perfectly destroyed he now most perfectly accepts across the gulf.

This is the beauty of Deerslayer, that he knows at last that there are two ways, two mysteries—the Red Man's and his own. He must remain true to his own way, his own mystery. But now at last he acknowledges perfectly and in full the opposite mystery —the mystery of the other.

Still, there is no physical mating for him—only the passage and consummation into death. And this is why Deerslayer must live in peril and conflict, live by his death-dealing rifle. For him the physical consummation is a consummation into death. Ecstasy after ecstasy of keen peril and terrible death-dealing passes through his frame, gradually, mystically reducing him, dissolving out his animate tissue, the tissue of his oldness, into death as a pearl dissolves in wine. This is his slow, perfect, sensual consummation, his ultimate mystic consummation into death. For as an individual and as a race unit he must pass utterly into death—dissolve out.

But even this is a process of futurity. It is the flower which burns down to mould, to liberate the new seed. And the lovely American landscape is the pure landscape of futurity: not of our present factory-smoked futurity, but of the true future of the as yet unborn, or scarcely born, race of Americans.

6. EDGAR ALLAN POE

6. Edgar Allan Poe

This essay appeared in the English Review *for April, 1919. Version 2, if it existed, is lost. Version 3 in the book of 1923 is of equal length. Both versions are divided into two parts: in the first part Lawrence discusses the bad influence of "spiritual love", proving this from the example of Ligeia. In the second part he analyses some of Poe's short-stories. In the essay "The Crown", parts of which appeared in* The Signature *in 1915 (printed complete in* Reflections on the Death of a Porcupine, *1925), Lawrence had said about "Ligeia" and "The Fall of the House of Usher": "The man seeks his own sensational reduction, but he disintegrates the woman even more, in the name of love." This idea occurs again in both versions of the essay on Poe. The introductory remarks about Poe's character are concentrated from two pages in version 1 into one page in version 3. The next six pages in version 1, represented by ten pages in version 3, are concerned with the tale "Ligeia". In version 3 Lawrence repeats all quotations from Poe which he had used in version 1 and in the same order, but his comments are often quite different. While he had been content with interpretation in version 1, he inserted whole pages of love-psychology in version 3. The second part of both versions correspond sometimes almost literally.*

In version 1 Lawrence keeps more closely to the theme. In version 3 he is too much occupied with his views about

love and the Holy Ghost. Lawrence did not try, as in the
case of Cooper and Crèvecoeur, to explain Poe from the
ambiguity of his character. He is content to identify Poe
with the figures in his tales. The only improvement in ver-
sion 3 consists in some humorous parenthetical comments.

I T SEEMS a long way from Fenimore Cooper to Poe. But in
fact it is only a step. Leatherstocking is the last instance of
the integral, progressive, soul of the white man in America.
In the last conjunction between Leatherstocking and Chingachgook we see the passing out into the darkness of the interim, as
a seed falls into the dark interval of winter. What remains is the
old tree withering and seething down to the crisis of winter-
death, the great white race in America keenly disintegrating,
seething back in electric decomposition, back to that crisis where
the old soul, the old era, perishes in the denuded frame of man,
and the first throb of a new year sets in.

The process of the decomposition of the body after death is
slow and mysterious, a life process of post-mortem activity. In
the same way, the great psyche, which we have evolved through
two thousand years of effort, must die, and not only die, must
be reduced back to its elements by a long, slow process of disintegration, living disintegration.

This is the clue to Edgar Allan Poe, and to the art that
succeeds him, in America. When a tree withers, at the end of a
year, then the whole life of the year is gradually driven out until
the tissue remains elemental and almost null. Yet it is only
reduced to that crisis of perfect quiescence which *must* intervene
between life-cycle and life-cycle. Poe shows us the first vivid,
seething reduction of the psyche, the first convulsive spasm that
sets-in in the human soul, when the last impulse of creative love,

creative conjunction, is finished. It is like a tree whose fruits are perfected, writhing now in the grip of the first frost.

For men who are born at the end of a great era or epoch nothing remains but the seething reduction back to the elements; just as for a tree in autumn nothing remains but the strangling-off of the leaves and the strange decomposition and arrest of the sap. It is useless to ask for perpetual spring and summer. Poe had to lead on to that winter-crisis when the soul is, as it were, denuded of itself, reduced back to the elemental state of a naked, arrested tree in midwinter. Man must be stripped of himself. And the process is slow and bitter and beautiful, too. But the beauty has its spark in anguish; it is the strange, expiring cry, the phosphorescence of decay.

Poe is a man writhing in the mystery of his own undoing. He is a great dead soul, progressing terribly down the long process of post-mortem activity in disintegration. This is how the dead bury their dead. This is how man must bury his own dead self : in pang after pang of vital, explosive self-reduction, back to the elements. This is how the seed must fall into the ground and perish before it can bring forth new life. For Poe the process was one of perishing in the old body, the old psyche, the old self. He leads us back, through pang after pang of disintegrative sensation, back towards the end of all things, where the beginning is : just as the year begins where the year is utterly dead. It is only perfect courage which can carry us through the extremity of death, through the crisis of our own nullification, the midwinter which is the end of the end and the beginning of the beginning.

Yet Poe is hardly an artist. He is rather a supreme scientist. Art displays the movements of the pristine self, the living conjunction or communion between the self and its context. Even in tragedy self meets self in supreme conjunction, a communion of passionate or creative death. But in Poe the self is finished, already stark. It would be true to say that Poe had no soul. He lives in the post-mortem reality, a living dead. He reveals the

I

after-effects of life, the processes of organic disintegration. Arrested in himself, he cannot realise self or soul in any other human being. For him, the vital world is the sensational world. He is not sensual, he is sensational. The difference between these two is a difference between growth and decay. In Poe, sensationalism is a process of explosive disintegration, phosphorescent, electric, refracted. In him, sensation is that momentaneous state of consciousness which concurs with the sudden combustion and reduction of vital tissue. The combustion of his own most vital plasm liberates the white gleam of his sensational consciousness. Hence his addiction to alcohol and drugs, which are the common agents of reductive combustion.

It is for this reason that we would class the "tales" as science rather than art : because they reveal the workings of the great inorganic forces, disruptive within the organic psyche. The central soul or self is in arrest. And for this reason we cannot speak of the tales as stories or novels. A tale is a concatenation of scientific cause and effect. But in a story the movement depends on the sudden appearance of spontaneous emotion or gesture, causeless, arising out of the living self.

Yet the chief of Poe's tales depend upon the passion of love. The central stories, "Ligeia" and "The Fall of the House of Usher" *are* almost stories; there is in these almost a relation of soul to soul. These are the two stories where love is still recognisable as the driving force.

Love is the mysterious force which brings beings together in creative conjunction or communion. But it is also the force which brings them together in frictional disruption. Love is the great force which causes disintegration as well as new life, and corruption as well as procreation. It brings life together with life, either for production or for destruction, down to the last extremes of existence.

And in Poe, love is purely a frictional, destructive force. In him, the mystic, spontaneous self is replaced by the self-determined ego. He is a unit of will rather than a unit of being.

And the force of love acts in him almost as an electric attraction rather than as a communion between self and self. He is a lodestone, the woman is the soft metal. Each draws the other mechanically. Such attraction, increasing and intensifying in conjunction, does not set up a cycle of rest and creation. The one life draws the other life with a terrible pressure. Each presses on the other intolerably till one is bound to disappear : one or both.

The story of this process of magnetic, self-less pressure of love is told in the story of "Ligeia", and this story we may take to be the clue to Poe's own love-tragedy. The motto to the tale is a quotation from Joseph Glanville : "And the will therein lieth which dieth not. Who knoweth the mysteries of the will, with its vigour? For God is but a great will pervading all things by nature of its intentness. Man doth not yield himself to the angels, nor unto death utterly, save only through the weakness of his feeble will."

If God is a great will, then the universe is a great machine, for the will is a fixed principle. But God is not a will. God is a mystery, from which creation mysteriously proceeds. So is the self a unit of creative mystery. But the will is the greatest of all control-principles, the greatest machine-principle.

So Poe establishes himself in the will, self-less and determined. Then he enters the great process of destructive love, which in the end works out to be a battle of wills as to which can hold out longest.

The story is told in a slow method of musing abstraction, most subtle yet most accurate. Ligeia is never a free person. She is just a phenomenon with which Poe strives in ill-omened love. She is not a woman. She is just a re-agent, a re-acting force, chimerical almost. "In stature she was tall, somewhat slender, and, in her later days, even emaciated. I would in vain attempt to portray the majesty, the quiet ease, of her demeanour, or the incomprehensible lightness and elasticity of her footfall. I was never made aware of her entrance into my closed study save by the dear music of her low, sweet voice as she placed her marble hand upon my shoulder."

Perhaps it is hardly fair to quote fragments of Poe's prose, for the careful style shows up a little meretricious. It is for their scientific progress in sensation that the tales should be studied, not as art.

When Poe comes to the clue of Ligeia he leaves a blank. He paints her portrait till he comes to the very look in her eyes. This he never meets, never knows. His soul never goes out to her in that strange conjunction where self greets self, beautiful and unspeakable. He only analyses her till he comes to the un-analysable, the very quick of her.

Speaking of her eyes, he goes on: "They were, I must believe, far larger than the ordinary eyes of our own race. They were even fuller than the fullest of the gazelle eyes of the tribe of Nourjahad . . . . The hue of the orbs was the most brilliant of black, and, far over them, hung pretty lashes of great length. The brows, slightly irregular in outline, had the same tint. The *strangeness*, however, which I found in the eyes was of a nature distinct from the formation, or the colour, or the brilliancy of the features, and must, after all, be referred to the *expression*. Ah, word of no meaning! behind whose vast latitude of sound we intrench our ignorance of so much of the spiritual. The expression of the eyes of Ligeia! How for long hours have I pondered upon it! How have I, through the whole of a midsummer night, struggled to fathom it! What was it—that something more profound than the well of Democritus—which lay far within the pupils of my beloved? What *was* it? I was possessed with a passion to discover . . . . "

This is the same old effort, to analyse and possess and know the secret of the soul, the living self. It is the supreme lust of possession. But the soul can never be analysed any more than living protoplasm can be analysed. The moment we start we have dead protoplasm. We may, with our own soul, behold and know the soul of the other. Look can meet look in pure recognition and communion. And this communion can be conveyed again in speech. But ever didactically. It is a motion of the whole soul in its entirety, whereas scientific knowledge is never more than a post-mortem residuum.

Of a piece with this craving to analyse the being of the beloved, to be scientifically master of the mystery of the other being, is the whole passion for knowledge which fills these two. The learning of Ligeia was immense, we are told, such as has never before been known in woman. It shows the unspeakable craving of those whose souls are arrested, to gain mastery over the world through knowledge. This is one of the temptations of Christ, when Satan offers him the world. To possess the world in deliberate, scientific knowledge, this is one of the cravings of the unrebuked human heart. It cannot be done. We can only know in full when we *are* in full. In the fulness of our own being we are at one with the mystery; in the deepest and most beautiful sense we know it. But as creatures of exact knowledge and deliberate will we exist in the world of post-mortem reality. Life is beyond us for ever, even as the strangeness of the eyes of Ligeia was beyond the man's probing and fathoming. He seemed so often *on the verge,* thrillingly, awfully. But that was all.

He decided that the clue to the strangeness was in the mystery of will. "And the will therein lieth, which dieth not . . . . " Ligeia had a "gigantic volition." . . . "An *intensity* in thought, action, or speech was possibly, in her, a result, or at least an index, of that gigantic volition which, during our long intercourse, failed to give other and more immediate evidence of its existence. Of all the women whom I have ever known, she, the outwardly calm, the ever-placid Ligeia, was the most violently a prey to the tumultuous vultures of stern passion. And of such passion I could form no estimate, save by the miraculous expansion of those eyes which at once so delighted and appalled me—by the almost magical melody, modulation, distinctness, and placidity of her very low voice—and by the fierce energy (rendered doubly effective by contrast with her manner of utterance) of the wild words which she habitually uttered."

Having recognised the clue to Ligeia in her gigantic volition, there must inevitably ensue the struggle of wills. But Ligeia, true to the great traditions, remains passive or submissive, womanly, to the man; he is the active agent, she the recipient. To this her gigantic volition fixes her also. Hence, moreover, her conquest of the stern vultures of passion.

The stress of inordinate love goes on, the consuming into a oneness. And it is Ligeia who is consumed. The process of such love is inevitable consumption. In creative love there is a recognition of each soul by the other, a mutual kiss, and then the balance in equilibrium which is the peace and beauty of love. But in Poe and Ligeia such balance is impossible. Each is possessed with the craving to search out and *know* the other, entirely; to know, to have, to possess, to be identified with the other. They are two units madly urging together towards a fusion which must break down the very being of one or both of them. Ligeia craves to be identified with her husband, he with her. And not until too late does she realise that such identification is death.

"That she loved me I should not have doubted; and I might have been easily aware that, in a bosom such as hers, love would have reigned no ordinary passion. But in death only was I fully impressed with the strength of her affection. For long hours, detaining my hand, would she pour out before me the overflowing of a heart whose more than passionate devotion amounted to idolatry. How had I deserved to be blessed by such confessions? How had I deserved to be cursed with the removal of my beloved in the hour of her making them? But upon this subject I cannot bear to dilate. Let me say only that in Ligeia's more than womanly abandonment to a love, alas! all unmerited, all unworthily bestowed, I at length recognised the principle of her longing with so wildly earnest a desire for the life which was now fleeing so rapidly away. It is this wild longing—it is this vehement desire for life—*but* for life—that I have no power to portray—no utterance capable of expressing."

Thus Ligeia is defeated in her terrible desire to be identified with her husband, and live, just as he is defeated in his desire, living, to grasp the clue of her in his own hand.

On the last day of her existence Ligeia dictates to her husband the memorable poem, which concludes : —

> "Out—out are all the lights—out all!
>   And over each quivering form
> The curtain, a funeral pall,
>   Comes down with the rush of a storm,
> And the angels, all pallid and wan,
>   Uprising, unveiling, affirm
> That the play is the tragedy 'Man,'
>   And its hero the Conqueror Worm."

" 'O God!' half shrieked Ligeia, leaping to her feet and extending her arms aloft with a spasmodic movement, as I made an end of these lines, 'O God! O Divine Father!—shall these things be undeviatingly so? Shall this conqueror be not once conquered? Are we not part and parcel in Thee? Who—who knoweth the mysteries of the will with its vigour? Man doth not yield him to the angels, *nor unto death utterly,* save only through the weakness of his feeble will.' "

So Ligeia dies. Herself a creature of will and finished consciousness, she sees everything collapse before the devouring worm. But shall her will collapse?

The husband comes to ancient England, takes a gloomy, grand old abbey, puts it into some sort of repair, and, converting it into a dwelling, furnishes it with exotic, mysterious splendour. As an artist Poe is unfailingly in bad taste—always in bad taste. He seeks a sensation from every phrase or object, and the effect is vulgar.

In the story the man marries the fair-haired, blue-eyed Lady Rowena Trevanion, of Tremaine.

"In halls such as these—in a bridal chamber such as this—I passed, with the Lady of Tremaine, the unhallowed hours of the first month of our marriage—passed them with but little disquietude. That my wife dreaded the fierce moodiness of my

temper—that she shunned me and loved me but little—I could
not help perceiving; but it gave me rather pleasure than otherwise. I loathed her with a hatred belonging rather to a demon
than to a man. My memory flew back (Oh, with what intensity
of regret!) to Ligeia, the beloved, the august, the entombed. I
revelled in recollections of her purity," etc.

The love which had been a wild craving for identification with
Ligeia, a love inevitably deadly and consuming, now in the man
has become definitely destructive, devouring, subtly murderous.
He will slowly and subtly consume the life of the fated Rowena.
It is his vampire lust.

In the second month of the marriage the Lady Rowena fell
ill. It is Ligeia whose presence hangs destructive over her; it
is the ghostly Ligeia who pours poison into Rowena's cup. It is
Ligeia, active and unsatisfied within the soul of her husband,
who destroys the other woman. The will of Ligeia is not yet
broken. She wants to live. And she wants to live to finish her
process, to satisfy her unbearable craving to be identified with
the man. All the time, in his marriage with Rowena, the husband
is only using the new bride as a substitute for Ligeia. As a substitute for Ligeia he possesses her. And at last from the corpse
of Rowena Ligeia rises fulfilled. When the corpse opens its eyes,
at last the two are identified, Ligeia with the man she so loved.
Henceforth the two are one, and neither exists. They are consumed into an inscrutable oneness.

"Eleanora", the next story, is a fantasy revealing the sensational delights of the man in his early marriage with the young
and tender bride. They dwelt, he, his cousin and her mother, in
the sequestered Valley of Many-coloured Grass, the valley of
prismatic sensation, where everything seems spectrum-coloured.
They looked down at their own images in the River of Silence,
and drew the God Eros from that wave. This is a description
of the life of introspection and of the love which is begotten by
the self in the self, the self-made love. The trees are like serpents
worshipping the sun. That is, they represent the phallic passion

in its poisonous or destructive activity. The symbolism of Poe's parables is easy, too easy, almost mechanical.

In "Berenice" the man must go down to the sepulchre of his beloved and take her thirty-two small white teeth, which he carries in a box with him. It is repulsive and gloating. The teeth are the instruments of biting, of resistance, of antagonism. They often become symbols of opposition, little instruments or entities of crushing and destroying. Hence the dragon's teeth in the myth. Hence the man in "Berenice" must take possession of the irreducible part of his mistress. "Toutes ses dents étaient des idées," he says. Then they are little fixed ideas of mordant hate, of which he possesses himself.

The other great story somewhat connected with this group is "The Fall of the House of Usher". Here the love is between brother and sister. When the self is broken, and the mystery of the recognition of *otherness* fails, then the longing for identification with the beloved becomes a lust. And it is this longing for identification, utter merging, which is at the base of the incest problem. In psychoanalysis almost every trouble in the psyche is traced to an incest-desire. But this will not do. The incest-desire is only one of the manifestations of the self-less desire for merging. It is obvious that this desire for merging, or unification, or identification of the man with the woman, or the woman with the man, finds its gratification most readily in the merging of those things which are already near—mother with son, brother with sister, father with daughter. But it is not enough to say, as Jung does, that all life is a matter of lapsing towards, or struggling away from, mother-incest. It is necessary to see what lies at the back of this helpless craving for utter merging or identification with a beloved.

The motto to "The Fall of the House of Usher" is a couple of lines from De Béranger.

"Son coeur est un luth suspendu;
Sitôt qu'on le touche il résonne."

We have all the trappings of Poe's rather overdone vulgar
fantasy. "I reined my horse to the precipitous brink of a black
and lurid tarn that lay in unruffled lustre by the dwelling, and
gazed down—but with a shudder even more thrilling than before
—upon the remodelled and inverted images of the grey sedge,
and the ghastly tree-stems, and the vacant and eye-like windows."
The House of Usher, both dwelling and family, was very old.
Minute fungi overspread the exterior of the house, hanging in
festoons from the eaves. Gothic archways, a valet of stealthy
step, sombre tapestries, ebon black floors, a profusion of tattered
and antique furniture, feeble gleams of encrimsoned light
through latticed panes, and over all "an air of stern, deep, irre-
deemable gloom"—this makes up the interior.

The inmates of the house, Roderick and Madeline Usher, are
the last remnants of their incomparably ancient and decayed race.
Roderick has the same large, luminous eye, the same slightly
arched nose of delicate Hebrew model, as characterised Ligeia.
He is ill with the nervous malady of his family. It is he whose
nerves are so strung that they vibrate to the unknown quiverings
of the ether. He, too, has lost his self, his living soul, and become
a sensitised instrument of the external influences; his nerves are
verily like an aeolian harp which must vibrate. He lives in "some
struggle with the grim phantasm, Fear," for he is only the physical, post-mortem reality of a living being.

It is a question how much, once the rich centrality of the self
is broken, the instrumental consciousness of man can register.
When man becomes self-less, wafting instrumental like a harp in
an open window, how much can his elemental consciousness express? It is probable that even the blood as it runs has its own
sympathies and responses to the material world, quite apart from
seeing. And the nerves we know vibrate all the while to unseen
presences, unseen forces. So Roderick Usher quivers on the edge
of dissolution.

It is this mechanical consciousness which gives "the fervid
facility of his impromptus." It is the same thing that gives Poe

his extraordinary facility in versification. The absence of real central or impulsive being in himself leaves him inordinately mechanically sensitive to sounds and effects, associations of sounds, association of rhyme, for example—mechanical, facile, having no root in any passion. It is all a secondary, meretricious process.   So we get Roderick Usher's poem, "The Haunted Palace," with its swift yet mechanical subtleties of rhyme and rhythm, its vulgarity of epithet. It is all a sort of dream-process, where the association between parts is mechanical, accidental as far as passional meaning goes.

Usher thought that all vegetable things had sentience. Surely all material things have a form of sentience, even the inorganic : surely they all exist in some subtle and complicated tension of vibration which makes them sensitive to external influence and causes them to have an influence on other external objects, irrespective of contact. It is of this vibrational or inorganic consciousness that Poe is master : the sleep-consciousness. Thus Roderick Usher was convinced that his whole surroundings, the stones of the house, the fungi, the water in the tarn, the very reflected image of the whole, was woven into a physical oneness with the family, condensed, as it were, into one atmosphere—the special atmosphere in which alone the Ushers could live. And it was this atmosphere which had moulded the destinies of his family.

In the human realm, Roderick had one connection : his sister Madeline. She, too, was dying of a mysterious disorder, nervous, cataleptic. The brother and sister loved each other passionately and exclusively. They were twins, almost identical in looks. It was the same absorbing love between them, where human creatures are absorbed away from themselves, into a unification in death. So Madeline was gradually absorbed into her brother; the one life absorbed the other in a long anguish of love.

Madeline died and was carried down by her brother into the deep vaults of the house. But she was not dead. Her brother roamed about in incipient madness—a madness of unspeakable terror and guilt. After eight days they were suddenly startled

by a clash of metal, then a distinct, hollow, metallic, and clangor-
ous, yet apparently muffled, reverberation. Then Roderick Usher,
gibbering, began to express himself : *"We have put her living
into the tomb* ! Said I not that my senses were acute? *I now*
tell you that I heard her first feeble movements in the hollow
coffin. I heard them—many, many days ago—yet I dared not—
I dared not speak."

It is again the old theme of "each man kills the thing he
loves." He knew his love had killed her. He knew she died at
last, like Ligeia, unwilling and unappeased. So, she rose again
upon him. "But then without those doors there *did* stand the
lofty and enshrouded figure of the Lady Madeline of Usher.
There was blood upon her white robes, and the evidence of some
bitter struggle upon every portion of her emaciated frame. For a
moment she remained trembling and reeling to and fro upon
the threshold, then, with a low moaning cry, fell heavily inward
upon the person of her brother, and in her violent and now final
death-agonies bore him to the floor a corpse, and a victim to
the terrors he had anticipated."

It is lurid and melodramatic, but it really is a symbolic truth
of what happens in the last stages of this inordinate love, which
can recognise none of the sacred mystery of *otherness,* but must
unite into unspeakable identification, oneness in death. Brother
and sister go down together, made one in the unspeakable mystery
of death. It is the world-long incest problem, arising inevitably
when man, through insistence of his will in one passion or
aspiration, breaks the polarity of himself.

The best tales all have the same burden. Hate is as inordinate
as love, and as slowly consuming, as secret, as underground, as
subtle. All this underground vault business in Poe only symbolises
that which takes place *beneath* the consciousness. On top, all is
fair-spoken. Beneath, there is the awful murderous extremity of
burying alive. Fortunato, in "The Cask of Amontillado," is
buried alive out of perfect hatred, as the Lady Madeline of
Usher is buried alive out of love. The lust of hate is the inordinate

desire to consume and unspeakably possess the soul of the hated one, just as the lust of love is the desire to possess, or to be possessed by, the beloved, utterly. But in either case the result is the dissolution of both souls, each losing itself in transgressing its own bounds.

The lust of Montresor is to devour utterly the soul of Fortunato. It would be no use killing him outright. If a man is killed outright his soul remains integral, free to return into the bosom of some beloved, where it can enact itself. In walling-up his enemy in the vault, Montresor seeks to bring about the indescribable capitulation of the man's soul, so that he, the victor, can possess himself of the very being of the vanquished. Perhaps this can actually be done. Perhaps, in the attempt, the victor breaks the bounds of his own identity, and collapses into nothingness, or into the infinite.

What holds good for inordinate hate holds good for inordinate love. The motto, *Nemo me impune lacessit,* might just as well be *Nemo me impune amat.*

In "William Wilson" we are given a rather unsubtle account of the attempt of a man to kill his own soul. William Wilson, the mechanical, lustful ego succeeds in killing William Wilson, the living self. The lustful ego lives on, gradually reducing itself towards the dust of the infinite.

In the "Murders in the Rue Morgue" and "The Gold Bug" we have those mechanical tales where the interest lies in following out a subtle chain of cause and effect. The interest is scientific rather than artistic, a study in psychologic reactions.

The fascination of murder itself is curious. Murder is not just killing. Murder is a lust utterly to possess the soul of the murdered—hence the stealth and the frequent morbid dismemberment of the corpse, the attempt to get at the very quick of the murdered being, to find the quick and to possess it. It is curious that the two men fascinated by the art of murder, though in different ways, should have been De Quincey and Poe, men so different in ways of life, yet perhaps not so widely different in nature. In each of them is traceable that strange lust for extreme love and extreme hate, possession by mystic violence of the other soul, or violent deathly surrender of the soul in the self.

Inquisition and torture are akin to murder: the same lust. It is a combat between conqueror and victim for the possession of the soul after death. A soul can be conquered only when it is forced to abdicate from its own being. A heretic may be burned at the stake, his ashes scattered on the winds as a symbol that his soul is now broken by torture and dissolved. And yet, as often as not, the brave heretic dies integral in being; his soul re-enters into the bosom of the living, indestructible.

So the mystery goes on. La Bruyère says that all our human unhappiness *vient de ne pouvoir être seuls.* As long as man lives he will be subject to the incalculable influence of love or of hate, which is only inverted love. The necessity to love is probably the source of all our unhappiness; but since it is the source of everything it is foolish to particularise. Probably even gravitation is only one of the lowest manifestations of the mystic force of love. But the triumph of love, which is the triumph of life and creation, does not lie in merging, mingling, in absolute identification of the lover with the beloved. It lies in the communion of beings, who, in the very perfection of communion, recognise and allow the mutual otherness. There is no desire to transgress the bounds of being. Each self remains utterly itself—becomes, indeed, most burningly and transcendently itself in the uttermost embrace or communion with the other. One self may yield honourable precedence to the other, may pledge itself to undying service, and in so doing become fulfilled in its own nature. For the highest achievement of some souls lies in perfect service. But the giving and the taking of service does not obliterate the mystery of otherness, the being-in-singleness, either in master or servant. On the other hand, slavery is an avowed obliteration of the singleness of being.

7. NATHANIEL HAWTHORNE I

7. Nathaniel Hawthorne I

The essay below is divided into two parts. Part one appeared in the English Review *for May, 1919. A combined typescript and manuscript of this essay with the heading "Nathaniel Hawthorne" is extant. On the first page there is the note "English Review," and the first and last pages bear the name of the printer for the* English Review, *"Richard Clay, April 4th, 1919." Lawrence probably received proofs of the first part of this essay, but the text appeared with negligible changes.*

The manuscript-typescript extends over 28 pages, the essay in the English Review *corresponding with the first 16½ pages of the manuscript. The 28 page manuscript was much longer than the other essays about American literature, and Austin Harrison, the editor of the* English Review, *cut out the last 11½ pages which have never been published. The first part of the essay below corresponds with the portion which appeared in the* English Review, *the second part with the rest of the manuscript. Both parts together represent the complete essay on Hawthorne in its first version.*

In length this essay is almost equal to the two essays on Hawthorne in the book of 1923 (version 3). But content and wording differ considerably. Lawrence asserts that the Eve-myth symbolises the birth of the upper mind. This leads to an outbreak against "knowing" in version 3. According to Lawrence, the sin of Adam and Eve was that they observed their instincts consciously: "No wonder the Lord kicked

133

them out of the Garden. Dirty hypocrites." The half-page on this theme in version 1 becomes four pages in version 3 where Lawrence replaces Adam and Eve by Americans in general doing everything from their nerves instead of doing it from their blood. Jesus was the first who shed his blood to become "mind-conscious". "Shed the blood, and you become mind-conscious. Eat the body and drink the blood, self-cannibalizing, and you become extremely conscious, like Americans and some Hindus." Such hysterical outbreaks generally run parallel with personal confessions in Lawrence's writings: "My father hated books, hated the sight of anyone reading or writing.

"My mother hated the thought that any of her sons should be condemned to manual labour. Her sons must have something higher than that.

"She won. But she died first."

In version 1 Lawrence compares Hester to the Blessed Virgin Mary. In version 3 Mary is mentioned in connection with the letter "A" on Hester's breast. Some of the meanings of the scarlet letter, which Lawrence mentions, are taken from Stuart P. Sherman's Americans *(1922), a book which Lawrence had reviewed* (Dial, *May, 1923).*

Version 1 is, as usual, objective, logical and to the point. Lawrence uses his method of distinguishing between the author's conscious and unconscious intentions convincingly. Version 3, in contrast, is Lawrence at his poorest—nervous, excited, noisy, once more grinding his axe against America.

I

BEFORE BEGINNING the study of Hawthorne it is necessary again to consider the bases of the human consciousness.

Man has two distinct fields of consciousness, two living minds. First, there is the physical or primary mind, a perfect and spontaneous consciousness centralising in the great plexuses and ganglia of the nervous system and in the hind brain. Secondly, there is the ideal consciousness, which we recognise as mental, located in the brain. We are mistaken when we conceive of the nerves and the blood as mere vehicles or media of the mental consciousness. The blood itself is self-conscious. And the great nerve-centres of the body are centres of perfect primary cognition.

What we call "instinct" in creatures such as bees, or ants, or whales, or foxes, or larks, is the sure and perfect working of the primary mind in these creatures. All the tissue of the body is all the time aware. The blood is awake : the whole blood-system of the body is a great field of primal consciousness. But in the nervous system the primary consciousness is localised and specialised. Each great nerve-centre has its own peculiar consciousness, its own peculiar mind, its own primary percepts and concepts, its own spontaneous desires and ideas. The singing of a lark is direct expression from the whole primary or dynamic mind. When a bee leaves its hive and circles round to sense the locality, it is attending with the primary mind to the surrounding objects, establishing a primary *rapport* between its own very tissue and the tissue of the adjacent objects. A process of rapid *physical* thought takes place, an act of the primary, not the cerebral mind : the sensational, not the ideal consciousness. That is, there is a rapid sensual association within the body of the bee, equivalent to the process of reasoning; sensation develops sensation and sums up to a conclusion, a completed sum of sensations which we may call a sensual concept.

All thought and mental cognition is but a sublimation of the great primary, sensual knowledge located in the tissues of the physique and centred in the nervous ganglia. It is like the flowering of those water-weeds which live entirely below the surface, and only push their blossoms at one particular moment into the light and the air above water.

The process of sensual reasoning, the processes of the primary mind, go on all the time, even when the upper or cerebral mind is asleep. During sleep the first-mind thinks and makes its momentous conclusions—sensual and sensational conclusions, which are the *real* bases of all our actions, no matter what our mental ideas and opinions and decisions may be.

In the highest art, the primary mind expresses itself direct, in direct dynamic pulsating communication. But this expression is harmonious with the outer or cerebral consciousness.

At the beginning, however, of a civilisation, the upper mind cannot adequately deal with the tremendous conclusions of the physical or primary mind. The great dynamic concepts can find no reasonable utterance. Then we have myths; after myths, legends; after legends, romance; and after romance, pure art, where the sensual mind is harmonious with the ideal mind.

Myth, legend, romance, drama, these forms of utterance merge off into one another by imperceptible degrees. The primary or sensual mind of man expresses itself most profoundly in myth. At the same time, myth is most repugnant to reason. Myth is the huge, concrete expression wherein the dynamic psyche utters its first great passional concepts of the genesis of the human cosmos, the inception of the human species. Following myth comes legend, giving utterance to the genesis of a race psyche. Beyond legend is romance, where the individual psyche struggles into dynamic being, still impersonal. When we enter the personal plane we enter the field of art proper—dramatic, lyric, emotional.

Myth, legend, romance, these are all utterances in defiance of reason. They are none the less most profoundly, passionally reasonable. The field of the primary sensual mind is so immense that the attempt to reduce myth or legend to one consistent rational interpretation is futile. It is worse than useless to bring down every great primary myth to cosmic terms, sun myth, thunder myth, and so on. It is still more useless to see the phallic, procreative, and parturitive meaning only. Myth is the utterance of the primary self-knowledge of the dynamic psyche of man. The dynamic or primary or sensual psyche utters, in terms more or less monstrous, its own fundamental knowledge of its own genesis. Owing to the great coordination of everything in the universe, the genesis of the psyche of the human species is at the same time the genesis of the sun, the moon, and the thunderbolt : indeed, the genesis of everything. So that, in one sense, a great primary myth means everything, and all our interpretations are only particularisations from a colossal root-whole.

For the clue or quick of the universe lies in the creative mystery. And the clue or active quick of the creative mystery lies in the human psyche. Hence, paradoxical as it may seem, if we conceive of God we must conceive of Him in personal terms. But the test of wisdom lies in abstaining from the attempt to make a presentation of God. We must start from what seems to be nullity, the unknowable, the inexpressible, the creative mystery wherein we are established. We cannot become more exact than this without introducing falsehood. But we know that the quick of the creative mystery lies, for us at least, in the human soul, the human psyche, the human anima. Hence the only form of worship is *to be* : each man to be his own self, that which has issue from the mystery and takes form as an inscrutable self. In the soul, the self, the very man unto himself, the god-mystery is active and evident first and foremost.

The progression of man's conscious understanding is dual. The primary or sensual mind begins with the huge, profound, passional generalities of myth, and proceeds through legend and romance to pure, personal art. Parallel to this, the reasoning mind starts from the great cosmic theories of the ancient world, and proceeds, by a progress in particularisation, to establish great laws, physical and ethical, then to discover the exact and minute scientific relation between particular bodies or substances and the great laws, and finally to gain an inkling of the connection be-

tween scientific reality and creative, personal reality. The progress
is a progression towards harmony between the two halves of the
psyche. The approach is towards a pure unison between religion
and science. The monstrosity of myth is most repugnant to
reason. In the same way, the monstrosity of scientific cosmogony
and cosmogenesis is most repugnant to the passional psyche. But
the progress of religion is to remove all that is repugnant to
reason, and the progress of science is towards a reconciliation with
the personal, passional soul. The last steps remain to be taken,
and then man can really begin to be free, really to live his whole
self, his whole life, in fulness.

The nearest approach of the passional psyche to scientific or
rational reality is in art. In art we have perfect dynamic utterance. The nearest approach of the rational psyche towards passional truth is in philosophy. Philosophy is the perfect static
utterance. When the unison between art and philosophy is complete, then knowledge will be in full, not always in part, as it is
now.

Hawthorne is a philosopher as well as an artist. He attempts
to understand as deeply as he feels. He does not succeed. There
is a discrepancy between his conscious understanding and his
passional understanding. To cover this discrepancy he calls his
work romance. Now, it is evident that Hawthorne is not a
romanticist in the strict sense. Romance is the utterance of the
primary individual mind, in defiance of reason. The two forms
of romance are heroic and idyllic, Arthurian romance and "As
You Like It." In heroic romance magic is substituted to symbolise the powers of the psyche. A magic weapon such as the
sword Excalibur symbolises some primal, dynamic power of the
heroic psyche over the ordinary psyche. To give the sword a
necessary phallic reference, as some of the popular symbologists
do to-day, is false and arbitrary. In idyllic romance, all external
conditions are made subservient to the will of the human psyche :
everything occurs as you like it.

It is evident that Hawthorne belongs to neither of these categories. Yet he is not, at least in his greatest work, a realist, nor even a novelist. He is not working in the *personal* plane. His great characters, Hester Prynne, Dimmesdale, Chillingworth, in *The Scarlet Letter,* are not presented spontaneously as persons. They are abstracted beyond the personal plane. They are not even types. They represent the human soul in its passional abstraction, as it exists in its first abstract nakedness, as a great dynamic mystery, nakedly ethical, nakedly procreative. *The Scarlet Letter* is, in truth, a legendary myth. It contains the abstract of the fall of the white race. It is the inverse of the Eve myth, in the Book of Genesis. It contains the passional or primary account of the collapse of the human psyche in the white race. Hawthorne tries to keep up a parallel rational exposition of this fall. But here he fails.

The Eve myth symbolises the birth of the upper mind, the upper consciousness which, the moment it becomes self-conscious, rebels against the physical being, and is sensible of shame because of its own helpless connection with the passional body. The serpent is the symbol of division in the psyche, the knife, the dagger, the ray of burning or malevolent light, the undulating line of the waters of the flood, the divider, which sets spiritual being against sensual being, man against woman, sex against sex, the introducer of the hostile duality into the human psyche. But the era of Christianity is the era in which the rational or upper or spiritual mind has risen superior to the primary or sensual being. It is the era, when, in the white race particularly, spirit has triumphed over flesh, mind over matter. The great triumph of the one half over the other half is effected.

And then comes the fall. *The Scarlet Letter* contains a precise and accurate account of this Fall, dynamically logical in its exactitude. The book scarcely belongs to the realm of art. It belongs to the realm of primary or passional ethics and ethnology, the realm of the myth and the morality play.

It is the worship, upon the scaffold, of the Mother of the Maculate Conception. It is a worship of Astarte, the Magna

Mater, the great mother of physical fecundity. Only it has this
strange difference : that the great mother is exposed on the
scaffold and worshipped as an object of *sin*. This introduces the
peculiar voluptuous complication.

In Christian mythology, Mary enthroned is the Mother of the
Sacred Heart, pierced with seven wounds. This has many meanings. But the most obvious is that here we have the mother of
the sensual and primary body pierced in her seven sensual or
physical connections, pierced, destroyed, the spiritual remainder
deified. This is Mary of the Sacred Heart, with the strange
symbol on her breast of the scarlet, bleeding heart and the sword
rays. It is the sensual body pierced in its seven profound sense-
activities, pierced through the seven gates of the body, in the
seven great passional centres.

Hester Prynne, on the scaffold, has a scarlet symbol on her
breast. It burns and flashes with rays, sword-rays or sun-rays
of golden thread. Here is Mary of the Bleeding Heart standing
enthroned in the dark, puritanical New England.

But the scarlet letter is not a bleeding heart. It is the burning
symbol of the sensual mystery, the mystery of the sensual, primal
psyche, angry now, in its hostility flashing like a conflagration.
This is the great A, the Alpha of Adam, now the Alpha of
America. It flashes with the great revenge of the serpent, as the
primary or sensual psyche, which was perfectly subjected,
humiliated, turns under the heel like the servant of wrath, and
bites back. Woman is wasted into abstraction, as Ligeia was wasted, gone in a mental activity and a spiritual purity. Then behold,
suddenly, she turns, and we have the Scarlet Woman, the Magna
Mater, with her fiery insignia of the sensual self in revolt, presented for worship upon the scaffold, worship in contumely and
blame. The revelation is subtle. The almost insane malice of the
situation, the malicious duplicity which exalts in shame that
which it worships in lust, is conveyed by Hawthorne acutely
enough.

"Had there been a Papist among the crowd of Puritans, he

might have seen in this beautiful woman, so picturesque in her attire and mien, and with the infant at her bosom, an object to remind him of the image of Divine Maternity, which so many illustrious painters have vied with one another to represent; something which should remind him, indeed, but only by contrast, of that sacred image of sinless motherhood, whose infant was to redeem the world. Here, there was a taint of deepest sin in the most sacred quality of human life, working such effect that the world was only the darker for this woman's beauty, and the more lost for the infant that she had borne."

Hawthorne is a master of symbology, and, further, a master of serpent subtility. His pious blame is subtle commendation to himself. He longs, like the serpent, for revenge, even upon himself. He is divided against himself. Openly he stands for the upper, spiritual, reasoned being. Secretly he lusts in the sensual imagination, in bruising the heel of this spiritual self and laming it for ever. All his reasoned exposition is a pious fraud, kept up to satisfy his own upper or outward self.

Hester Prynne is the successor of Ligeia. In Ligeia the primary or sensual self was utterly submitted, and in its submission it was tortured and ground to death by the triumphant husband, the spirit-worshipping or mind-worshipping male; Ligeia herself worshipped the conscious mind. She herself submitted the body of her own primary being to deliberate disintegration, attempting to sublimate it altogether into mind-stuff. Then she shrieks because she must die, leaving the destructive mental being in the man triumphant. The stern vultures of passion in Ligeia are the angry heavings of revolt, in her primary or sensual soul, against its prostitution to the upper or spiritual or mental ego. But she suppresses this revolt with all her will. She *keeps* the primary, sensual psyche utterly prostitute till it is worn away, devoured, by the spiritual psyche. Then she shrieks in a frenzy of despair, and deliberately sets herself to persist in the after-death, malevolently destructive still of the thing she hates so much, the very first reality of being, the sensual or primary self

in woman. Ligeia's after death malevolence destroys the body
and life of Rowena, and then spends itself. Ligeia is spent and
gone. And now, as from the tomb, rises the murdered body of
the woman, the murdered first-principle of being: just as the
Lady Madeline of Usher rose from the tomb and brought down
her vampire brother Roderick—Roderick, who loved her to such
a deathly extremity, in spiritual or mental love: and who destroyed her.

Hester Prynne is the great nemesis of woman. She, too, is born
utterly subject. She, too, loves the ultra-spiritual being, Arthur
Dimmesdale, the young, saintly, almost miraculous preacher.
Arthur Dimmesdale is the very asphodel of spiritual perfection,
refined till he is almost translucent and glassy. He is far more
refined than Angel Clare in *Tess,* perfect as a moonstone emit-
ting the white and sacred beam of the spirit and the holy mind.
He is so spiritual and inspired that he becomes impossible; he
is a pure lambent flame sucking up and consuming the very life-
stuff of mankind. But particularly he sucks up the life-stuff of the
woman who loves him. Without this nourishment from her consumed, prostituted being his flame would fade out, for he belongs
no more to earth. Unless the woman will be holy prostitute to
him in sacred spiritual love, given to him as wax is given to the
candle-flame, to be consumed into light, he is done, for his own
substance is spent. Therefore, the woman gives herself in sacred,
virgin prostitution, and is consumed. It is what happens all the
time with spiritual clergymen and their female devotees. The
true being in woman is prostitute to the ghastly spiritual effulgence.

But not for ever. The hour for revenge comes. Subtly, with
extreme serpent subtlety, having been held down and wasted
long enough into the spiritual effulgence of Arthur Dimmesdale,
the woman in Hester Prynne recoils, turns in rich, lurid revenge.
She seduces the saint, and the saint is seduced. Mystically he is
killed, as he must be killed. The child born of him is a little
serpent, a poison blossom.

Now at last the spiritual era is at an end, but only at the beginning of the end. This is the disaster of disasters, when the woman suddenly recoils from her union with man, and strikes back at him like a serpent, secretly, from an infuriated, tormented primary soul. Through two thousand years man, the leader, has been slaying the dragon of the primary self, the sensual psyche, and the woman has been with him. But the hour of triumph is the hour of the end. In the hour of triumph the slain rises up in revenge and the destroyer is destroyed.

When Hester Prynne seduces Arthur Dimmesdale we have the beginning of the end: but not the end by a long way. In the creative union between man and woman, man must take the lead, though woman gives the first suggestion. When man, holding woman still in the bond of union, leads into prostitution and death, as man has led all humanity into the nacreous, sanctified vampiredom of pure spiritual or intellectual being, then the bond of union breaks between the sexes. Then the deep, subconscious, primary self in woman recoils in antagonism. But it is a recoil of long, secret destructiveness, nihilism, subtle, serpentlike, outwardly submissive. Man must either lead or be destroyed. Woman cannot lead. She can only be at one with man in the creative union, whilst he leads; or, failing this, she can destroy by undermining, by striking the heel of the male. The woman isolate or in advance of man is always mystically destructive. When man falls before woman, and she must become alone and self-responsible, she goes on and on in destruction, till all is death or till man can rise anew and take his place. When the woman takes the responsible place in the conjunction between man and woman, then the mystic creative union is reversed; it becomes a union of negation and undoing. Whatever the outward profession and action may be, when woman is the leader or dominant in the sex relationship, and in the human progress, then the activity of mankind is an activity of disintegration and undoing. And it is woman who gives the first suggestion, starts the first impulse of the undoing.

Man falls before woman because he has led on into a ghastly bog of falsehood. He then clings to the woman like a child, and she becomes the responsible party. But woe betide her; her triumph is a bitter one. Every stride she takes is a stride of further death. With all her passion she cherishes and nourishes her man, and yet her cherishing and nourishing only destroy him more. With all her soul she tries to save life. And the greatness of her effort only further saps the root of life, weakens the soul of man, destroys him, and drives him into an insanity of self-destruction. Such is the Age of Woman. Such it always has been, and always will be. It is the age of cowardly, false, destructive men. It is the age of fatal, suffocating love, love which kills like a Laocoon snake.

Woman cannot take the creative lead; she can only give the creative radiation. From her, as from Eve, must come the first suggestion or impulse of new being. When, however, she recoils from man's leadership and takes matters in her own hands, she recoils in mystic destruction. She cannot make a beginning, go on ahead. She can only prompt man, not knowing herself to what she prompts him. When he will not be prompted, woman becomes a devastating influence. She has no way of her own. She can only follow in exaggeration the old creed. This is evident in Hester Prynne. Hester Prynne has struck the blow that will kill for ever the triumphant spiritual being in man. And yet, in her living, she can only exaggerate the old life of self-abnegation and spiritual purity. She becomes a sister of mercy.

This is the puzzling anomaly of the present day. In the old days, when woman turned in her terrible recoil, she became Astarte, the Syria Dea, Aphrodite Syriaca, the Scarlet Woman. To-day, in her recoil the Scarlet Woman becomes a Sister of Mercy. She cannot help it. She must, in her upper mind, keep true to the old faith that man has given her, the belief in love and self-sacrifice. To this she is, as it were, hypnotized or condemned. Yet, all the while, her potent self is utterly at outs with this faith and this sacrifice. Darkly, she bites the heel of selfless humanity.

It is the fate of woman, that what she is she is darkly and helplessly. What woman *knows*, she knows because man has taught it to her. What she *is*, this is another matter. She can never give expression to the profound movements of her own being. These movements can only find an expression through a man. Man is the utterer, woman is the first cause. Whatever God there is made it so.

Hester, however, urges Dimmesdale to go away with her to a new country, to begin a new life. But it is doubtful if she was any more ready for this step than he. When a man responds to the prompting of a woman towards a new life, he has not only to face the world itself, but a great reaction in the very woman he takes. In her conscious self woman is almost inhumanly conservative, reactionary. Anna Karenin, Hester Prynne, Sue in *Jude the Obscure*, these women are never satisfied till they have shattered the man who responded to them. If Dimmesdale had fled with Hester they would have felt themselves social outcasts. And then they would have had to live in secret hatred of mankind, like criminal accomplices; or they would have felt isolated, cut off, two lost creatures, a man meaningless except as the agent, or tool, or creature of the possessive woman; and when a man loses his meaning, the woman one way or other destroys him. She kills him by her very possessive love itself. It would have been necessary for Dimmesdale in some way to conquer society with a new spirit and a new idea. And this was impossible. The time was by no means ripe. The old idea must be slowly undermined : slowly and secretly undermined. Dimmesdale in his confession struck his blow at the old idea. But he could not survive. And it was for this reason he hated Hester at the last.

She outlived him. But she went on with the work of secretly undermining the established form of Society. Her duplicity was purely unconscious. In all her conscious passion she desired to be pure and good, a true sister of mercy. But the primal soul is in-

exorable. Hawthorne gives the picture in all its details, introducing the suggestion of witchcraft. The ancients were not
altogether fools in their belief in witchcraft. When the profound,
subconscious soul of woman recoils from its creative union with
man it can exact a tremendous invisible destructive influence.
This malevolent force can invisibly press upon the sources of life
in any hated individual—or perhaps much more so on any
loved individual—pressing, sapping, shattering life unknowably
at its very sources.   There is a terrible effluence from the reactionary human soul, and this effluence acts as a destructive
electricity upon the centres of primary life in man, and destroys
the flow, the very life itself, at those centres. The activity is so
intensely powerful, yet so invisible, often even involuntary on
the part of the agent, that it produces ghastly and magical results.
And it is the frenzy of people harried and pressed by the destructive power emitted from the hateful soul of an individual,
woman or man, who is possessed by this reaction against all
creative union, that drives communities into a sudden frenzied
seeking for a victim. Then we have the burning of witches and
wizards. No passion of the human soul is *utterly* misguided. And
the old witch-lady, Mistress Hibbins, claims Hester as a witch.

Hawthorne says of Hester : "She had in her nature a rich,
voluptuous, oriental characteristic—a taste for the gorgeously
beautiful." This is the aboriginal American principle working in
her, the Aztec principle. She repressed it. Even she would not
allow herself the luxury of labouring at fine, delicate stitchery.
But she dressed the little Pearl vividly, and the scarlet letter was
gorgeously embroidered. These were her Hecate or Astarte
insignia. For the rest she was the sternest, most ascetic Puritan.

All the while we can *see* that she is the pivot, the mystic centre
of the most implacable destruction of Dimmesdale, of his white
sanctity and of his spiritual effulgence. Nay, of more than this :
she, the grey nurse, the sister of mercy and charity, she was a
centre of mystic obstruction to the creative activity of all life.
She destroyed the Puritan being from within. "The poor, whom

she sought out to be the objects of her bounty, often reviled the
hand that was stretched forth to succour them." We know for
ourselves that her succour was her helpless attempt to cover her
implacable hate, and the poor responded intuitively. "She was
patient—a martyr indeed," Hawthorne continues, "but she for-
bore to pray for her enemies, lest, in spite of her forgiving
aspirations, the words of the blessing should stubbornly twist
themselves into a curse."

Yet she is not a hypocrite. Only the serpent has turned in her
soul. She invests herself in the sternest righteousness to escape
the doom of her own being. But it is no good. At the very quick
she is in revolt; she is a destroyer, her heart is a source of the
malevolent Hecate electricity, flashing with serpent rays.

"She grew to have a dread of children; for they had imbibed
from their parents a vague idea of something horrible in this
dreary woman gliding silently through the town, with never any
companion but only one child."

The Astarte or Hecate principle has in it a necessary antagonism to life itself, the very issue of life : it contains the element
of blood sacrifice of children, in its darker, destructive mood; just
as it worships procreative child-birth, in its productive mood.
The motion from the productive to the destructive activity of the
Hecate principle is only a progression in intensity : intensity
reached either through triumph and overweening, as in the old
religions, or through opposition and repression, as in modern
life.

"But sometimes, once in many days, or perchance in many
months, she felt an eye—a human eye—upon the ignominious
brand, that seemed to give a momentary relief, as if half her
agony were shared. The next instant, back it all rushed again,
with a still deeper throb of pain; for in that brief interval she
had sinned again. Had Hester sinned alone?"

Hawthorne is a sorcerer, a real seer of darkness. He knows,
admittedly, what it is to meet in a crowd two eyes dark with the
same instant, dreadful mystery of unfathomable, indomitable,

destructive passion—eyes that answer in instant, mystic, deadly understanding, as the eye of a gipsy will sometimes answer, out of a crowd.

Hester's real, vital activity, however, lies in her unconscious struggle with Dimmesdale, who is polarised against her in the mystic conjunction and opposition. Once she has destroyed him, her dreadful spirit is more or less appeased. After his death it comes to pass that the "A" on her breast is said to stand for "Abel." There is a devilish, unconscious satire—a dream irony —in this also. She is appeased. But she lives on, a lonely, grey, dreadful woman, one of the shades of the underworld.

She is appeased, but her spirit lives on in Pearl. Pearl is the scarlet letter incarnate, as the book says. There was that in the child "which often impelled Hester to ask, in bitterness of heart, whether it were for good or ill that the poor little creature had been born at all."

In her relation to Pearl, there is the same horrible division in Hester's heart. The child is the scarlet letter incarnate. Once she is compared to the demon of plague or scarlet fever—a demoniacal little creature, in her red dress. Then again she is tender and loving—but always uncertain. The subtle, steely pallid mockery is never absent from her eyes. The strange Judas principle, of betrayal, of the neutralisation of the one impulsive self against the other, this is purely expressed in Pearl. She can love with clinging tenderness—only that she may draw away and hit the mouth that kisses her, with a mocking laugh. She can hate with dark passion—only to turn again with easy, indifferent friendliness, more insulting than rage. Her principle is the truly deadly principle of betrayal for betrayal's sake—the real demon principle, which just neutralises the sensual impulse with a spiritual gesture, and neutralises the spiritual impulse with a sensual gesture, creates a perfect frustration, neutralisation, and laughs with recurrent mockery. This is the one single motive of Pearl's being, this motive of neutralisation into nothingness. And her triumph is in her jeering laugh. In the end, very fitly, she marries an Italian nobleman. But we are not told whether she outmatched him, or he her, in diabolic opposition.

Hester, inevitably, *hates* something that Pearl is. And as well she cherishes the child as her one precious treasure. Pearl is the continuing of her terrible revenge on all life. "The child could not be made amenable to rules. In giving her existence a great law had been broken; and the result was a being whose elements were perhaps beautiful and brilliant, but all in disorder, or with an order peculiar to themselves, amidst which the point of variety and arrangement was difficult or impossible to be discovered."

This is Hawthorne's diagnosis. He did not choose to discover too much, openly. But he gives us all the data. He goes on to describe the peculiar look in her eyes—"a look so intelligent, yet inexplicable, so perverse, sometimes so malicious, but generally accompanied by a wild flow of spirits, that Hester could not help questioning at such moments whether Pearl was a human child." To answer that question Hester would have had to define what she meant by human. Pearl by the very openness of her perversity, was at least straightforward. She answers downright that she has no Heavenly Father. She mocks and tortures Dimmesdale with a subtlety rarer even than her mother's, and more exquisitely poisonous. But even in this she has a sort of reckless gallantry, the pride of her own deadly being. We cannot help regarding the phenomenon of Pearl with wonder, and fear, and amazement, and respect. For surely nowhere in literature is the spirit of much of modern childhood so profoundly, almost magically revealed.

II.

The triangle of disruption, between Hester and Chillingworth and Dimmesdale, is explicitly drawn. Chillingworth represents

K

the sensual male being in complete subordination, as we have him in modern life. His principle is the sensual serpent, full of wisdom, but subjected and dangerous. It is the subjected, even enslaved sensual male that captures the representative female : the affinity is between these two. The accidents of poverty and the like, which Hawthorne introduces for the sake of probability, only make up the chain of inevitability. Hester inevitably marries the learned old Chillingworth, who also is skilled in medicine and the art of healing. The physician is the deadly hater. The physician and the Sister of Mercy, these are the dark psyche in revolt, the subtle destroyers. Chillingworth is skilled in the arts of the Golden Hermes, Hermes of the Underworld, the undoer. He knows the subtle sensual reactions, such as are contained in the science of magic. He is a twisted old scholar—but potent in the sensual underworld, and diabolic there.

Still, he is humble, subjected—in symbolism, crippled and elderly; he is under the dominion of the triumphant spiritual principle; dominated, cringing, but unsubdued, malevolent in his soul. Francis Bacon is his prototype.

He marries Hester. Outwardly she believes in him as a wise, good old scholar. His taking her is a kind of theft. But inwardly she knows his principle. She enters into a tacit conspiracy—a conspiracy against the spiritual being who dominates them both. At the very beginning, Hester swears an oath of silence to Chillingworth : their oath of allegiance. For they are the two prime conspirators.

" 'Why dost thou smile so at me?' inquired Hester . . . . 'Art thou like the Black Man that haunts the forest round about us? Hast thou enticed me into a bond that will prove the ruin of my soul?'

" 'Not thy soul,' he answered, with another smile. 'No, not thine.' "

The Black Man of the American forests is the aboriginal spirit of the primary, sensual psche. The first settlers were all very conscious of this Black Man, their enemy.

Chillingworth, Hester, Dimmesdale, these are the triangle of destruction. Hester has thrown down the spiritual being from his pure pre-eminence. Chillingworth, the physician, the male sensual psyche subjected and turned back in recoil, must proceed with the minister's undoing. It goes on subtly and horribly. And yet Dimmesdale finally robs Chillingworth of the triumph. The spiritual being saves itself by confession upon the scaffold. The end is not yet.

As Chillingworth says : " . . . it has all been a dark necessity." Yet even he dates the dark necessity from Hester's "sin." It dates from much further back—far back as Christ himself. It dates from the beginning of the triumph of the one half of the psyche, over the other half.

The ruin of Dimmesdale is horrible. He cannot conceive that his fall with Hester is not a sin. The whole world, and his whole psyche, would have to be shattered before such a conception could enter. He cannot yield to the woman, commit himself to her, and flee away with her. He still holds his own.

But now there is the torture of his awakened sensual self. What is he to do with this sensual self? The old perfect flow, wherein the lower or primary self flows in gradual sublimation upwards towards a spiritual transmutation and expression, is broken. The old circuit of positive spiritual being and negative sensual being is broken for ever. The two halves are in antagonism.

Dimmesdale now hates his body with morbid hate. He lusts to destroy it. He practises horrible secret tortures, wounding himself with thorns, cutting himself with whips, searing himself. It is a common phenomenon, a lust of self-torture. He is the Inquisition unto himself. He has a hideous voluptuous satisfaction in the process. He is his own prostitute.

His vital belief in what he stands for is gone. All that remains is a will to preservation of his appearances. Underneath, the most horrible blasphemous mockery sets in.

Right to the very end, Dimmesdale must have his saintly

triumphs. He must preach his Election Sermon, and win his last saintly applause. At the same time he has an almost imbecile, epileptic impulse to defile the religious reality he exists in. In Dimmesdale at this period lies the whole clue to Dostoevsky.

This saintly minister of New England meets one of his hoary-headed deacons in the road, just before the time of the Election Sermon, and "it was only by the most careful self-control that the former could refrain from uttering certain blasphemous suggestions that rose into his mind respecting the communion-supper." And again, as an old widow stops him for a word of comfort, he longs to whisper into her ear "a brief, pithy, and, as it then appeared to him, unanswerable argument against the immortality of the human soul." Once more, as he sees a girl, "fair and pure as a lily that had bloomed in Paradise," approaching him, he must cover his face in his cloak to pass by, because he knows he could not help giving her one look, full of evil suggestion, that would blight all her innocence.

It is the fatal, imbecile or epileptic state of soul, such as Dostoevsky's, which makes the one half of the psyche malevolently act against its other half, in leering, malignant progress of futility.

In his very last words Dimmesdale is an actor, subtly malevolent and vicious.

" 'Shall we not meet again?' whispered she, bending her face down close to his. 'Surely, surely, we have ransomed one another, with all this woe! Thou lookest far into eternity, with those bright dying eyes. Then, tell me what thou seest?'

" 'Hush, Hester, hush!' said he, with tremulous solemnity. 'The law we broke!—the sin here so awfully revealed!—let these alone be in thy thoughts. I fear! I fear!' "

So, with a last bit of pulpit rhetoric, the perfect exemplar of the spiritual way dies, in America. The pathos, and the malignant satire, in Hawthorne's double language, his perfect, marvellous exposition of the very deepest soul processes, make this book one of the wonder-books of the world. And yet it is somewhat detestable, because of its duplicity. All the way, there is the pious preaching of the conventional creed, on the ostentatious surface, whilst underneath is the lurid lust in sin, the gloating in the overthrow of that which is so praised.

After *The Scarlet Letter,* some of the *Tales* are wonderful in their two-faced reality. *The House of the Seven Gables* is again a dark romance of the mystic revenge, mixed with the ugliness of the coming generation, commercial and vulgar. Only *The Blithedale Romance* is really personal.

Here we have Hawthorne's waking reality, touched up with lurid dream-colours. *The Blithedale Romance* is an account, more or less, of the Brook Farm experiment. A number of the most advanced spirits of America, wishing to set the perfect social example, and start the real utopia, bought a farm, and settled themselves in, a company of advanced transcendentalists, to live in common and till the land and be perfectly at one with all things, through their common labour and their common transcendence in the Oversoul. Hawthorne stood it for a few weeks. Then he shrugged his shoulders and departed.

The Brook Farm experiment is the legitimate descendant of Crèvecoeur's dreams. It is the attempt to work the sensual body from the spiritual centres. But the attempt never works.

The Brook Farmers wanted to triumph purely in the spiritual being : they wanted to be transcendentally at one with all things. Their "social experiment" was a new flight into oneness and perfection. The physical or brute self must be spiritualised by labour in common, the soul must be perfected by bringing the body into line, in a brotherhood of selfless, productive toil. But it was hopeless to introduce brute physical labour. Brute labour, the brute struggle with earth and herds, *must* rouse the dark, sensual centres, darken the mind, isolate the being in heavy-blooded separateness. Then there is an end of spiritual oneness and transcendence.

Moreover, the clue to the movement lay in the desire to subject or disintegrate the primary sensual self. It was an attempt to perform by pleasant means what Dimmesdale, in his physical

self-tortures, attempted by unpleasant means. The reduction of
the primary, spontaneous self to pure subordination, however, is
never pleasant. And the process of the reduction is a process of
disintegration of the primal self. And human beings engaged in
the toils of such disintegration must react, sooner or later, against
the spiritual bond of union that is superimposed. So the Brook
Farm experiment was a failure.

The individuals of *The Blithedale Romance* present a four-
square group, of two triangles. There are two men : Hawthorne,
the I, the refined spiritual being, comparable to Dimmesdale;
then Hollingsworth, the deep-voiced ex-blacksmith, the patron
of criminals; then Zenobia, superb, like Hester Prynne, or like
Judith Hutter; and, fourthly, a white lily, a white weed of a
sickly lily, called Priscilla, a little forlorn sempstress who turns
out to be half-sister to the rich, superb Zenobia, just as Hetty
Hutter was sister to Judith, or the White Lily was sister to Cora.

Now all these four are idealists, creatures of the spiritual one
way. And they are all secretly seeking for the sensual satisfaction. Hawthorne is the spiritual being secretly worshipping the
sensual mysteries, the next generation after Dimmesdale.
Hollingsworth is a descendant of Chillingworth : a dark, black-
bearded monomaniac. His monomania is criminals : his one end
in life is to build an asylum for criminals, of which he will be
the head, the reformer. This Hephaestos of the underworld
stubbornly adheres to his spiritual assertion. He will reform all
criminals. But his passion, it is obvious, is to be in communion
with criminals. Potentially a criminal, the actual criminals of
the state fix him like a lodestone. He is Chillingworth without
Chillingworth's intellect : Chillingworth more subject than ever,
but criminally polarised.

The criminal is the man who, like Roger Chillingworth, is
abject and down-trodden in his sensual self, by the spiritual or
social domination, and who turns round secretly on life, to bite
it and poison it and mutilate it. There is a genuine *passion* at
the bottom of the ultra-social individual, for criminal gratifica-

tion. De Quincey in his essay on "Murder as a Fine Art" reveals this terrible reality. And this passion is Hollingsworth's passion. But he maintains his spiritual dominion, and seeks to gratify his passion, and vindicate his triumphal spiritual being, in reforming criminals.

The connection between the two men is like that between Dimmesdale and Chillingworth. Hawthorne falls sick at Brook Farm, and Hollingsworth nurses him. There is a strong love and blood-tenderness between the two men. Hawthorne, helpless and passive between the strong, but unspeakably gentle hands of the blacksmith, is lulled in sheer self-gratification.

But his love turns to hate. Hollingsworth wants absolute, monomaniac dominion over him, to use him. And Hawthorne will not be either dominated or used. After all, he is the finer and stronger soul of the two. And he detests and despises the monomaniac blacksmith, who has really a lust to consume and use the other man. He is like Chillingworth, who heals in order to consume his partner.

Then there is the criss-cross of love between the men and women. Hawthorne admires, even loves the superb Zenobia, with the exotic flower in her hair, but he has no real *desire* for her. Hollingsworth also seems to love Zenobia. But he does not love her. He hates her, really. He only wants her money. Zenobia would outmatch Hollingsworth in the sensual conflict. She would beat him at his own game. The serpent in her is stronger than the serpent in him. And for this he hates her. He needs to be predominant, because, actually, he is the sensual-subjugate being, and he craves to arrogate.

Zenobia, however, loves Hollingsworth madly. She has a sister-love for Hawthorne. They understand each other. Hollingsworth almost marries her, for the money, for his criminal scheme. But poor Zenobia drowns herself.

Priscilla, the little frail sempstress, captures both men. This white, weak, ingenuous little creature has been used as a spiritualistic medium in the public shows that were then the rage in

America. She has been veiled in a white veil, set on a public platform and made to answer, as a medium, the questions of a ghastly corrupt person who turns out to be Zenobia's unconfessed husband.

Priscilla is interesting as a phenomenon. She is a real "medium." In this, she is almost like a degenerate descendant of Ligeia. Ligeia triumphs in her unspeakable submissiveness to the man, her husband. She is the passive pole of his love.

Now if we carry this process of unutterable passivity, and destructive submission, a little further, we go beyond death, and we get the little "medium", Priscilla. In Priscilla, the mystic seal of integrity, the integrity of being, is broken. She is strictly a thing, a mystic prostitute, or an imbecile. She has no being, no true waking reality, only a sleeping, automatic reality.

The covering her up with the white veil symbolises the abstracting of the upper or wakeful consciousness, leaving the under-dream consciousness free and active. It is the same as the clairvoyant gazing into the crystal. The gazing into the crystal is a process of annulling or abstracting the whole waking consciousness, leaving the mechanical dream-consciousness in possession of the being. But in the wakeful consciousness the *being* has its presence. By destroying this consciousness—and it is a process of destruction, not of suspension, as in sleep—the core and centre and pivot of the being is gradually destroyed, and the being becomes a thing, an incontestably marvellous *transmitter,* like a telephone apparatus, of the great *natural-mechanical* vibrations in the ether, vibrations of mechanical cause and effect. Priscilla, covered with the veil, is abstracted from conscious being—she is a pure passive medium. The director puts the questions, not to her mind, but automatically, to her sensory-conscious *mechanical* reason. And, as a little unutterably delicate machine, she answers automatically. There is no correspondence of telepathy or thought transmission, or even mesmerism. It is a process of after-death, when the being is annulled, and the unimaginably sensitive sensory machine remains vibrating in the flow of the great invisible forces, mechanical, psychic, animistic, the uttermost spiritualism of material being. The whole process, however, is so inordinately delicate and difficult, that the base tricks of mesmerism and thought-transmission must form the greatest part of any public show. No medium, no clairvoyant, however, can, granted the maximum of success, transmit more than the *mechanical* possibilities of past, present, or future, those things which depend on cause and effect, in the mechanical or casual world. In the spontaneous or creative world, they do not exist—they have forfeited existence. They are things, not beings.

Now both men love Priscilla. Hawthorne confesses it at the very end of his book, pops it out as if it were some wonderful secret. But Hollingsworth gets her: she marries him: and they live in a little cottage, and he walks, leaning on her arm, queer and aged.

It is inevitable that both men should love Priscilla. She is the only being who will so submit to them, as to give them the last horrible thrills of sensual experience, in the direct *destruction* of the sensual body, pure prostitution. Priscilla, passive, mediumistic, almost imbecile, is profoundly strong. Once the real living integrity of being is broken in her, once she becomes will-less, she is stronger, less destructible than any living being. Will-less, clinging, unspeakably passive, she forms, almost like an imbecile, a pole of obscene negative passion. Towards her the overweening sensual electricity runs in violent destructive flow, the flow of not-being. It destroys at the very quick the correspondent. Hollingsworth, the powerful dark blacksmith, becomes quite soon tottering and shaky, when he has married Priscilla—and she is stronger, alert, active. In her last mystery of not-being, the dream existence, the somnabulist, mechanical, infernal reality such as is suggested by the old legends of were-wolves and metamorphoses, she is established and triumphant, and, by her very presence, almost without contact, she so draws the vital electricity from the male, in a horrible sensual-disintegrative flow, that she destroys his being as by magic. This is the meaning of the were-wolf and witch stories. Apuleius, with his metamorphoses, and Petronius, with his *Satyricon,* these are not so very different, in *substance,* from Hawthorne. The obscene metamorphoses of beings into elementals and hell-principles is described more perfectly, though less explicity, in Priscilla and Dimmesdale and Pearl, than in these old authors.

Hollingsworth *wants* this obscene polarity with the almost imbecile Priscilla, a polarity in sheer disintegration into nought. His sensual sensations are those that he desires—the acute sensual-electric experience in the sacral ganglion. It is an experience that immediately suggests the crackling and sparkling of electricity from a battery in which it is generated. And this acute vibratory motion is set up intensely in the sacral region of the nerves of the human being, in the last processes of mystic disintegration out of being. The last lust is for this indescribable sensation—whose light we can see in the eyes of a tiger, or a a wolf.

8. NATHANIEL HAWTHORNE II

8. Nathaniel Hawthorne II

The essay below has never been published and is reprinted from a typescript. It carries the title "Nathaniel Hawthorne's Blithedale Romance." *On the title-page this is crossed out and the title "Nathaniel Hawthorne's* The Scarlet Letter" *was written in by hand. "Nathaniel Hawthorne" was also crossed out again, and* "The Scarlet Letter" *alone remained as a title. The name and address of Robert Mountsier, Lawrence's American agent, and, above, evidently stamped in later, the name and address of Curtis Brown, the English agent, appear on the title-page. The essay quite clearly is version 2.*

This essay covers the same topics in the same order as the second part of "Nathaniel Hawthorne I". It is, indeed, a revision of the 11½ pages not printed in the English Review. *Lawrence evidently still wanted to make use of those 11½ pages; he rewrote them and, at first, titled the essay "Nathaniel Hawthorne's* Blithedale Romance" *because a part of the essay was concerned with this novel, but only the smaller part. Most of it still treats of the characters in* The Scarlet Letter. *That is probably the reason why he did not let the title stand.*

This essay originally began like this: "The character in the allegory of The Scarlet Letter *we have not mentioned."* [sic]. *This essay continues exactly where the essay in the* English Review *had ended. Lawrence crossed out this sentence and began as reproduced in the essay below. This leads us to believe very strongly that Lawrence, in the Sicily revision, did not—or only slightly—revise the material which had already appeared in the* English Review. *But he completely rewrote the unpublished second part of the essay on Hawthorne, and revised, though probably to a lesser extent, the essay on Whitman and the two essays on Melville.*

In version 3 (in the book of 1923) Lawrence has two essays on Hawthorne: "Nathaniel Hawthorne and The Scarlet Letter" *and* "Hawthorne's Blithedale Romance." *He shortened the seven pages on Chillingworth (in version 2) to two pages which he inserted at the end of the essay on* The Scarlet Letter *where they belong.* "Hawthorne's Blithedale Romance" *is an expansion of the rest of version 2. The first four pages about the Divine Father and the Holy Ghost have no equivalent in version 1 or version 2. They are another attack against* "America, you Pearl, you Pearl without a blemish!" *and specifically against spiritual women,* "Particularly American women."

This essay is quite different from the corresponding parts in version 1 and 3. Compared to the complete manuscript of version 1 it does not bring in anything new, except that the character of Chillingworth is more extensively analyzed. As in "Whitman" *(version 2) the tone is quiet, somewhat subdued, without the force, spontaneity and conviction of version 1. On the other hand this essay is free of the savage humour and hysterical outbreaks of version 3.*

R OGER CHILLINGWORTH in the allegory of *The Scarlet Letter,* the actual husband of Hester, appears as the evil figure in the trinity. A physician, he belongs to the old mediaeval school of medicine and alchemy rather than to modern

science. Mysterious herbs and black magic seem to be his instruments of healing.

He is an old man, older than Hester, with a grey beard and
a twisted body—the magician of old. But he is the magician on
the verge of modern science, like Francis Bacon, his great prototype.

We are apt to assume that there is only one mode of science
—our own. We have decided that, because the old Hermetic
science and alchemy and astrology are all displaced to-day, they
were therefore quite fallacious. But if we choose to see only the
failure and the fraud in the alchemistic sciences, and only the
success of our own, it is our own affair.

Is there, indeed, no way of examining the phenomena of the
world except our own way? A true act of scientific study or dis-
covery is to-day an act of submission. The true scientist divests
himself of his own assurance and devotes himself inde-
fatigably to the phenomenon he wishes to analyse and
comprehend, until such time as he receives the desired
enlightenment. Our true scientific process is the same as our
religious process, a pure self-abnegation on the part of the postulant. This reverential humility, this extreme devotion to the
phenomenon under investigation is the pure act of the upper
or spiritual consciousness. The lower or sensual centres are
abnegated. And when the scientist, through pure *inward* submission to the unresolved phenomenon, has at last apprehended
its actual nature, he can then, by another act of self-abnegation
proceed to convert his new knowledge into power, power for the
common good.

In ancient science, of which alchemy and astrology and the
Hermetic science are only mutilated remains, the process was
just the opposite. Instead of the act of supreme self-denial and
devotion before his object, the alchemist sought to perform the
supreme act of authority and command. He would not humbly,
religiously *seek;* he would *compel* the material world to yield up
its secret to him. There is a world of difference between the two

processes, and between the results obtained. The alchemistic knowledge was *de facto* esoteric. It *could not* be common knowledge. It *must* be secret, private, by its very nature.

We imagine that, because our humility has brought us such great gain, we have exhausted the field of science and knowledge. We imagine that our exoteric knowledge, held by us all in common, having given us such immense power over the natural forces, is the one and the true knowledge. But as a matter of fact we are driven at last to conclude that all our knowledge is only half-knowledge, all our power is only a half of power, and an inferior half at that.

If we think a moment we realise that our whole science assumes the subordination of life to the great mechanistic forces. The great forces, the great planets, these are abiding and unchanging. Life is a flux, a sort of atmosphere depending on the planets, a mere product of the forces. Life is the subordinate reality : Force, Matter, the eternal planets, these are primordial. That is the true scientific opinion to-day. Our science tends all the time to the assertion that life is a mere outcome of certain conjunction of specific forces : a made thing, manufactured in the great and fascinating factory of the cosmos, at a certain point in time.

Now the ancient science held just the opposite. Let us repeat that the alchemy and astrology which dribbled on into our era was but a distorted remains. And still at its core we can discern a central truth different from the truth that sustains all our knowledge. To the ancient scientist, *life* was the first mover. It was life which produced the universe, not the universe which produced life. Life certainly must precede death : there could be no death if there were no life. And to the far-off pagan scientists the universe as we have it is only the great permanent death-result from the great preceding life-phases. Dead life is Matter and Force. All matter was once, in some way, alive, just as the dust of a dead man's bones was once alive. All dust was once bones and flesh. All Matter was once tissue. But in the great post-mortem reaction between the shed dust and the shed, naked elements of fire and water, the material universe has been set up.

Though this material universe is set up in apparent independence of the living, it is not even now dependent of life. The life-mystery still has the final sway over the mechanistic forces and the material universe. The independence of the material universe is an illusion. The illusion comes owning to the fact that the life-power in *one individual* cannot easily affect the motion of the natural phenomena. But, though the phenomenal universe has its own fixed laws, these laws themselves are subject ultimately to direct life-control.

Our science has reached the point of declaring that all laws are immutable, and can be brought to the service of man through their very immutability. Man submits, and in submission triumphs.

The ancient scientist held the opposite. He held that even the sun is but a cast-off burning breath of life, cast away like a breath emitted, but still not exempt from life. All is part of life, and therefore subject to change. For in life, nothing is immutable. And, therefore, since the great sun is still within the bounds of life, he may be arrested in his course and made to stand still in midheaven, if such be the life-will: that is, if it be the supreme will of the *living*. If it be the supreme will of the living that the sun should stand still in heaven, then the sun will stand still. For life means the living: nothing else. How then exert this supreme will?

This was the basis and the problem of the enormous prehistoric science of the world: how to use, to exert the supreme will. To us it seems nonsense. The sun will not stand still, even if we *will* our heads off. But that, the ancients would tell us, is because we are fools who know nothing about the sacred powers of the life-will which is in us. In the ancient sense, we have no will: none of that tremendous Old-Testament power which moved worlds. We have only the will which to them was unholy, the will to submission, and triumph through submission.

L

Now Roger Chillingworth was of the old order: what we call the order of sensual knowledge and power, which has become for us mere abracadabra. He was mediaeval, a descendant from the pagan world through Simon Magus and Roger Bacon, to the point where old Francis Bacon left off. He believed in the powers of the sensual will. Modern science also has come to the point where it must grant a supreme and terrifying power to *will*. But with us, as with Nietzsche, will is something conscious, or at least selfless, spiritual: a form of triumph through supreme transcending of self through abnegation, as in Christ. Even the hypnotist, though he hypnotises his patient, makes a sacrifice also of himself. The Germans went to war in a spirit of self-immolation which they intended should raise them to the highest power. The supreme will of to-day is like the will in Ligeia. The supreme will of the Pharaohs was just the opposite: an all-extension of the centripetal self, all-powerful, magical, in our sense mindless. It was not *actually* mindless: it had a great science of its own, embodied in the priesthood. But according to our conception of mind and of science, it was mindless and futile.

The old way of sensual understanding and power fell into disrepute with the Greeks, and with the Christians [it became] the one supreme sin of pride. Naturally, therefore, those remnants of the sensual understanding which lived on in the Christian era lived on stigmatised. And this is Roger Chillingworth: he persists, but he is stigmatised. His slight physical deformity is the symbol. He is the serpent of the Creation myth. Woman bruises his head, but he bruises her heel: for he is the indestructible reality of our sensual being, which always strikes at us through woman.

In this myth of the second Fall, it is the serpent who marries Eve, it is the spiritual Adam who is brought down to prostitution. Hester marries Chillingworth: the woman gives herself to the stigmatised one, the dark alchemist who must needs masquerade as a healer. It is the reversal of the great order of our era. The mother is now enthroned upon the Serpent again, not upon the dove or the cloud of light.

Hester swears her oath with him to the end. She is his great accomplice in the pulling-down of the spiritual man.

"Why dost thou smile so at me?—Art thou not like the Black Man that haunts the forest around us? Hast thou enticed me into a bond which will prove the ruin of my soul?"

"Not thy soul!" he answered with another smile. "No, not thine."

The close fight goes on between the two men, Dimmesdale the pure preacher, and the old Roger. Each of them is fixed in his own way, the one ancient, stigmatised, sensual, the other exalted and spiritual. Each of them represents the fatal old doctrine, "Pereat Mundus—"

It is a satanic hatred, closely akin to love. The men, through their sheer oppositeness of mode and being, gravitate together in a helpless attraction of mutual hate and mutual love. Dimmesdale will suffer all tortures rather than admit he has fallen. He will suffer all destruction if he may still vindicate the old triumph of spirit over death, the triumph of immortality in selfless love. But it is already too late. Chillingworth holds the one drop of poison that can darken the sun of spiritual immortality : man's irremediable being in sensuality.

Christ made the great revelation that passive power is greater than active power. Passive power has been accumulating through a long era; is still accumulating. But mystically, essentially, it is already broken. The world is like Dimmesdale, it has its Chillingworth in the dark races. It has had its Hester in Germany.

But like Dimmesdale, it persists even after it has fallen. Nothing is more horrible than the distintegration that sets in in the minister's soul. He becomes obscene and dreadful, all the while preserving his sanctified mode. The fatal self-division takes place in his psyche, incipient epilepsy or imbecility, the desire to defile most horribly the thing he holds most holy. Dostoevsky's whole essence is in these last days of Arthur Dimmesdale.

At the last the saintly minister cheats the satanic physician. By *confessing* his fall he expiates, he throws himself at the feet of mercy, he leaves the great *ideal* intact. He refutes the woman, the sensual union with her.

" 'Shall we not meet again?' whispered she, bending her face down close to him. 'Shall we not spend our immortal life together? Surely, surely we have ransomed one another with all this woe! Thou lookest far into eternity with those bright dying eyes. Then, tell me what thou seest!'

" ' Hush, Hester, hush,' said he, with tremulous solemnity. 'The law we broke!—the sin here so awfully revealed!—let these alone be in thy thoughts. I fear! I fear!' "

So he dies, and both Chillingworth and Hester are cheated of their triumph. Woman still has no place save as the Mater Dolorosa, and the sensual being no acceptance save as the hated serpent.

The Scarlet Letter is a profound and wonderful book, one of the eternal revelations. Those who look for realism and personal thrills may jeer at it. It is not thrilling in the vulgar way. But for those who talk about the profundities of Dostoevsky, it is far more profound than the epileptic Russian, and for those who talk about the perfection of the French novel, it is more perfect than any work of fiction in French. True, Hawthorne classes it as a romance, and thus puts it almost in line with the Morte D'Arthur. But as a matter of fact, it is greater than any romance, and its concentrated *perfection* is a matter of wonder to any artist. It is a romance as much as the Book of Job or the Book of Ruth is a romance, and as little as Don Quixote. It is the lasting representative book of American literature. If it displeases us in any particular, it is in the way the ethical Hawthorne embroiders over the artist Hawthorne. The deepest joy is the pride of sin: and all the preaching is so lugubrious and moral. This touch of cant or falseness, duplicity, is however absolutely essential to the fallen Puritan psyche, and therefore artistically true. The lust of sin goes simultaneous with the solemn condemnation of sin.

Which is peculiarly American. And this book is the myth of the fallen Puritan psyche, in the New World.

The Scarlet Letter is a profound and wonderful book, an eternal revelation. No other work of Hawthorne's is supreme. *The House of the Seven Gables* is a tale of the passing of the dark old Chillingworth order, which was mediaeval, touched with the supernatural. The magic spends itself, the black old proud blood perishes. The young generations are reconciled in a glow of commercial prosperity, modern America.

These are wonderful stories in *Twice Told Tales*. But *The Blithedale Romance* has another element. Here Hawthorne approaches actuality, his own actual doings. The story opens with a more or less true picture of Brook Farm, where the American transcendentalists made their famous experiment. A number of the great idealists, wishing to initiate the social Utopia, bought a farm and united to live in common, to till the ground and eat the bread their own hands had raised, at the same time lifting their souls to that perfect harmony with the Oversoul which was for them the goal of life.

The experiment was in direct line from Crèvecoeur : nature sweet and pure, and brotherhood in toil. It was the old attempt to idealise that which you cannot idealise, heavy physical work and physical, sensual reaction. You cannot dig the ground with the spirit. In the long run, you realise you are fighting the natural elements. The very act of stooping and thrusting the heavy earth calls into play the dark sensual centres in a man, at last, that old Adam which is the eternal opposite of the spiritual or ideal being. Brute labour, the brute struggle with the beast and herd, must rouse into activity the primary centres, darken the mind, induce a state of animal mindlessness, and pivot a man in his own heavy-blooded isolation. That is what the transcendentalists wanted, but in an ideal manner. Which is as good as saying they wanted fire which did not burn.

The real clue to the movement lay in this desire of the self-conscious idealists for the sensual unconsciousness of the peasant.

They thought they could get it ideally, or idyllically—like Marie
Antoinette playing dairymaid. They went for it in earnest. And
some enjoyed it. But the experiment was a failure, like all the
others of the same sort. The temper of an idealist is too frictional.
He is too much engaged in sublimating the natural brute in himself—which is a frictional, reducing process—to be able to live in
physical contact with others. Hawthorne at once knew the falseness of the attempt. Never, he says, did he feel himself more
spectral than when he was winding the horn to summon the
labourers to their tasks. A more self-conscious scarecrow never
stood in a field than the author of *The Scarlet Letter*. No doubt
he would have quite liked to be a brute, in the healthy sense of
the word, if he could have been it without forfeiting his whole
established ideal nature.

The characters in the tale present a four-square group—of
two triangles. There is the superb Zenobia, with her tropic flower
in her hair, her proud voluptuousness; there is a forlorn little
sempstress called Priscilla, another festering White Lily; there is
the I, the teller of the story, the sensitive, idealist young man; and
there is Hollingsworth, the ex-blacksmith, deep-voiced, black-
bearded, patron of criminals.

We have something of the same four-square group as in Deerslayer. Zenobia is lurid with a suggestion of sin, Priscilla is
touched with imbecility. But in Hollingsworth is a new element.
He is a monomaniac, fascinated by criminals. His one aim in
life is to build an asylum for criminals, which he shall super-
intend. It is strictly the criminal in himself, the dark luster, taking
on a beneficent form.

Hollingsworth is the sensual type, stigmatised, but rising now
to self-arrogance and revenge. He is dark, passionate, obscure—a
blacksmith. The sensitive young man is nursed by him, tenderly.
Hollingsworth has the strong blood-gentleness, the frail newcomer
is lapped in warmth and restoration. So that the two men love
each other warmly, at first. The young, frail, thoughtful man, the
I of the story, feels a deep love for his sombre nurse. Which love

turns to hate, when he realises that Hollingsworth wants to dominate him absolutely, with monomaniac overbearing. He will not be dominated. He turns at last in anger and contempt from the Hephaestus of the underworld, finds him unintelligent and stupidly overbearing, criminal really.

Both men pretend to love Zenobia, the lurid woman who has become a sort of tropic idealist. And Zenobia has a passion for the criminal-saving blacksmith, who only cares for her because her money will build his asylum.

Both men, we are told, actually love Priscilla. The story is worthy of Poe, should really, after the beautiful opening, have been carried out in Poe's manner. Priscilla is a degenerate descendant of Ligeia. In her the will-to-submission is carried to obscenity. She has been used as a spiritualistic medium by a corrupt person who turns out to be Zenobia's husband. Priscilla is the famous Veiled Lady of the public spiritualist shows at that time so popular in America. Poe should have dealt with all this part of the story.

Priscilla is the psychic prostitute. In her the integral being is gone, leaving her a sort of thing or instrument, repulsive really. When she is covered with the white veil, in the public shows, her trivial upper consciousness is obliterated, she remains an automatic instrument. Apart from her subjectivity to the suggestion which comes from the "professor," she is actually a medium.

Which means, that she exists under the cloth as a sort of wireless instrument. The apparatus of the human consciousness is much more delicate than any telegraphic apparatus. It can register vibrations which no wireless can register. It can report from the unseen. It does so all the time, in our deep pre-conscious soul. But it can register direct in isolate *mental* messages. On one condition only, however.

That the central being is obliterated in the medium herself, leaving her only an instrument. And when she is reduced to this mere telegraphic apparatus, what is it she can report? Nothing but *things*: items of consciousness which exist as wireless messages exist, in vibrations and impressions upon the so-called ether. Should we expect souls to communicate to each other through a medium? Should we expect the dead to need a telephone to speak to us? It is absurd. The dead, if they die and rest, enter into a oneness with life, they are made so *at one* with us, that the thought of a medium is a mere vulgar profanity. And those dead who die are not at rest, are they going to ring us up on the faulty and silly telephone of a medium like Priscilla? They too can speak *direct*, within us, as they do.

A medium can tell us *nothing* from the dead or the living. What she can do, and all she can do, is to report the scattered pieces of *detached* consciousness which are littered, like torn bits of paper, upon the impressible ether—or electricity, call it what you will. She communicates nothing. She only picks up random bits of thought-impression from her atmosphere.

Another thing a medium *might* do—is what the oracles tried to do. Supposing that the whole universe of time and phenomena were a remorseless chain of cause and effect, then a medium might, by the subtlest transmission and interpretation of the vibrations in the vital ether, forecast an event in the future. But the universe of time and phenomena is *not* a chain of cause-and-effect. It depends, as we know, upon the life-mystery. And the life-mystery knows no absolute cause and effect. It can vary any law at any minute, it does actually create *new fate* every moment. So that mediumistic foretelling of event, though not absolutely nonsensical, must forever be a chancy business. Life itself sets the limit to all enquiry beyond life. The living soul, in its own fulness, contains all it needs to know. Impertinent inquiry is forever made useless by the perfect immediacy of all things which are in life, and by the eternal incalculability of life, and hence of phenomena.

9. THE TWO PRINCIPLES

9. The Two Principles

This essay appeared as number eight of the Studies in Classic American Literature *in the* English Review, *June, 1919. As is evident from the opening paragraphs, it was intended as an introduction to the essays on Dana and Melville. It has, however, nothing whatever to do with literature. Lawrence is concerned with Biblical events, Genesis, chemistry, the meaning of symbols; in short, with his "philosophy". The essay has not been reprinted and has never been published in book-form, but it still serves its purpose: several startling passages in the essay on Dana, even in its third version, can be more easily understood if the reader has first made himself familiar with the contents of this essay.*

AFTER HAWTHORNE come the books of the sea. In Dana and Herman Melville the human relationship is no longer the chief interest. The sea enters as the great protagonist.

The sea is a cosmic element, and the relation between the sea and the human psyche is impersonal and elemental. The sea that we dream of, the sea that fills us with hate or with bliss, is a primal influence upon us beyond the personal range.

We need to find some terms to express such elemental con-

nections as between the ocean and the human soul. We need to
put off our personality, even our individuality, and enter the
region of the elements.

There certainly does exist a subtle and complex sympathy,
correspondence between the plasm of the human body, which is
identical with the primary human psyche, and the material
elements outside. The primary human psyche is a complex
plasm, which quivers, sense-conscious, in contact with the circumambient cosmos. Our plasmic psyche is radio-active, con-
necting with all things, and having first-knowledge of all things.

The religious systems of the pagan world did what Christianity
has never tried to do : they gave the true correspondence between
the material cosmos and the human soul. The ancient cosmic
theories were exact, and apparently perfect. In them science and
religion were in accord.

When we postulate a beginning, we only do so to fix a starting-
point for our thought. There never was a beginning, and there
never will be an end of the universe. The creative mystery, which
is life itself, always was and always will be. It unfolds itself in
pure living creatures.

Following the obsolete language, we repeat that in the beginning was the creative reality, living and substantial, although
apparently void and dark. The living cosmos divided itself, and
there was Heaven and Earth : by which we mean, not the sky
and the terrestrial globe, for the Earth was still void and dark;
but an inexplicable first duality, a division in the cosmos. Between
the two great valves of the primordial universe, moved "The
Spirit of God," one unbroken and indivisible heart of creative
being. So that, as two great wings that are spread, the living
cosmos stretched out the first Heaven and the first Earth, terms
of the inexplicable primordial duality.

Then the Spirit of God moved upon the face of the waters.
As no "waters" are yet created, we may perhaps take the mystic
"Earth" to be the same as the Waters. The mystic Earth is the
cosmic Waters, and the mystic Heaven the dark cosmic Fire.

The Spirit of God, moving between the two great cosmic principles, the mysterious universal dark Waters and the invisible,
unnameable cosmic Fire, brought forth the first created apparition, Light. From the darkness of primordial fire, and the darkness of primordial waters, light is born, through the intermediacy
of creative presence.

Surely this is true, scientifically, of the birth of light.

After this, the waters are divided by the firmament. If we
conceive of the first division in Chaos, so-called, as being perpen-
dicular, the inexplicable division into the first duality, then this
next division, when the line of the firmament is drawn, we can
consider as horizontal: thus we have the $\bigoplus$, the elements of the
Rosy Cross, and the first enclosed appearance of that tremendous
symbol, which has dominated our era, the Cross itself.

The universe at the end of the Second Day of Creation is,
therefore, as the Rosy Cross, a fourfold division. The mystic
Heaven, the cosmic dark Fire is not spoken of. But the firmament
of light divides the waters of the unfathomable heights from the
unfathomable deeps of the other half of chaos, the still unformed
earth. These strange unfathomable waters breathe back and
forth, as the earliest Greek philosophers say, from one realm to
the other.

Central within the fourfold division is the creative reality itself,
like the body of a four-winged bird. It has thrown forth from
itself two great wings of opposite Waters, two great wings of
opposite Fire. Then the universal motion begins, the cosmos begins to revolve, the eternal flight is launched.

Changing the metaphors and attending to the material
universe only, we may say that sun and space are now born.
Those waters and that dark fire which are drawn together
in the creative spell impinge into one centre in the sun; those
waters and that fire which flee asunder in the creative spell form
space.

So that we have a fourfold division in the cosmos, and a fourfold travelling. We have the waters under the firmament and the

waters above the firmament : we have the fire to the left hand and
the fire to the right hand of the firmament; and we have each
travelling back and forth across the firmament. Which means,
scientifically, that invisible waters steal towards the sun, right
up to feed the sun, whilst new waters are shed away from the
sun, into space; whilst invisible dark fire rolls its waves to the
sun, and new fire floods out into space. The sun is the great
mystery-centre where the invisible fires and the invisible waters
roll together, brought together in the magnificence of the creative
spell of opposition, to wrestle and consummate in the formation
of the orb of light. Night, on the other hand, is Space presented
to our consciousness, that space or infinite which is the travelling
asunder of the primordial elements, and which we recognise in
the living darkness.

So the ancient cosmology, always so perfect theoretically, becomes, by the help of our scientific knowledge, physically, actually perfect. The great fourfold division, the establishment of the
Cross, which has so thrilled the soul of man from ages far back
before Christianity, far back in pagan America, as well as in the
Old World, becomes real to our reason as well as to our instinct.

Cosmology, however, considers only the creation of the
material universe, and according to the scientific idea life itself
is but a product of reactions in the material universe. This is
palpably wrong.

When we repeat that on the First Day of Creation God made
Heaven and Earth we do not suggest that God disappeared between the two great valves of the cosmos once these were created.
Yet this is the modern, scientific attitude. Science supposes that
once the first forces were in existence, and the first motion set
up, the universe produced itself automatically, throwing off life
as a by-product, at a certain stage.

It is such an idea which has brought about the materialization
and emptiness of life. When God made Heaven and Earth, that
is, in the beginning when the unthinkable living cosmos divided
itself, God did not disappear. If we try to conceive of God, in this

instance, we must conceive some homogenous rare *living* plasm, a *living* self-conscious ether, which filled the universe. The living ether divided itself as an egg-shell divides. There is a mysterious duality, life divides itself, and yet life is indivisible. When life divides itself, there is no division in life. It is a new life-state, a new being which appears. So it is when an egg divides. There is no split in life. Only a new life-stage is created. This is the eternal oneness and magnificence of life, that it moves creatively on in progressive being, each state of being whole, integral, complete.

But as life moves on in creative singleness, its substance divides and subdivides into multiplicity. When the egg divides itself, a new stage of creation is reached, a new oneness of living being; but there appears also a new differentiation in inanimate substance. From the new life-being a new motion takes place : the inanimate reacts in its pure polarity, and a third stage of creation is reached. Life has now achieved a third state of being, a third creative singleness appears in the universe; and at the same time, inanimate substance has re-divided and brought forth from itself a new creation in the material world.

So creation goes on. At each new impulse from the creative body, All comes together with All : that is, the one half of the cosmos comes together with the other half, with a dual result. First issues the new oneness, the new singleness, the new life-state, the new being, the new individual; and secondly, from the locked opposition of inanimate dual matter, another singleness is born, another creation takes place, new matter, a new chemical element appears. Dual all the time is the creative activity : first comes forth the living apparition of new being, the perfect and indescribable singleness; and this embodies the single beauty of a new substance, gold or chlorine or sulphur. So it has been since time began. The gems of being were created simultaneously with the gems of matter, the latter inherent in the former.

Every new thing is born from the consummation of the two halves of the universe, the two great halves being the cosmic

waters and the cosmic fire of the First Day. In procreation, the
two germs of the male and female epitomise the two cosmic
principles, as these are held within the life-spell. In the sun and
the material waters the two principles exist as independent
elements. Life-plasm mysteriously corresponds with inanimate
matter. But life-plasm, in that it lives, is itself identical with being, inseparable from the singleness of a living being, the
indivisible oneness.

Life can never be produced or made. Life as an unbroken
oneness, indivisible. The mystery of creation is that new and
indivisible being appears forever within the oneness of life.

In the cosmic theories of the creation of the world it has been
customary for science to treat of life as a product of the material
universe, whilst religion treats of the material universe as having
been deliberately created by some will or idea, some sheer
abstraction. Surely the universe has arisen from some universal
living self-conscious plasm, plasm which has no origin and no
end, but is life eternal and identical, bringing forth the infinite
creatures of being and existence, living creatures embodying
inanimate substance. There is no utterly immaterial existence, no
spirit. The distinction is between living plasm and inanimate
matter. Inanimate matter is released from the dead body of the
world's creatures. It is the static residue of the living conscious
plasm, like feathers of birds.

When the living cosmos divided itself, on the First Day, then
the living plasm became twofold, twofold supporting a new state
of singleness, new being; at the same time, the two fold living
plasm contained the finite duality of the two unliving, material
cosmic elements. In the transmutation of the plasm, in the interval of death, the inanimate elements are liberated into separate
existence. The inanimate material universe is born through death
from the living universe, to co-exist with it for ever.

We know that in its essence the living plasm is twofold. In
the same way the dynamic elements of material existence are
dual, the fire and the water. These two cosmic elements are pure

mutual opposites, and on their opposition the material universal is established. The attraction of the two, mutually opposite, sets up the revolution of the universe and forms the blazing heart of the sun. The sun is formed by the impinging of the cosmic water upon the cosmic fire, in the stress of opposition. This causes the central blaze of the universe.

In the same way, mid-way, the lesser worlds are formed, as the two universal elements become entangled, swirling on their way to the great central conjunction. The core of the worlds and stars is a blaze of the two elements as they rage interlocked into con-summation. And from the fiery and moist consummation of the two elements all the material substances are finally born, perfected.

This goes on however, mechanically now, according to fixed, physical laws. The plasm of life, the state of living potentially exists still central, as the body of a bird between the wings, and spontaneously brings forth the living forms we know. Ultimately, or primarily, the creative plasm has no laws. But as it takes form and multiple wonderful being, it keeps up a perfect law-abiding relationship with that other half of itself, the material inanimate universe. And the first and greatest law of creation is that all creation, even life itself, exists within the strange and incalculable balance of the two elements. In the living creature, fire and water must exquisitely balance, commingle, and consummate, this in continued mysterious process.

So we must look for life midway between fire and water. For where fire is purest, this is a sign that life has withdrawn itself, and is withheld. And the same with water. For by pure water we do not mean that bright liquid rain or dew or fountain stream. Water in its purest is water most abstracted from fire, as fire in its purest must be abstracted from water. And so, water becomes more essential as we progress through the rare crystals of snow and ice, on to that infinitely suspended invisible element which travels between us and the sun, inscrutable water such as life can know nothing of, for where it is, all life has long ceased

M

to be. This is the true cosmic element. Our material water, as our fire, is still a mixture of fire and water.

It may be argued that water is proved to be a chemical compound, composed of two gases, hydrogen and oxygen. But is it not more true that hydrogen and oxygen are the first naked products of the two parent-elements, water and fire. In all our efforts to decompose water we do but introduce fire into the water, in some naked form or other, and this introduction of naked fire into naked water *produces* hydrogen and oxygen, given the proper conditions of chemical procreation. Hydrogen and oxygen are the first-fruits of fire and water. This is the alchemistic air. But from the conjunction of fire and water within the living plasm arose the first matter, the Prima Materia of a living body, which, in its dead state, is the alchemistic Earth.

Thus, at the end of what is called the Second Day of Creation, the alchemistic Four Elements of Earth, Air, Fire, and Water have come into existence: the Air and the Earth born from the conjunction of Fire and Water within the creative plasm. Air is a final product. Earth is the incalculable and indefinite residuum of the living plasm. All other substance is born by the mechanical consummation of fire and water within this Earth. So no doubt it is the fire and water of the swirling universe, acting upon that Earth or dead plasm which results at the end of each life-phase, that has brought the solid globes into being, invested them with rock and metal.

The birth of the chemical elements from the grain of Earth, through the consummation of fire with water, is as magical, as incalculable as the birth of men. For from the material consummation may come forth a superb and enduring element, such as gold or platinum, or such strange, unstable elements as sulphur or phosphorus, phosphorus, a sheer apparition of water, and sulphur a netted flame. In phosphorus the watery principle is so barely held that at a touch the mystic union will break, whilst sulphur only waits to depart into fire. Bring these two unstable elements together, and a slight friction will cause them to burst spontaneously asunder, fire leaping out; or the phosphorus will pass off in watery smoke. The natives of Zoruba, in West Africa, having the shattered fragments of a great pagan culture in their memory, call sulphur the dung of thunder: the fire-dung, un-digested excrement of the fierce consummation between the upper waters and the invisible fire.

The cosmic elements, however, have a two-fold direction. When they move together, in the mystic attraction of mutual unknowing, then, in some host, some grain of Earth, or some grain of living plasm, they embrace and unite and the fountain of creation springs up, a new substance, or a new life-form. But there is also the great centrifugal motion, when the two flee asunder into space, into infinitude.

This fourfold activity is the root-activity of the universe. We have first the mystic dualism of pure otherness, that which science will not admit, and which Christianity has called "the impious doctrine of the two principles." This dualism extends through everything, even through the *soul* or *self* or *being* of any living creature. The self or soul is single, unique, and undivided, the gem of gems, the flower of flowers, the fulfilment of the universe. Yet *within* the self, which is single, the principle of dualism reigns. And then, consequent upon this principle of dual *other-ness*, comes the scientific dualism of polarity.

So we have in creation the two life-elements coming together within the living plasm, coming together softly and sweetly, the kiss of angels within the glimmering place. Then newly created life, new being arises. There comes a time, however, when the two life-elements go asunder, after the being has perfected itself. Then there is the seething and struggling of inscrutable life-disintegration. The individual form disappears, but the being remains implicit within the intangible life-plasm.

Parallel to this, in the material universe we have the productive coming-together of water and fire, to make the sun of light, the rainbow, and the perfect elements of Matter. Or we have the slow activity in disintegration, when substances resolve back towards the universal Prima Materia, primal inanimate ether.

Thus all creation depends upon the fourfold activity. And on this root of four is all law and understanding established. Following the perception of these supreme truths, the Pythagoreans made their philosophy, asserting that all is number, and seeking to search out the mystery of the roots of three, four, five, seven, stable throughout all the universe, in a chain of developing phenomena. But our science of mathematics still waits for its fulfilment, its union with life itself. For the truths of mathematics are only the skeleton fabric of the living universe.

Only symbolically do the numbers still live for us. In religion we still accept the four Gospel Natures, the four Evangels, with their symbols of man, eagle, lion, and bull, symbols parallel to the Four Elements, and to the Four Activities, and to the Four Natures. And the Cross, the epitome of all this fourfold division, still stirs us to the depths with unaccountable emotions, emotions which go much deeper than personality and the Christ drama.

The ancients said that their cosmic symbols had a sevenfold or a fivefold reference. The simplest symbol, the divided circle, ⊖, stands not only for the first division in the living cosmos and for the two cosmic elements, but also, within the realms of created life, for the sex mystery; then for the mystery of dual psyche, sensual and spiritual, within the individual being; then for the duality of thought and sensation—and so on, or otherwise, according to varying exposition. Having such a clue, we can begin to find the meanings of the Rosy Cross, the ⊕; and for the ankh, the famous Egyptian symbol, called the symbol of life, the cross or Tau beneath the circle ♀, the soul undivided resting upon division; and for the so-called symbol of Aphrodite, the circle resting upon the complete cross, ♀. These symbols too have their multiple reference, deep and far-reaching, embracing the cosmos and the indivisible soul, as well as the mysteries of function and production. How foolish it is to give these great signs a merely phallic indication!

The sex division is one of the Chinese three sacred mysteries. Vitally, it is a division of pure otherness, pure dualism. It is one of the first mysteries of creation. It is parallel with the mystery of the first division in chaos, and with the dualism of the two cosmic elements. This is not to say that the one sex is identical with fire, the other with water. And yet there is some indefinable connection. Aphrodite born of the waters, and Apollo the sun-god, these give some indication of the sex distinction. It is obvious, however, that some races, men and women alike, derive from the sun and have the fiery principle predominant in their constitution, whilst some, blonde, blue-eyed, northern, are evidently water-born, born along with the ice-crystals and blue, cold deeps, and yellow, ice-refracted sunshine. Nevertheless, if we must imagine the most perfect clue to eternal waters, we think of woman, and of man as the most perfect premiss of fire.

Be that as it may, the duality of sex, the mystery of creative *otherness,* is manifest, and given the sexual polarity, we have the fourfold motion. The coming-together of the sexes may be the soft, delicate union of pure creation, or it may be the tremendous conjunction of opposition, a vivid struggle, as fire struggles with water in the sun. From either of these consummations birth takes place. But in the first case it is the birth of a softly rising and budding soul, wherein the two principles commune in gentle union, so that the soul is harmonious and at one with itself. In the second case it is the birth of a disintegrative soul, wherein the two principles wrestle in their eternal opposition: a soul finite, momentaneous, active in the universe as a unit of sundering. The first kind of birth takes place in the youth of an era, in the mystery of accord; the second kind preponderates in the times of disintegration, the crumbling of an era. But at all times beings are born from the two ways, and life is made up of the duality.

The latter way, however, is a way of struggle into separation, isolation, psychic disintegration. It is a continual process of sun-

dering and reduction, each soul becoming more mechanical and
apart, reducing the great fabric of co-ordinate human life. In
this struggle the sexes act in the polarity of antagonism or mystic
opposition, the so-called sensual polarity, bringing tragedy. But
the struggle is progressive. And then at last the sexual polarity
breaks. The sexes have no more dynamic connection, only a
habitual or deliberate connection. The spell is broken. They are
not balanced any more even in opposition.

But life depends on duality and polarity. The duality, the
polarity now asserts itself within the individual psyche. Here, in
the individual, the fourfold creative activity takes place. Man is
divided, according to old-fashioned phraseology, into the upper
and lower man : that is, the spiritual and sensual being. And this
division is physical and actual. The upper body, breast and
throat and face, this is the spiritual body; the lower is the sensual.

By spiritual being we mean that state of being where the self
excels into the universe, and knows all things by passing into all
things. It is that blissful consciousness which glows upon the
flowers and trees and sky, so that I am sky and flowers, I, who
am myself. It is that movement towards a state of infinitude
wherein I experience my living oneness with all things.

By sensual being, on the other hand, we mean that state in
which the self is the magnificent centre wherein all life pivots,
and lapses, as all space passes into the core of the sun. It is a
magnificent central positivity, wherein the being sleeps upon the
strength of its own reality, as a wheel sleeps in speed on its
positive hub. It is a state portrayed in the great dark statues of
the seated lords of Egypt. The self is incontestable and unsurpassable.

Through the gates of the eyes and nose and mouth and ears,
through the delicate ports of the fingers, through the great window
of the yearning breast, we pass into our oneness with the universe,
our great extension of being, towards infinitude. But in the lower
part of the body there is darkness and pivotal pride. There in
the abdomen the contiguous universe is drunk into the blood,

assimilated, as a wheel's great speed is assimilated into the hub. There the great whirlpool of the dark blood revolves and assimilates all unto itself. Here is the world of living dark waters, where the fire is quenched in watery creation. Here, in the navel, flowers the water-born lotus, the soul of the water begotten by one germ of fire. And the lotus is the symbol of our perfected sensual first-being, which rises in blossom from the unfathomable waters.

In the feet we rock like the lotus, rooted in the undermud of earth. In the knees, in the thighs we sway with the dark motion of the flood, darkly water-conscious, like the thick, strong, swaying stems of the lotus that mindlessly answer the waves. It is in the lower body that we are chiefly blood-conscious.

For we assert that the blood has a perfect but untranslatable consciousness of its own, a consciousness of weight, of rich, downpouring motion, of powerful self-positivity. In the blood we have our strongest self-knowledge, our most powerful dark consicence. The ancients said the heart was the seat of understanding. And so it is : it is the seat of the primal sensual understanding, the seat of the passional self-consciousness.

In the nerves, on the other hand, we pass out and become the universe. But even this is dual. It seems as if from the tremendous sympathetic centres of the breast there ran out a fine, silvery emanation from the self, a fine silvery seeking which finds the universe, and by means of which we *become* the universe, we have our extended being. On the other hand, it seems as if in the great solar plexus of the abdomen were a dark whirlwind of pristine force, drawing, whirling all the world darkly into itself, not concerned to look out, or to consider beyond itself. It is from this perfect self-centrality that the lotus of the navel is born, according to oriental symbolism.

But beyond the great centres of breast and bowels, there is a deeper and higher duality. There are the wonderful plexuses of the face, where our being runs forth into space and finds its vastest realisation; and there is the deep living plexus of the loins, there where deep calls to deep. All the time, there is some great incomprehensible balance between the upper and lower centres, as when the kiss of the mouth accompanies the passionate embrace of the loins. In the face we live our glad life of seeing, perceiving, we pass in delight to our greater being, when we are one with all things. The face and breast belong to the heavens, the luminous infinite. But in the loins we have our unbreakable root, the root of the lotus. There we have our passionate self-possession, our unshakable and indomitable being. There deep calls unto deep. There in the sexual passion the very blood surges into communion, in the terrible sensual oneing. There all the darkness of the deeps, the primal flood, is perfected, as the two great waves of separated blood surge to consummation, the dark infinitude.

When there is balance in first-being between the breast and belly, the loins and face, then, and only then, when this fourfold consciousness is established within the body, then, and only then, do we come to full consciousness in the mind. For the mind is again the single in creation, perfecting its finite thought and idea as the chemical elements are perfected into finality from the flux. The mind brings forth its gold and its gems, finite beyond duality. So we have the sacred pentagon, with the mind as the conclusive apex.

In the body, however, as in all creative forms, there is the dual polarity as well as the mystic dualism of *otherness*. The great sympathetic activity of the human system has the opposite pole in the voluntary system. The front part of the body is open and receptive, the great valve to the universe. But the back is sealed, closed. And it is from the ganglia of the spinal system that the *will* acts in direct compulsion, outwards.

The great plexuses of the breast and face act in the motion of oneing, from these the soul goes forth in the spiritual oneing. Corresponding to this, the thoracic ganglion and the cervical ganglia are the great centres of spiritual compulsion or control or dominion, the great *second* or negative activity of the spiritual self. From these ganglia go forth the motions and commands which *force* the external universe into that state which accords with the spiritual will-to-unification, the will for equality. Equality, and religious agreement, and social virtue are enforced as well as found. And it is from the ganglia of the upper body that this compulsion to equality and virtue is enforced.

In the same way, from the lumbar ganglion and from the sacral ganglion acts the great sensual will to dominion. From these centres the soul goes forth haughty and indomitable, seeking for mastery. These are the great centres of activity in soldiers, fighters: as also in the tiger and the cat the power-centre is at the base of the spine, in the sacral ganglion. All the tremendous sense of power and mastery is located in these centres of volition, there where the back is walled and strong, set blank against life. These are the centres of negative polarity of our first-being.

So the division of the psychic body is fourfold. If we are divided horizontally at the diaphragm, we are divided also perpendicularly. The upright division gives us our polarity, our for and against, our mystery of right and left.

Any man who is perfect and fulfilled lives in fourfold activity. He knows the sweet spiritual communion, and he is at the same time a sword to enforce the spiritual level; he knows the tender unspeakable sensual communion, but he is a tiger against anyone who would abate his pride and his liberty.

10. DANA'S *TWO YEARS BEFORE THE MAST*

10. Dana's *Two Years Before the Mast*

This essay appeared in the book of Studies in Classic American Literature *in 1923. Version 1 and 2 have been lost. Internal evidence shows that version 1 and, probably, version 2 existed. Lawrence refers to the essay in version 1 of "The Two Principles" and in version 2 of "Walt Whitman". "The Two Principles" was planned as an introduction to the essays on Dana and Melville. In chapters eight and nine of his essay "Education of the People", written during the first World War and published in* Phoenix, *Lawrence had advocated that parents should beat their children as often as they felt furious and angry with them, because they were following sound instinct. So Lawrence had probably already been on the side of the captain in version 1.*

YOU CAN'T idealize brute labour. That is to say, you can't idealize brute labour, without coming undone, as an idealist.

You can't idealize brute labour.

That is to say, you can't idealize brute labour, without coming undone, as an idealist.

The soil! The great ideal of the soil. Novels like Thomas Hardy's and pictures like the Frenchman Millet's. The soil.

What happens when you idealize the soil, the mother-earth, and really go back to it? Then with overwhelming conviction it is borne in upon you, as it was upon Thomas Hardy, that the whole scheme of things is against you. The whole massive rolling of natural fate is coming down on you like a slow glacier, to crush you to extinction. As an idealist.

Thomas Hardy's pessimism is an absolutely true finding. It is the absolutely true statement of the idealist's last realization, as he wrestles with the bitter soil of beloved mother-earth. He loves her, loves her, loves her. And she just entangles and crushes him like a slow Laocoön snake. The idealist must perish, says mother earth. Then let him perish.

The great imaginative love of the soil itself! Tolstoi had it, and Thomas Hardy. And both are driven to a kind of fanatic denial of life, as a result.

You can't idealize mother earth. You can try. You can even succeed. But succeeding, you succumb. She will have no pure idealist sons. None.

If you are a child of mother earth, you must learn to discard your ideal self, in season, as you discard your clothes at night.

Americans have never loved the soil of America as Europeans have loved the soil of Europe. America has never been a blood-home-land. Only an ideal home-land. The home-land of the idea, of the *spirit*. And of the pocket. Not of the blood.

That has yet to come, when the idea and the spirit have collapsed from their false tyranny.

Europe has been loved with a blood love. That has made it beautiful.

In America, you have Fenimore Cooper's beautiful landscape : but that is wish-fulfilment, done from a distance. And you have Thoreau in Concord. But Thoreau sort of isolated his own bit of locality and put it under a lens, to examine it. He almost anatomized it, with his admiration.

America isn't a blood-home-land. For every American, the blood-home-land is Europe. The spirit home-land is America.

Transcendentalism. Transcend this home land business, exalt the idea of These States till you have made it a universal idea, says the true American. The oversoul is a world-soul, not a local thing.

So, in the next great move of imaginative conquest, Americans turned to the sea. Not to the land. Earth is too specific, too particular. Besides, the blood of white men is wine of no American soil. No, no.

But the blood of all men is ocean-born. We have our material universality, our blood-oneness, in the sea. The salt water.

You can't idealize the soil. But you've got to try. And trying, you reap a great imaginative reward. And the greatest reward is failure. To know you have failed, that you *must* fail. That is the greatest comfort of all, at last.

Tolstoi failed with the soil : Thomas Hardy too : and Giovanni Verga; the three greatest.

The further extreme, the greatest mother, is the sea. Love the great mother of the sea, the Magna Mater. And see how bitter it is. And see how you must fail to win her to your ideal : forever fail. Absolutely fail.

Swinburne tried in England. But the Americans made the greatest trial. The most vivid failure.

At a certain point, human life becomes uninteresting to men. What then ? They turn to some universal.

The greatest material mother of us all is the sea.

Dana's eyes failed him when he was studying at Harvard. And suddenly, he turned to the sea, the naked Mother. He went to sea as a common sailor before the mast.

You can't idealize brute labour. Yet you can. You can go through with brute labour, and *know* what it means. You can even meet and match the sea, and KNOW her.

This is what Dana wanted: a naked fighting experience with the sea.

KNOW THYSELF. That means, know the earth that is in your blood. Know the sea that is in your blood. The great elementals.

But we must repeat: KNOWING and BEING are opposite, antagonistic states. The more you know, exactly, the less you *are*. The more you *are,* in being, the less you know.

This is the great cross of man, his dualism. The blood-self, and the nerve-brain self.

Knowing, then, is the slow death of being. Man has his epochs of being, his epochs of knowing. It will always be a great oscillation. The goal is to know how not-to-know.

Dana took another great step in knowing: knowing the mother sea. But it was a step also in his own undoing. It was a new phase of dissolution of his own being. Afterwards, he would be a less human thing. He would be a knower: but more near to mechanism than before. That is our cross, our doom.

And so he writes, in his first days at sea, in winter, on the Atlantic: "Nothing can compare with the *early breaking of day* upon the wide, sad ocean. There is something in the first grey streaks stretching along the Eastern horizon, and throwing an indistinct light upon the face of the deep, which creates a feeling of loneliness, of dread, and of melancholy foreboding, which nothing else in nature can give."

So he ventures wakeful and alone into the great naked watery universe of the end of life, the twilight place where integral being lapses, and a warm life begins to give out. It is man moving on into the face of death, the great adventure, the great undoing, the strange extension of the consciousness. The same in his vision of the albatross. "But one of the finest sights that I have ever seen was an albatross asleep upon the water, off Cape Horn, when a heavy sea was running. There being no breeze, the surface of the water was unbroken, but a long, heavy swell was rolling, and we saw the fellow, all white, directly ahead of us, asleep upon the waves, with his head under his wing; now rising upon the top of a huge billow, and then falling slowly until he was lost in the hollow between. He was undisturbed for some time, until the noise of our bows, gradually approaching, roused him; when lifting his head, he stared upon us for a moment, and then spread his wide wings, and took his flight."

We must give Dana credit for a profound mystic vision. The best Americans are mystics by instinct. Simple and bare as his narrative is, it is deep with profound emotion and stark comprehension. He sees the last light-loving incarnation of life exposed upon the eternal waters: a speck, solitary upon the verge of the two naked principles, aerial and watery. And his own soul is as the soul of the albatross.

It is a storm-bird. And so is Dana. He has gone down to fight with the sea. It is a metaphysical, actual struggle of an integral soul with the vast, non-living, yet potent element. Dana never forgets, never ceases to watch. If Hawthorne was a spectre on the land, how much more is Dana a spectre at sea. But he must watch, he must know, he must conquer the sea in his consciousness. This is the poignant difference between him and the common sailor. The common sailor lapses from consciousness, becomes elemental like a seal, a creature. Tiny and alone Dana watches the great seas mount round his own small body. If he is swept away, some other man will have to take up what he has begun. For the sea must be mastered by the human consciousness, in the great fight of the human soul for mastery over life and death, in KNOWLEDGE. It is the last bitter necessity of the Tree. The Cross. Impartial, Dana beholds himself among the elements, calm and fatal. His style is great and hopeless, the style of a perfect tragic recorder.

"Between five and six the cry of 'All starbowlines ahoy!' summoned our watch on deck, and immediately all hands were called. A great cloud of a dark slate-colour was driving on us from the southwest; and we did our best to take in sail before we were in the midst of it. We had got the lightsails furled, the courses hauled up, and the top-sail reef tackles hauled out, and were

N

just mounting the fore-rigging when the storm struck us. In an instant the sea, which had been comparatively quiet, was running higher and higher; and it became almost as dark as night. The hail and sleet were harder than I had yet felt them, seeming almost to pin us down to the rigging."

It is in the dispassionate statement of plain material facts that Dana achieves his greatness. Dana writes from the remoter, non-emotional centres of being—not from the passional emotional self.

So the ship battles on, round Cape Horn, then into quieter seas. The island of Juan Fernandez, Crusoe's island, rises like a dream from the sea, like a green cloud, and like a ghost Dana watches it, feeling only a faint, ghostly pang of regret for the life that was.

But the strain of the long sea-voyage begins to tell. The sea is a great disintegrative force. Its tonic quality is its disintegrative quality. It burns down the tissue, liberates energy. And after a long time, this burning-down is destructive. The psyche becomes destroyed, irritable, frayed, almost dehumanized.

So there is trouble on board the ship, irritating discontent, friction unbearable, and at last a flogging. This flogging arouses Dana for the first and last time to human and ideal passion.

"Sam was by this time seized up—that is, placed against the shrouds, with his wrists made fast to the shrouds, his jacket off, and his back exposed. The captain stood on the break of the deck, a few feet from him, and a little raised, so as to have a good swing at him, and held in his hand a light, thick rope. The officers stood round, and the crew grouped together in the waist. All these preparations made me feel sick and faint, angry and excited as I was. A man—a human being made in God's likeness—fastened up and flogged like a beast! The first and almost uncontrollable impulse was resistance. But what could be done?—The time for it had gone by—"

So Mr. Dana couldn't act. He could only lean over the side of the ship and spue.

Whatever made him vomit?

Why shall man not be whipped?

As long as man has a bottom, he must surely be whipped. It is as if the Lord intended it so.

Why? For lots of reasons.

Man doth not live by bread alone, to absorb it and to evacuate it.

What is the breath of life? My dear, it is the strange current of interchange that flows between men and men, and men and women; and men and things. A constant current of interflow, a constant vibrating interchange. That is the breath of life.

And this interflow, this electric vibration is polarized. There is a positive and a negative polarity. This is a law of life, of vitalism.

Only ideas are final, finite, static, and single.

All life-interchange is a polarized communication. A circuit.

There are lots of circuits. Male and female, for example, and master and servant. The idea, the IDEA, that fixed gorgon monster and the IDEAL, that great stationary engine, these two gods-of-the-machine have been busy destroying all *natural* reciprocity and *natural* circuits, for centuries. IDEAS have played the very old Harry with sex relationship, that is, with the great circuit of man and woman. Turned the thing into a wheel on which the human being in both is broken. And the IDEAL has mangled the blood-reciprocity of master and servant into an abstract horror.

Master and servant-or master and man relationship is, essentially a polarized flow, like love. It is a circuit of vitalism which flows between master and man and forms a very precious nourishment to each, and keeps both in a state of subtle, quivering, vital equilibrium. Deny it as you like, it is so. But once you *abstract* both master and man, and make them both serve an *idea*: production, wage, efficiency, and so on: so that each looks on himself as an instrument performing a certain repeated evolution, then you have changed the vital, quivering circuit of master and

man into a mechanical machine unison. Just another way of life :
or anti-life.

You could never quite do this on a sailing ship. A master had to
be master, or it was hell. That is, there had to be this strange
interflow of master-and-man, the strange reciprocity of command and obedience.

The reciprocity of command and obedience is a state of unstable vital equilibrium. Everything vital, or natural, is unstable,
thank God.

The ship had been at sea many weeks. A great strain on
master and men. An increasing callous indifference in the men,
an increasing irritability in the master.

And then what?

A storm.

Don't expect me to say *why* storms must be. They just are.
Storms in the air, storms in the water, storms of thunder, storms
of anger. Storms just are.

Storms are a sort of violent readjustment in some polarised
flow. You have a polarized circuit, a circuit of unstable equilibrium. The instability increases till there is a crash. Everything
seems to break down. Thunder roars, lightning flashes. The
master roars, the whip whizzes. The sky sends down sweet rain.
The ship knows a new strange stillness, a readjustment, a re-
finding of equilibrium.

Ask the Lord Almighty why it is so. I don't know. I know it
is so.

But flogging? Why flogging? Why not use reason or take away
jam for tea?

Why not? Why not ask the thunder please to abstain from this
physical violence of crashing and thumping, please to swale
away like thawing snow.

Sometimes the thunder *does* swale away like thawing snow,
and then you hate it. Muggy, sluggish, inert, dreary sky.

Flogging.

You have a Sam, a fat slow fellow, who has got slower and

more slovenly as the weeks wear on. You have a master who has grown more irritable in his authority. Till Sam becomes simply wallowing in his slackness, makes your gorge rise. And the master is on red hot iron.

Now these two men, Captain and Sam, are there in a very unsteady equilibrium of command and obedience. A polarized flow. Definitely polarized.

The poles of will are the great ganglia of the voluntary nerve system, located beside the spinal column, in the back. From the poles of will in the backbone of the Captain, to the ganglia of will in the back of the sloucher Sam, runs a frazzled, jagged current, a staggering circuit of vital electricity. This circuit gets one jolt too many, and there is an explosion.

"Tie up that lousy swine!" roars the enraged Captain.

And whack! Whack! down on the bare back of that sloucher Sam comes the cat.

What does it do? By Jove, it goes like ice-cold water into his spine. Down these lashes runs the current of the Captain's rage, right into the blood and into the toneless ganglia of Sam's voluntary system. Crash! Crash! runs the lightning flame, right into the cores of the living nerves.

And the living nerves respond. They start to vibrate. They brace up. The blood begins to go quicker. The nerves begin to recover their vividness. It is their tonic. The man Sam has a new clear day of intelligence, and a smarty back. The Captain has a new relief, a new ease in his authority, and a sore heart.

There is a new equilibrium, and a fresh start. The *physical* intelligence of a Sam is restored, the turgidity is relieved from the veins of the Captain.

It is a natural form of human coition, interchange.

It is good for Sam to be flogged. It is good, on this occasion, for the Captain to have Sam flogged. I say so. Because they were both in that physical condition.

Spare the rod and spoil the *physical* child.

Use the rod and spoil the *ideal* child.

There you are.

Dana, as an idealist, refusing the blood-contact of life, leaned over the side of the ship powerless, and vomited : or wanted to. His solar plexus was getting a bit of its own back. To him, Sam was an "ideal" being, who should have been approached through the mind, the reason, and the spirit. That lump of a Sam !

But there was another idealist on board, the seaman John, a Swede. He wasn't named John for nothing, this Jack-tar of the Logos, John felt himself called upon to play Mediator, Intercedor, Saviour, on this occasion. The popular Paraclete.

"Why are you whipping this man, sir?"

But the Captain had got his dander up. He wasn't going to have his natural passion judged and interfered with by these long-nosed salvationist Johannuses. So he had nosey John hauled up and whipped as well.

For which I am very glad.

Alas, however, the Captain got the worst of it in the end. He smirks longest who smirks last. The Captain wasn't wary enough. Natural anger, natural passion has its unremitting enemy in the idealist. And the ship was already tainted with idealism. A good deal more so, apparently, than Herman Melville's ships were.

Which reminds us that Melville was once going to be flogged. In *White Jacket*. And he, too, would have taken it as the last insult.

In my opinion, there are worse insults than floggings. I would rather be flogged than have most people "like" me.

Melville too had an Intercedor : a quiet, self-respecting man, not a saviour. The man spoke in the name of Justice. Melville was to be unjustly whipped. The man spoke honestly and quietly. Not in any salvationist spirit. And the whipping did not take place.

Justice is a great and manly thing. Saviourism is a despicable thing.

Sam was justly whipped. It was a passional justice.

But Melville's whipping would have been a cold, disciplinary injustice. A foul thing. Mechanical *justice* even is a foul thing. For true justice makes the heart's fibres quiver. You can't be cold in a matter of real justice.

Already in those days it was no fun to be a captain. You had to learn already to abstract yourself into a machine part, exerting machine-control. And it is a good deal bitterer to exert machine-control, selfless, ideal control, than it is to have to obey, mechanically. Because the idealists who mechanically obey almost always hate the *man* who must give the orders. Their idealism rarely allows them to exonerate the man for the office.

Dana's captain was one of the real old-fashioned sort. He gave himself away terribly. He should have been more wary, knowing he confronted a shipful of enemies and at least two cold and deadly idealists, who hated all "masters" on principle.

"As he went on, his passion increased, and he danced about on the deck, calling out as he swung the rope, 'If you want to know what I flog you for, I'll tell you. It's because I like to do it!—Because I like to do it!—It suits me. That's what I do it for!'

"The man writhed under the pain. My blood ran cold, I could look no longer. Disgusted, sick and horror-stricken, I turned away and leaned over the rail and looked down in the water. A few rapid thoughts of my own situation, and the prospect of future revenge, crossed my mind; but the falling of the blows, and the cries of the man called me back at once. At length they ceased, and, turning round, I found that the Mate, at a signal from the captain, had cut him down."

After all, it was not so terrible. The captain evidently did not exceed the ordinary measure. Sam got no more than he asked for. It was a natural event. All would have been well, save for the *moral* verdict. And this came from theoretic idealists like Dana and the seaman John, rather than from the sailors themselves. The sailors understood spontaneous *passional* morality, not the artificial ethical. They respected the violent readjustments of the naked force, in man as in nature.

"The flogging was seldom, if ever, alluded to by us in the forecastle. If anyone was inclined to talk about it, the other, with a delicacy which I hardly expected to find among them, always stopped him, or turned the subject."

Two men had been flogged: the second and the elder, John, for interfering and asking the captain why he flogged Sam. It is while flogging John that the captain shouts, "If you want to know what I flog you for, I'll tell you—"

"But the behaviour of the two men who were flogged," Dana continues, "toward one another, showed a delicacy and a sense of honour which would have been worthy of admiration in the highest walks of life. Sam knew that the other had suffered solely on his account, and in all his complaints he said that if he alone had been flogged it would have been nothing, but that he could never see that man without thinking that he had been the means of bringing that disgrace upon him: and John never, by word or deed, let anything escape him to remind the other that it was by interfering to save his shipmate that he had suffered."

As a matter of fact, it was John who ought to have been ashamed for bringing confusion and false feeling into a clear issue. Conventional morality apart, John is the reprehensible party, not Sam or the captain. The case was one of passional readjustment, nothing abnormal. And who was the sententious Johannus, that he should interfere in this? And if Mr. Dana had a weak stomach as well as weak eyes, let him have it. But let this pair of idealists abstain from making all the other men feel uncomfortable and fuzzy about a thing they would have left to its natural course, if they had been allowed. No, your Johannuses and your Danas have to be creating "public opinion," and mugging up the life-issues with their sententiousness. O, idealism!

The vessel arrives at the Pacific coast, and the swell of the rollers falls in our blood—the weary coast stretches wonderful, on the brink of the unknown.

"Not a human being but ourselves for miles—the steep hill rising like a wall, and cutting us off from all the world—but the 'world of waters.' I separated myself from the rest, and sat down on a rock, just where the sea ran in and formed a fine spouting-horn. Compared with the dull, plain sand-beach of the rest of the coast, this grandeur was as refreshing as a great rock in a weary land. It was almost the first time I had been positively alone .... My better nature returned strong upon me. I experienced a glow of pleasure at finding that what of poetry and romance I had ever had in me had not been entirely deadened in the labor-ious life I had been lately leading. Nearly an hour did I sit, almost lost in the luxury of this entire new scene of the play in which I was acting, when I was aroused by the distant shouts of my companions."

So Dana sits and Hamletizes by the Pacific—chief actor in the play of his own existence. But in him, self-consciousness is almost nearing the mark of scientific indifference to self.

He gives us a pretty picture of the then wild, unknown bay of San Francisco.—"The tide leaving us, we came to anchor near the mouth of the bay, under a high and beautifully sloping hill, upon which herds of hundreds of red deer, and the stag, with his high-branching antlers were bounding about, looking at us for a moment, and then starting off affrighted at the noises we made for the purpose of seeing the variety of their beautiful attitudes and motions—"

Think of it now, and the Presidio! The idiotic guns.

Two moments of strong human emotion Dana experiences: one moment of strong but impotent hate for the captain, one strong impulse of pitying love for the Kanaka boy, Hope—a beautiful South Sea Islander sick of a white man's disease, phthisis or syphilis. Of him Dana writes—"but the other, who was my friend, and aikane—Hope—was the most dreadful object I had ever seen in my life; his hands looking like claws; a dread-ful cough, which seemed to rack his whole shattered system; a hollow, whispering voice, and an entire inability to move himself. There he lay, upon a mat on the ground, which was the only floor of the oven, with no medicine, no comforts, and no one to care for or help him but a few Kanakas, who were willing enough, but could do nothing. The sight of him made me sick and faint. Poor fellow! During the four months that I lived upon the beach we were continually together, both in work and in our excursions in the woods and upon the water. I really felt a strong affection for him, and preferred him to any of my own country-men there. When I came into the oven he looked at me, held out his hand and said in a low voice, but with a delightful smile, 'Aloha, Aikane! Aloha nui!' I comforted him as well as I could, and promised to ask the captain to help him from the medicine chest."

We have felt the pulse of hate for the captain—now the pulse of Saviour—like love for the bright-eyed man of the Pacific, a real child of the ocean, full of the mystery-being of that great sea. Hope is for a moment to Dana what Chingachgook is to Cooper—the hearts-brother, the answerer. But only for an ephemeral moment. And even then his love was largely pity, tinged with philanthropy. The inevitable saviourism. The ideal being.

Dana was mad to leave the California coast, to be back in the civilized east. Yet he feels the poignancy of departure when at last the ship draws off. The Pacific is his glamour-world: the eastern States his world of actuality, scientific, materially real. He is a servant of civilization, an idealist, a democrat, a hater of master, a KNOWER. Conscious and self-conscious, without ever forgetting.

"When all sail had been set and the decks cleared up the *California* was a speck in the horizon, and the coast lay like a low cloud along the north-east. At sunset they were both out of sight, and we were once more upon the ocean, where sky and water meet."

The description of the voyage home is wonderful. It is as if the sea rose up to prevent the escape of this subtle explorer. Dana seems to pass into another world, another life, not of this earth. There is first the sense of apprehension, then the passing right into the black deeps. Then the waters almost swallow him up, with his triumphant consciousness.

"The days became shorter and shorter, the sun running lower in its course each day, and giving less and less heat, and the nights so cold as to prevent our sleeping on deck; the Magellan Clouds in sight of a clear night; the skies looking cold and angry; and at times a long, heavy, ugly sea, setting in from the Southward, told us what we were coming to."

They were approaching Cape Horn, in the southern winter, passing into the strange, dread regions of the violent waters.

"And there lay, floating in the ocean, several miles off, an immense irregular mass, its top and points covered with snow, its centre a deep indigo. This was an iceberg, and of the largest size. As far as the eye could reach the sea in every direction was of a deep blue colour, the waves running high and fresh, and sparkling in the light; and in the midst lay this immense mountain-island, its cavities and valleys thrown into deep shade, and its points and pinnacles glittering in the sun. But no description can give any idea of the strangeness, splendour, and, really, the sublimity of the sight. Its great size—for it must have been two or three miles in circumference, and several hundred feet in height; its slow motion, as its base rose and sunk in the water and its points nodded against the clouds; the lashing of the waves upon it, which, breaking high with foam, lined its base with a white crust; and the thundering sound of the cracking of the mass, and the breaking and the tumbling down of huge pieces; together with its nearness and approach, which added a slight element of fear—all combined to give it the character of true sublimity—"

But as the ship ran further and further into trouble, Dana became ill. First it is a slight toothache. Ice and exposure cause the pains to take hold of all his head and face. And then the face so swelled, that he could not open his mouth to eat, and was in danger of lock-jaw. In this state he was forced to keep his bunk for three or four days. "At the end of the third day, the ice was very thick; a complete fog-bank covered the ship. It blew a tremendous gale from the eastward, with sleet and snow, and there was every promise of a dangerous and fatiguing night. At dark, the captain called the hands aft, and told them that not a man was to leave the deck that night; that the ship was in the greatest danger; any cake of ice might knock a hole in her, or she might run on an island and go to pieces. The look-outs were then set, and every man was put in his station. When I heard what was the state of things, I began to put on my things, to stand it out with the rest of them, when the mate came below, and looking at my face ordered me back to my berth, saying if we went down we should all go down together, but if I went on deck I might lay myself up for life. In obedience to the mate's orders, I went back to my berth; but a more miserable night I never wish to spend."

It is the story of a man pitted in conflict against the sea, the vast, almost omnipotent element. In contest with this cosmic enemy, man finds his further ratification, his further ideal vindication. He comes out victorious, but not till the sea has tortured his living, integral body, and made him pay something for his triumph in consciousness.

The horrific struggle round Cape Horn, homewards, is the crisis of the Dana history. It is an entry into chaos, a heaven of sleet and black ice-rain, a sea of ice and iron-like water. Man fights the element in all its roused, mystic hostility to conscious life. This fight is the inward crisis and triumph of Dana's soul. He goes through it all consciously, enduring, *knowing*. It is not a mere overcoming of obstacles. It is a pitting of the deliberate consciousness against all the roused, hostile, anti-life waters of the Pole.

After this fight, Dana has achieved his success. He knows. He knows what the sea is. He knows what the Cape Horn is. He knows what work is, work before the mast. He knows, he knows a great deal. He has carried his consciousness open-eyed through it all. He has won through. The ideal being.

And from his book, we know too, He has lived this great experience for us, we owe him homage.

The ship passes through the strait, strikes the polar death-mystery, and turns northward, home. She seems to fly with new strong plumage, free. "Every rope-yarn seemed stretched to the utmost, and every thread of the canvas; and with this sail added to her the ship sprang through the water like a thing possessed. The sail being nearly all forward, it lifted her out of the water, and she seemed actually to jump from sea to sea."

Beautifully the sailing-ship nodalizes the forces of sea and wind, converting them to her purpose. There is no violation, as in a steam-ship, only a winged centrality. It is this perfect adjusting of ourselves to the elements, the perfect equipoise between them and us, which gives us a great part of our life-joy. The more we intervene machinery between us and the naked forces the more we numb and atrophy our own senses. Every time we turn on a tap to have water, every time we turn a handle to have fire or light, we deny ourselves and annul our being. The great elements, the earth, air, fire, water are there like some great mistress whom we woo and struggle with, whom we heave and wrestle with. And all our appliances do but deny us these fine embraces, take the miracle of life away from us. The machine is the great neuter. It is the eunuch of eunuchs. In the end it emasculates us all. When we balance the sticks and kindle a fire, we partake of the mysteries. But when we turn on an electric tap there is as it were a wad between us and the dynamic universe. We do not know what we lose by all our labour-saving appliances. Of the two evils it would be much the lesser to lose all machinery, every bit, rather than to have, as we have, hopelessly too much.

When we study the pagan gods, we find they have now one meaning, now another. Now they belong to the creative essence, and now to the material-dynamic world. First they have one aspect, then another. The greatest god has both aspects. First he is the source of life. Then he is mystic dynamic lord of the elemental physical forces. So Zeus is Father, and Thunderer.

Nations that worship the material-dynamic world, as all nations do in their decadence, seem to come inevitably to worship the Thunderer. He is Ammon, Zeus, Wotan and Thor, Shango of the West Africans. As the creator of man himself, the Father is greatest in the creative world, the Thunderer is greatest in the material world. He is the god of force and of earthly blessing, the god of the bolt and of sweet rain.

So that electricity seems to be the first, intrinsic principle among the Forces. It has a mystic power of readjustment. It seems to be the overlord of the two naked elements, fire and water, capable of mysteriously enchaining them, and of mysteriously sundering them from their connections. When the two great elements become hopelessly clogged, entangled, the sword of the lightning can separate them. The crash of thunder is really not the clapping together of waves of air. Thunder is the noise of the explosion which takes place when the waters are loosed from the elemental fire, when old vapours are suddenly decomposed in the upper air by the electric force. Then fire flies fluid, and the waters roll off in purity. It is the liberation of the elements from hopeless conjunction. Thunder, the electric force, is the counterpart in the material-dynamic world of the life-force, the creative mystery, itself, in the creative world.

Dana gives a wonderful description of a tropical thunderstorm.

"When our watch came on deck at twelve o'clock it was as black as Erebus; not a breath was stirring; the sails hung heavy and motionless from the yards; and the perfect stillness, and the darkness, which was almost palpable, were truly appalling. Not a word was spoken, but everyone stood as though waiting for something to happen. In a few minutes the mate came forward, and in a low tone which was almost a whisper, gave the command to haul down the jib.—When we got down we found all hands looking aloft, and then, directly over where we had been standing, upon the main top-gallant masthead, was a ball of light, which the sailors name a corposant (*corpus sancti*). They were all watching it carefully, for sailors have a notion that if the corposant rises in the rigging, it is a sign of fair weather, but if it comes lower down, there will be a storm. Unfortunately, as an omen, it came down and showed itself on the top-gallant yard.

"In a few minutes it disappeared and showed itself again on the fore top-gallant-yard, and, after playing about for some time, disappeared again, when the man on the forecastle pointed to it upon the flying-jib-boom-end. But our attention was drawn from watching this by the falling of some drops of rain. In a few minutes low growling thunder was heard, and some random flashes of lightning came from the southwest. Every sail was taken in but the top-sail. A few puffs lifted the top-sails, but they fell again to the mast, and all was as still as ever. A minute more, and a terrific flash and peal broke simultaneously upon us, and a cloud appeared to open directly over our heads and let down the water in one body like a falling ocean. We stood motionless and almost stupefied, yet nothing had been struck. Peal after peal rattled over our heads with a sound which actually seemed to stop the breath in the body. The violent fall of the rain lasted but a few minutes, and was succeeded by occasional drops and showers; but the lightning continued incessant for several hours, breaking the midnight darkness with irregular and blinding flashes.

"During all this time hardly a word was spoken, no bell was struck, and the wheel was silently relieved. The rain fell at intervals in heavy showers, and we stood drenched through, and blinded by the flashes, which broke the Egyptian darkness with a brightness which seemed almost malignant, while the thunder rolled in peals, the concussion of which appeared to shake the very ocean. A ship is not often injured by lightning, for the electricity is separated by the number of points she presents, and the quality of iron which she has scattered in various parts. The electric fluid ran over our anchors, topsail-sheets and ties; yet no harm was done to us. We went below at four o'clock, leaving things in the same state."

Dana is wonderful at relating these mechanical, or dynamic-physical events. He could not tell about the being of men : only about the forces. He gives another curious instance of the process of recreation, as it takes place within the very corpuscles of the blood. It is *salt* this time which arrests the life-activity, causing a static arrest in Matter, after a certain sundering of water from the fire of the warm-substantial body.

"The scurvy had begun to show itself on board. One man had it so badly as to be disabled and off duty; and the English lad, Ben, was in a dreadful state, and was gradually growing worse. His legs swelled and pained him so that he could not walk; his flesh lost its elasticity, so that if it were pressed in, it would not return to its shape; and his gums swelled until he could not open his mouth. His breath, too, became very offensive; he lost all strength and spirit; could eat nothing; grew worse every day; and, in fact, unless something was done for him, would be a dead man in a week at the rate at which he was sinking. The medicines were all gone, or nearly all gone; and if we had had a chestfull, they would have been of no use; for nothing but fresh provisions and terra firma has any effect upon the scurvy."

However, a boat-load of potatoes and onions was obtained from a passing ship. These the men ate raw.

"The freshness and crispness of the raw onion, with the earthy state, give it a great relish to one who has been a long time on salt provisions. We were perfectly ravenous after them. We ate them at every meal, by the dozen; and filled our pockets with them, to eat on the watch on deck. The chief use, however, of the fresh provisions was for the men with scurvy. One was able to eat, and he soon brought himself to by gnawing upon raw potatoes; but the other, by this time, was hardly able to open his mouth; and the cook took the potatoes raw, pounded them in a mortar, and gave him the juice to suck. The strong earthy taste and smell of this extract of the raw potatoes at first produced a shuddering through his whole frame, and after drinking it, an acute pain, which ran through all parts of his body; but knowing by this that it was taking strong hold, he persevered, drinking a spoonful every hour or so, until, by the effect of this drink, and of his own restored hope, he became so well as to be able to move about, and open his mouth enough to eat the raw potatoes and onions pounded into a soft pulp. This course soon restored his appetite and strength; and ten days after we spoke the *Solon,* so rapid was his recovery that, from lying help-less and almost hopeless in his berth, he was at the masthead, furling a royal."

This is the strange result of the disintegrating effect of the sea, and of salt food. We are all sea-born, science tells us. The moon, and the sea, and salt, and phosphorus, and us: it is a long chain of connection. And then the earth: mother-earth. Dana talks of the relish which the *earthy* taste of the onion gives. The taste of created juice, the living milk of Gea. And limes, which taste of the sun.

How much stranger is the interplay of *life* among the elements, than any chemical interplay among the elements themselves. Life—and salt—and phosphorus—and the sea—and the moon. Life—and sulphur—and carbon—and volcanoes—and the sun. The way up, and the way down. The strange ways of life.

But Dana went home, to be a lawyer, and a rather dull and distinguished citizen. He was once almost an ambassador. And pre-eminently respectable.

He had been. He KNEW. He had even told us. It is a great achievement.

And then what?—Why, nothing. The old vulgar hum-drum. That's the worst of knowledge. It leaves one only the more life-less. Dana lived his bit in two years, and knew, and drummed out the rest. Dreary lawyer's years, afterwards.

We know enough. We know too much. We know nothing.

Let us smash something. Ourselves included. But the machine above all.

o

Dana's small book is a very great book: contains a great extreme of knowledge, knowledge of the great element.

And after all, we have to know all before we can know that knowing is nothing.

Imaginatively, we have to know all: even the elemental waters. And know and know on, until knowledge suddenly shrivels and we know that forever we don't know.

Then there is a sort of peace, and we can start afresh, knowing we don't know.

11. HERMAN MELVILLE'S *TYPEE* AND *OMOO*.

11. Herman Melville's *Typee* and *Omoo*

The essay below has never been published and is reprinted from a typescript. The typescript is 12½ pages long and carries the address of Robert Mountsier, Lawrence's American agent. Internal evidence (author's mood, structure of sentences, vocabulary used, interpunctuation, ideas expressed) shows that it is very probably version 2.

The manuscript carries the title "Studies in Classic American Literature (XI)."[1] In version 1 (containing one essay on Hawthorne) this essay would have been number X. It is very improbable that the essay on Moby Dick *would have preceded the one on* Typee and Omoo. *"Whitman" definitely was number XII. In version 3 the essay is again number X ("The Two Principles" left out, but two essays on Hawthorne this time). It is quite clear that for version 2 Lawrence divided the essay on Hawthorne (the published part on* The Scarlet Letter; *and the unpublished part, partly on* The Blithedale Romance). *Probably he had not deleted the essay on "The Two Principles" (as he had not yet written his two books on psychology). Therefore, the essay below would be number XI of version 2.*

---

[1] The title-pages of the other two manuscripts of version 2 ("Hawthorne II", "Herman Melville's *Moby Dick*") carry no numbers but the addresses of both agents.

217

When Lawrence rewrote the essay in America for the book of 1923 (version 3), he had this essay at hand. From time to time a paragraph begins with the same thought, sometimes with the same words. Nevertheless, both versions are entirely different, in wording and content. Lawrence does not use one single quotation from Melville. Before writing version 3, he read Weaver's book on Melville, White Jacket *and, possibly,* Pierre.

Though the essay below is objective and logical, version 3 was again full of axe-grinding. That Melville did not want to stay with the Typees gives Lawrence another opportunity to attack Mabel Dodge: "The truth of the matter is, one cannot go back. Some men can: renegade . . . But we cannot turn the current of our life backwards, back towards their soft warm twilight and uncreate mud. Not for a moment. If we do it for a moment, it makes us sick.

"We can only do it when we are renegade. The renegade hates life itself. He wants the death of life. So these many 'reformers' and 'idealists' who glorify the savages in America. They are death-birds, life-haters. Renegades."

The last two pages, concerned with human relationships, were not in the typescript and must have been added in America. These pessimistic passages were probably inspired by the failure of Lawrence's friendship with J. M. Murry, and, to a lesser degree, by his disillusionment with Mabel Dodge and the other people at Taos.

Harry T. Moore says that, "in taking Melville seriously, Lawrence was one of the first voices in the great Melville revival" *(The Intelligent Heart, p. 227). While version 3 is again full of personal spite and hatred against America and Americans, the essay below represents Lawrence the critic at his best. This version loses nothing by being only two-thirds of the length of version 3.*

THE GREATEST seer and poet of the sea, perhaps in all the world, is Herman Melville. His vision is more real than that of Swinburne, for he does not personify or humanise, and more profound than that of Conrad, for he does not emotionalise. Melville belongs to the sea, like one of its own birds. Like a sea-bird, he seems to have nothing of the land in him. He does not pit himself against the ocean, he is of it. And so he has that strange inscrutable magic and mystery of the sea-creatures, the same untranslatable speech, and, oddly, the same curious repulsiveness, or inferiority of order. One cannot help feeling that he is lapsing from the central order of life into an order of lower degree, or of external importance : moving towards the inanimate in one of the last flights of the consciousness, away into the boundless, where it loses itself.

There is also something about Melville which reminds us of the Vikings, inhuman, like sea-birds, creatures of the watery mystery who sailed from their settlements in Greenland down past Labrador to Nova Scotia, and even to Florida. They were Northmen, ocean-born, seeking the sun. Some met and mingled with the dark, earth-rich fiery creation of the South. Some lapsed in extreme ice. Some persisted unchanged. The blue-eyed, water-mystic people of the North have not yet lost their allegiance and origin. They are not yet fused into being. Creatures of the one preponderant principle, they are almost elementals, not being [sic] wonderful, primordial to us. The dead Viking chiefs are pushed out in flames into the ocean, given in death to the fire-consummation. And the living either seek the sun which will perfect them, or they return to the seas from whence they were derived, fire being the death-flame.

Melville is like one pushed out in flames again to the sea. But also he seeks the Southern sun. The sea claims him, as its own. The sea never quite loses its spell over the blue-eyed people. They love it, as the dark-eyed hate it. For the dark-eyed people are people of an old creation, created under the sun from the waters, sun-children. Their brown eyes are brown like the earth, which is tissue of bygone life, complicated, compound. The sun-spell is the stronger. They belong more to the fire-mystery, the earth-mystery quick with fire. The water is inherent in them too. But the fire preponderates. They are children of the old, old world.

Melville makes the great return. He would really melt him-self, an elemental, back into his vast beloved element, material though it is. All his fire he would carry down, quench in the sea. It is time for the sea to receive back her own, into the pale, bluish underworld of the watery after-life. He is like a Viking going home to the sea, encumbered with age and memories, and a sort of accomplished despair, almost madness. The great Northern cycle of which he is the returning unit has completed its round, accomplished itself, flowered from the waters like forget-me-nots and sea-poppies, and now returns into the sea, giving back its consciousness and its being to the vast material element, burying its flames in the deeps, self-conscious and deliberate. So blue flax and yellow, horned sea-poppies fall into the waters and give back their created sun-stuff to the watery end, the watery infinite.

It is to the Pacific Ocean Melville returns: the great, original ocean, fire-impregnated. This is the first of all the waters, im-memorial. Its mysteries are grander, profounder, *older* than those of the Atlantic. Without doubt the great era of the previous world perfected itself about the Pacific. Without doubt the Pacific has known a vast previous civilisation, before the geological cata-clysms. Without doubt its sleep is vastly impregnated with dreams unfathomable to us, it holds a great quenched epoch within itself. The China, the Japan, those lands historically known to us, they are only echoes of what went before, the vast Pacific civilisation, [about which] we can never know anything. The geological cataclysms intervene.

For many thousands of years the Pacific lands have been passing through the process of disturbing dreams, some good, mostly bad, dreams of the great sensual-mystic civilisations which once were theirs, and which are now ten times forgotten by the very peoples themselves. Egypt and India no doubt are young civilisations, forerunners of Europe. But China, Japan, the Aztecs, Maya, Incas, Polynesians—surely these are all only echoes and re-echoings of what is immemorially bygone, re-echoed a million times, each time fainter.

There must have been some universal body of knowledge over the world in the unknown past, just as there is now. There must have been intercommunication over all the globe, as there is now, and a universal understanding, as potentially, as there is now. The Pacific Ocean must have been the vast cradle of the civilisation of that geologically-incomprehensible world, and what is now Europe must have been the hinterland.

But all exact knowledge is gone forever. We have some fragments, almost barren remains, curious forms of an almost mathematical cosmology, found in Korea, native Argentine, the Soudan, similar abstract forms; also degraded mythologies. How much is survival, how much is legend, who knows? The surviving mythologies tell us almost less than nothing of the great sensual understanding these people had. And we lack the proper intelligence to understand.

Something similar happens much closer to us. We do not know how completely we have lost all comprehension of even Mediaeval Christianity. We shall soon have lost the *mystery* of Christianity altogether, even while we keep dogmas and ethical creeds and ritual services intact. Already we *cannot understand* what happened to St. Francis when he fell at the feet of the peasant. We have lost the faculty for experiencing the terrible shock of the revelation of present *otherness,* the crash of submission, and the subsequent gush of relaxation into the impersonal love, which sweeps the individual away in an unconsciousness or super-consciousness, bears him like a piece of flotsam on the flood, in that motion of uniting which is the gesture of new creation. This is the very crisis of Christian experience, and already we have lost all conception, or *even remembrance* of it. It has passed from

our range of passional experience, and becomes a verbal term.
The same with the mystery of the Eucharist. Since the transubstantiation disputes, and the rationalising of the sacrament, the
Holy Communion has become really a barren performance. The
profound, passional *experience* it was to the mediaeval Christian
is beyond our comprehension. We do not even choose to know.
Because we do not choose to admit the sensual apprehension. We
do not choose that the blood shall act in its own massive, inscrutable consciousness. We are artificial little idealists, really.

The Pacific Ocean holds the dream of immemorial centuries :
in the same way it is nascent with a new world. It is the great
blue twilight of the vastest of all evenings, the most wonderful
of all dawns. This great ocean, with its peoples, is still latent
with the coming unknown. The Atlantic is again superseded.
Never was so vast a reality as the Pacific swung down into disintegration. Its waters are surcharged with the blue, ghostly end
of immemorial peoples. But it rolls also latent with all the unborn
issues of the coming world of man.

It was to this Pacific Ocean, then, that Melville returned, the
great bourne, the heaven under the wave, like the Celtic Tir-na-
Og. And he went to the center of the Pacific, to the South Sea
Islands : the center of the seas, under the sun. Among these
islands he wanders like an uneasy ghost seeking its rest, and never
finding it. For he cannot yet identify himself with the great sea,
he cannot yet escape his European self, ideal and ethical as it
is, chain-bound.

At the very center of the old primeval world sleeps the living
and forgetting of the South Sea Isles, Samoa, Tahiti, Nukuheva,
places with the magic names. Wordsworth hints at the sleep-
forgotten past magnificence of human history in his "trailing
clouds of glory do we come." Tahiti, Samoa, Nukuheva, the very
names are clouds of glory. They are echoes from the world once
splendid in the fulness of the other way of knowledge.

But Samoa, Tahiti, Nukuheva are the sleep and the forgetting
of this great life, the very body of dreams. To which dream

Melville helplessly returns. He enters first in *Typee*. Nothing is
more startling, at once actual and dream-mystical, than his
descent down the gorges to the valley of the dreadful Typee.
Down this narrow, steep, horrible dark gorge he slides and
struggles as we struggle in a dream, or in the act of birth, to
emerge in the green Eden of the first, or last era, the valley of
the timeless savages. He had dreaded this entry acutely, for the
men of Typee had a cannibal reputation. But they are good and
gentle with him, he finds himself at once in a pure, mysterious
world, pristine.

It is absurd to speak of savages as "children," young, rudimentary people. To look among them for the link between us
and the ape is laughably absurd. Of all childish things,
science is one of the most childish and amusing. The savages, we
may say *all* savages, are remnants of the once civilised world-
people, who had their splendour and their being for countless
centuries in the way of sensual knowledge, that conservative way
which Egypt shows us at its conclusion, mysterious and long-
enduring. It is we from the North, starting new centers of life in
ourselves, who have become young. The savages have grown
older and older. No man can look at the African grotesque carv-
ings, for example, or the decoration patterns of the Oceanic
islanders, without seeing in them the infinitely sophisticated soul
which produces distortion from its own distorted psyche, a psyche
distorted through myriad generations of degeneration.

No one can fail to see the quenched spark of a once superb
understanding. The savages are not children practising. They are
old, grotesque people, dreaming over their once wide-awake
realities, and in each dream producing a new distortion. It is a
real dream-process, a process of continuing almost mechanically
in life long after creative living has ceased : a sort of slow, infinitely slow degeneration, towards Matter and Force. It is something like the long, thousand-year sleep of toads. Any man
reading the Bushman folk-lore, as we have it now literally rendered, must feel horror-struck, catching the sounds of myriad

age-long contractions and age-long repetitions in human communication, communication become now unintelligible, yet in its
incomprehensibility most terrifyingly resonant of so far-off a past,
that the soul faintly re-echoes in horror. The ideographs are so
complicated, the sound-groups must convey so many unspeakable, unfeelable meanings, all at once, in one stroke, that it needs
myriads of ages to achieve such unbearable concentration. The
savages are not simple. It is we who are simple. They are unutterably complicated, every feeling, every term of theirs is un-
translatably agglomerate. So with the African fetishes. They are
timelessly-repeated dream-degradations of some once perfect,
sensual-mystic images, and each distortion contains centuries of
strange, slow experience, for which we have no reference.

So Melville's life among the Typee. It is inconceivable to think
of that life in Nukuheva as "savage." It is refined, and concentrated, and self-understood to a degree which makes our life
laughably crude. True, it is unscientific. But subjectively, it is
beyond us.

Melville brings against them nothing save their lack of European morals, the wildness of their warfare, and their cannibalism.
Their lack of morals he does not mind. The cannibalism fills him
with a fear and horror to an unaccountable degree. For surely
he must have assisted at the Christian Communion-Supper, he
must have heard the words, "This is my body, take, and eat."
After all, cannibalism seems everywhere to have primarily a
ritualistic, sacramental meaning. It is no doubt the remains of
the mystic Eucharist of the sensual religions, the very counterpart of our Eucharist. "This is thy body which I take from thee
and eat," says the sensual communicant, in his ecstasy of consummation in might. The savage may have forgotten the mystery
implied in his observance: but, to judge from the traveller's
reports, even then not so much as we have forgotten *our* mystery.
The savage seems to know the sacred, passional reality of the
act. In Typee they observed the strictest secrecy. There was
evidently a real passional comprehension of the sacrament, the

mystery of *oneing* which takes place when the communicant partakes of the body of his vanquished enemy. It is the mystery of final unification, ultimate oneing, as in our sacrament. The act is only reversed. Frobenius, after travelling in Africa, says: "All the tribes of Inner Africa associate quite a distinctive frame of mind with the consumption of human flesh, and as far as this refers to the territories I myself have travelled through, I am bound to regard it as a misrepresentation of facts for any traveller to say that the Africans of the interior eat human flesh with the same sensation which a beefsteak gives to us. This is not the truth, because, even if a negro has human meat upon his board several times a week, his enjoyment of it in these countries will always be connected with a definite emotion."

Melville found in Typee almost what he wanted to find, what every man dreams of finding: a perfect home among timeless, unspoiled savages. There, in Nukuheva, the European psyche, with its ideals and its limitations, had no place. Our artificial ethical laws had never existed. There was naked simplicity of life, with subtle, but non-mental understanding, *rapport* between human beings. And it was too much for the American Melville, idealist of all idealists still. For him, life must be an *idea,* essentially an idea. It must be a progression towards an ideal: a life dedicated to some process or goal of consciousness. He could never let be. He could never really let go. His will was always clinched, forcing life in some direction or other, the direction of ideal transcendence. Man must be an ideal consciousness: this was a fixed principle in him.

And therefore, beautiful, free as it was, the life in the island became torture to him. The very freedom was torture. If he had been *constrained,* he could have borne it. But he was free and cherished: only he might not depart. And so he spent all his energies contriving to escape.

One would have thought that now his gnawing restlessness would have ceased: that now his fretful spirit would be appeased. But no—on the contrary, he was mad to escape, mad to run back to that detestable America which he always had been driven to run away from : America of the increasing, insane, hateful industrialism, competition, fight for existence, idealism which was rooted in unbridled commercialism. He had to go back to it. it enshrined his ideal, hideous as it was, and he was an idealist. He needed the struggle, struggle, struggle into further ideal consciousness. The true spontaneous existence, though he longed for it achingly, was yet a torture and a *nullification* to him. This is the quandary of the idealist, the man who stakes all his being on his upper consciousness. He cannot be free and full, and he cannot be made free. He cannot even enjoy his own being. He can only delight in striving after some fixed, external goal, which is no goal when he gets there.

So Melville. He loved his savage hosts. But he never knew the sacred reality of their lives, lived in mindless, naked spontaneity. Such a life of spontaneity was null to him, just nothing. He could only understand forcing in some direction.

He had not fulfilled his own destiny. And so, escape he must, or die. Whilst in Typee he had a strange malady in his leg, which would never heal. Such maladies are due to an interruption in the vital circuit. The poles of his vital flow were broken. The escaping current destroyed him in his wound. The moment the poles were restored, the wound began to heal : that is, the moment he was on board a white ship again.

The white man must remain true to his own destiny. And therefore, later on in Omoo, Melville looked with horror on the renegade Englishman who had the blue shark tattooed across his brow, the mystic sign that he had gone over to the savages, accepted their life finally. Melville was horrified at the renegade. The white way of life, ideal and transcendent, was to him the only way.

Melville must remain true to his white destiny, the destiny of the Christian white races, of conquering life and death by submission and spiritual transcendence. This desire, this ideal, this conquest of life and death still possessed Melville. Man had sub-

mitted to man, in martyrdom and death, till at last the ideal
of meekness was established. Kings had fallen, men were equal,
a oneness in submission and humility and meek love was established, or at least accepted as the highest reality. Human life was
conquered, and the old world. Now the far-off savages must be
reduced to the same term of the upper consciousness, the great
oceans must be brought under. What Dana began, Melville must
finish: the conquest of the sea. Destiny did not permit him to
remain in the Eden of Nukuheva. He must strain away, after a
new conquest in spiritual consciousness. The malady in his leg
is a clear indication of his true destiny. He must go on.

Yet the moment he is free, and is actually sailing away, in a
voyage that will ultimately take him to America, oh, the acute
and intolerable nostalgia he feels for the island he is leaving. His
whole *desire* is that way: his aspiration is another way. Typee
is his paradise, that he longs for. But he is not ready for paradise.
The simple spontaneity of life itself, spontaneous being, this is the
goal of his desire but the prison of his aspiration. He must strive,
strict, strive in a given direction, towards a goal of triumphant
consciousness and self-extinction. Striving, his leg heals at once.

It is a great, necessary sacrifice, his giving himself up to the
conscious conquest of the sea. From such sacrifices we inherit our
possibility of grand freedom in the future. Having triumphed
over the universe, there is no further need to triumph: no need
for more of the insatiable striving. We can be confident and at
home in ourselves.

In *Omoo,* the book which succeeds *Typee,* Melville continues
his wanderings among the South Sea Islands. No man gives us
the Pacific as Melville does: and we feel that his is the *real*
Pacific. It is not emotional or even stupendous. It is just *there,*
immediate. If we cannot appreciate it, it is because we are not
far enough on, not abstracted, not sufficiently resolved. We are
still too much in our own practical, trivial world of machines
and arbitrary ideals. The Pacific has no ideals. It has no fixed

goal to strive after. There, each thing is itself, *arrivé*. And this
is what the European can't bear.

So Melville roams, sails, wanders, a vagabond, a hired land-
worker, a ship's hand. *Omoo* is a curious book. It has no unity
no purpose, no anything, and yet it is one of the most real, actual
books ever written about the South Seas. It seems like reality
itself. Melville, at his best, is the perfect life-accepter. At his
worst, he is a professional mystic and transcendentalist. At his
best, he is just a vivid man, accepting life. When we say just
a man, we don't mean a common anybody. Rarest of all things
to find is a man who can really accept life, without imposing
some theory or some arbitrary goal or some mechanistic vision.
Melville is no amateur at living. He is the perfect epicurean,
eating the world like a snipe, dirt and all baked in one *bonne
bouche*. He takes the crude, dirty realities along with the rest.
Essentially, he is one of the most cultured men that have ever
written. All the finicking niceties of "delicate" or "moral" individuals seem so cheap, so boorish in the end. That man is perfectly educated who knows how to meet life sensitively and
responsively in every one of its moods and aspects. Your picker
and chooser, your elegant and your Tolstoy are alike half-
educated, ill-bred, clownish.

Melville knows how to live, and living he *knows* life. This is
the highest pitch of culture. He has really no purpose in mind,
no scheme of life for himself. In his actual living he is quite spontaneous, non-moral. All the time he is the living quick of the
moment.

This is the free Melville, who has escaped from Typee. But he
is not ultimately free. A long, thin, fine chain is round his ankle,
the chain of the old Christian purpose, the purpose of the conquest of life and death, by meekness and "the spirit." He is curious: in his immediate living quite non-normal: and yet he keeps
the whole block of the Christian tenets intact at the back of his
mind, in a sort of cupboard. His brain, some part of it, is a tablet
of stone, on which the old ethic is engraved. No matter what

his first-consciousness may be : the spontaneous consciousness of
the blood which surges and returns, the first consciousness of the
great nerve-centers which are our physical, and basic first-minds,
this, the living reality of our waking being, can be annulled again
in a minute. The ethic fixed in his brain is like some fatal mill-
stone.

The old will, the old purpose is fixed in him. He, who seems
so truly spontaneous, is in reality a monomaniac, possessed by a
fixed idea of further spiritual triumph, further idealisation. The
end is not yet reached. Suddenly he starts from his peace and his
happy-go-lucky wandering, starts off on the old maniacal quest,
the quest of the infinite, the triumph over life and death. It seems
as if man will never be able to accept life and death, perfectly
and splendidly, till he has affected this triumph over life and
death, and proved his infinitude. Not till he has in real experience
accomplished his triumph and known his infinitude, will he
realise that infinitude is nothing, and automatic mastery over
life is less than nothing. To be able to live in sheer full spontaneity, because of the perfect harmony between the conscious
intelligence and the unconscious, pre-conscious prompting, urging
of the very life itself, the living soul-center itself, this is the whole
goal of our ambition, our education, our perfect culture. But this,
being the state of flowering in us, is hardest to come to. We have
first to go through all the processes of mastering life and mastering death, achieving the hollow triumph of our own nothingness,
before we can cease from such "triumphs," and be ourselves
from the center.

P

12. HERMAN MELVILLE'S
MOBY DICK

12. Herman Melville's
Moby Dick

The essay below was never published and is reprinted from a carbon-copy of a typescript found among Lawrence's papers. The typescript is 19 pages long. The title-page carries the handwritten address of Lawrence's American agent, Robert Mountsier, in the right bottom corner of the page. This address was later crossed out, and the stamp of Curtis Brown, Lawrence's London agent, covers part of the Mountsier text.

Lawrence had dismissed J. B. Pinker, his former London agent, in January, 1920. He finished revising the American essays in June, 1920 (Harry T. Moore: The Intelligent Heart, *p.* 267) *and sent them to Mountsier on August* 2, 1920 (*Lawrence's diary in E. W. Tedlock:* The Frieda Lawrence Collection of D. H. Lawrence Manuscripts). *Lawrence had no agent in England till April, 1921, when Curtis Brown began working for him. Mountsier visited Curtis Brown in May or June, 1920, and delivered to him manuscripts (or copies of manuscripts) which he had not been able to place in America, among them the essay on* Moby Dick *and the essay herein entitled "Nathaniel Hawthorne II", both carrying Mountsier's and Brown's name and address. It is very probable that Curtis Brown also received copies of "Herman Melville's* Typee *and* Omoo", "Dana's *Two Years Before the Mast", and "Whitman".*

Curtis Brown evidently tried hard to sell the five essays to periodicals. On July 25, 1921, we find Lawrence writing to him: *"Mountsier has just read me a list of Poems and Studies in* Classic Amer. Literature, *etc. that you have been sending out to the various papers. Will you please tell your magazine man to go slowly*: *not to send out anything unless it seems really likely to suit the miserable periodicals . . . I would rather sell* nothing *than have the goods hawked round and cheapened in the eyes of a lot of little people." It may have been a consequence of this letter that Curtis Brown kept the essays on Dana and Melville back, and that they were not published in periodicals before they appeared in book-form. But Curtis Brown had already sold the essay on Whitman to* The Nation *and* The Athenaeum *where it appeared on July 23, 1921.*

It is almost certain that this essay is version 2. Internal evidence leads to the same conclusion (style, sentence-structure, vocabulary, ideas expressed, interpunctuation, author's mood). Version 3, published in the book of 1923 is somewhat longer. More than half of the text in both versions is quotation from Melville. In both versions Lawrence uses the same quotations in the same order. His comments between the quotations are almost identical; only rarely does he change a word here or add a sentence there. However, the essays differ completely at the beginning and at the end. The last page of version 3 contains the interpretation of Moby Dick *as the "deepest blood-being", chased to death by the whole of humanity, but who, in the end, draws the spiritual humanity into destruction as well. This interpretation is much more carefully elaborated in the first six pages of the essay below. While version 3 starts with humorous and superficial lists of the three mates and the three harpooners, the first six pages of the essay below elaborate carefully the symbolic meaning of each of these figures. They are among the best pages of all of Lawrence's critical writings.*

HERMAN MELVILLE's biggest book is *Moby Dick,* or *The White Whale.* It is the story of the last hunt. The last hunt, the last conquest—what is it?

American art symbolises the destruction, decomposition, mechanizing of the fallen degrees of consciousness. Franklin and Crèvecoeur show the mechanizing of the shallowest instincts and passions, appetites; Cooper and Melville the deeper worship-through-contumely of the fallen sexual or sacral consciousness; Poe the direct decomposition of this consciousness; and Dana and Melville the final hunting of the same consciousness into the very Matter, the very watery material, last home of its existence, and its extinction there. Remains the entry into the last state, and into fulness, freedom.

St. John said, "there shall be no more sea." That was esoteric. Exoterically, Dana and Melville say the same. The Sea, the great Waters, is the material home of the deep sacral-sexual consciousness. To the very depths of this home Melville pursues the native consciousness in himself, and destroys it there. When he has really destroyed this sacral-sexual consciousness, destroyed or over-thrown it, then John's prophecy will be fulfilled. There will be no more sea.

Moby Dick is the story of this last symbolic hunt. Moby Dick is a great white whale, the Leviathan of the waters. He is old, hoary, monstrous and snow-white; unspeakably terrible in his wrath; having been repeatedly attacked, he swims now alone in the great, pathless seas.

He is the last warm-blooded tenant of the waters, the greatest and last. He is the deep, free sacral consciousness in man. He must be subdued.

In himself he is warm-blooded, even lovable. But he must be conquered. Curious are his counterparts in the world. The whole of the South Pacific seems to worship, in hate, the shark or the crocodile, the great cold-blooded tenants, lords of the water, fiendish and destructive lords. Curious how shark and crocodile patterns, with grinning teeth, dominate aboriginal decoration-designs in those regions. The same crocodile worship is found in Africa, very wide-spread. In China, however, the dragon, the Leviathan is the dragon of the sun : as the Mantis, surely another dragon of the sun, dominates the Bushmen. Is not this the inordinately ancient relic of the pre-Flood worship, a relic from that era when the upper consciousness was the anathema, and the glory and the triumph was all in the sensual understanding, incomprehensible to us now ?

Melville writes in the peculiar lurid, glamorous style which is natural to the great Americans. It gives us at first a sense of spuriousness. To some it merely seems wordy and meaningless, unreal. It comes, I think, from the violence native to the American Continent, where force is more powerful than consciousness, and so is never gracefully expressed. The life-force itself is so strong that it tends to come forth lurid and clumsy, obscure also. It causes also a savage desire to go to extremes, to hasten to extremes, whether of idealism or of violent action.

So, in beginning *Moby Dick,* we must be prepared for the curious lurid style, almost spurious, almost journalism, and yet *not* spurious : on the verge of falsity, still real. The book starts off with a semi-metaphysical effusion about water, and about the author's attraction to this element; it goes on with some clumsy humorisms, till it arrives in the sea-town of New Bedford. Then actual experience begins. It is curiously like cold material record, touched-up into journalese : neither veritable nor created. One cannot help feeling that the author is pretentious, and an amateur, wordy and shoddy. Yet something glimmers through all this : a glimmer of genuine reality. Not a reality of real, open-air experience. Yet it is a reality of what takes place in the dark

cellars of a man's soul, what the psychoanalysts call the unconscious. There is the old double set of values : the ostensible Melville, a sort of Emersonian transcendentalist, and the underneath
Melville, a sort of strange underworld, under-sea Yankee creature
looking with curious, lurid vision on the upper world. It is the
incongruous mixture of ideal heaven and the uncouth incoher-
ence of a self-conscious adolescent. The reality comes from the
adolescent, the uncouth, unformed creature, not from the
idealist.

It is no use pretending that Melville writes like a straightforward, whole human being. He is hardly a human being at all.
He gives events in the light of their extreme reality : mechanical,
material, a semi-incoherent dream-rendering. What the futurists
have tried hard to do, Dana and Melville have pretty well succeeded in doing for them. These two are masters of the sheer
movement of substance in its own paths, free from all human pos-
tulation or control. The result is nearly like artifice, a sort of rank
journalism. But we must restrain a too hasty judgment. The
author is never quite himself. He is always at the mercy of the
rank, self-conscious idealism which still rules white America, he
always has to handle artificial values.

Melville tries to square himself with the intellectual world by
dragging in deliberate transcendentalism, deliberate symbols and
"deeper meanings." All this is insufferably clumsy and in clownish bad taste : self-conscious and amateurish to a degree, the
worst side of American behavior. When however he forgets all
audience, and renders us his sheer apprehension of the world, he
is wonderful, his book commands a stillness in the soul, an awe.

Let us repeat that it is in rendering the sheer naked slidings
of the elements, and the curious mechanical cause-and-effect of
materials events, that he is a master. For near as he is to sheer
materialism, the central creative spark is still unquenched, the
integral soul is present, if alone. His mind lags far, far behind
his physical comprehension. His mind is cumbered up with a
hopeless aggregation of fixed ideas, which spin on together like

little wheels. But his bodily knowledge moves naked, a living quick among the stark elements. In sheer physical, vibrational sensitiveness, like a marvellous wireless-station, he registers the effects of the outer world. And he records also, almost beyond pain or pleasure, the extreme transitions of the isolated, far-driven soul, the soul which is now alone, without human connection.

The first days in New Bedford introduce the only human being who at all enters into the soul of Ishmael, the "I" of the book. This is Queequeg, the tattooed, powerful South Sea harpooner, whom Melville loves as Dana loves "Hope". The advent of Ishmael's bed-mate is amusing and unforgettable. But later the two swear "marriage," in the language of the savages. For Queequeg has opened again the flood-gates of love and human connection in Ishmael.

"As I sat there in that now lonely room, the fire burning low, in that mild stage when, after its first intensity has warmed the air, it then only glows to be looked at; the evening shades and phantoms gathering round the casements, and peering in upon us silent, solitary twain: I began to be sensible of strange feelings. I felt a melting in me. No more my splintered hand and maddened heart was turned against the wolfish world. This soothing savage had redeemed it. There he sat, his very indifference speaking a nature in which there lurked no civilized hypocrisies and bland deceits. Wild he was; a very sight of sights to see; yet I began to feel myself mysteriously drawn towards him." So they smoke together, and are clasped in each other's arms. The friendship is finally sealed when Ishmael offers sacrifice to Queequeg's little idol, Gogo.

"I was a good Christian, born and bred in the bosom of the infallible Presbyterian Church. How then could I unite with the idolater in worshipping his piece of wood? But what is worship?—to do the will of God—*that* is worship. And what is the will of God?—to do to my fellow man what I would have my fellow man do to me—*that* is the will of God. Now Queequeg is my fellow man. And what do I wish that this Queequeg would do to me? Why, unite with me in my particular Presbyterian form of worship. Consequently, I must then unite with him; ergo, I must turn idolater. So I kindled the shavings; helped prop up the innocent little idol; offered him burnt biscuit with Queequeg; salaamed before him twice or thrice; kissed his nose; and that done, we undressed and went to bed, at peace with our own consciences and all the world. But we did not go to sleep without some little chat. How it is I know not; but there is no place like bed for confidential disclosures between friends. Man and wife, they say, open the very bottom of their souls to each other; and some old couples often lie and chat over old times till nearly morning. Thus, then, lay I and Queequeg—a cosy, loving pair—" The sophistry with which he justifies his act of idolatry is amusing, and very characteristic of Melville. He continually spins an idea logic to fit his new acts. The ideal logic is apt to be boring. Plainly, he cared nothing about worship, and he loved Queequeg. Elsewhere he says he loved the savage's "large, deep eyes, fiery black and bold."

The two men go over from New Bedford to Nantucket, and there sign on for the Quaker whaling-ship, the *Pequod*. It is all strangely fantastic, phantasmagoric. Yet is it unreal? We pass on into the midst of the sea with this strange ship and its incredible crew. It is a mythical, mystical voyage, as any Argonaut voyage ever was. Sometimes its forced fantasy is irritating. And yet, after all, it is curiously *actual*. This is the beauty—the identity of daily experience with profound mystic experience. The blemish is the self-conscious posturing about it.

The voyage begins, like Dana's, in the winter-time, strange and dark at first. There is a mystery about the captain—he keeps hidden. The secret gradually emerges. The Quaker Ahab, the captain, a man in the prime of life, is a prey to monomania. He walks with an ivory stump, made from the sea-ivory. For Moby Dick, the great white whale, tore off his leg at the knee. So Ahab is now a monomaniac, and the ship is out on a maniacal cruise, the hunt of the almost mythical white whale.

It would be too long to unravel the amazing symbolisms of the book.—Starbuck, the first mate, is another Quaker Nantucketer, long, earnest, steadfast, prudent. He is a man of reason and forethought, intrepid, yet wise enough to say—"I will have no man in my boat who is not afraid of a whale." At the bottom of him is a sense of fatality, rooted in a great fear. This makes him succumb at last, in spite of himself, to Ahab's criminal madness.

Stubb, the second mate, is a man of spontaneous courage and jollity—"fearless as fire, and as mechanical," Ahab says of him. He is a mindless sailor delighting in sensation for sensation's sake. After a brief tussle, he too becomes a mere instrument of Ahab's hunt; a perfect instrument moreover. Flask, the third mate, is stubborn, obstinate, distinguished for his tenacity. He has no imagination, no vision at all. To him, "the wondrous whale was but a species of magnified mouse, or water-rat—This ignorant, unconscious fearlessness of his made him a little waggish in the matter of it—" None the less he is an admirable whalesman.

These three mates symbolise the three parts of the psyche, reason, impulsive passion, and blind will. But all these three elements are subject to the monomaniac in Ahab. Ahab is the force which drives them on the fearful, fatal chase.

Melville cannot always have known what his own symbols meant. He used them half-deliberately : never *quite* sure. Then again, he forgets them and moves into pure actuality. It is curious how actuality, of itself, in deep issues, becomes symbolic.

The three harpooners, Queeque, the Polynesian, Tashtego, the North-American Indian, and Daggoo, the great, black negro, are of three races.—Then, strangely and secretly, far more strangely than in Conrad, is introduced a boat's crew of fire-worshipping Parsees, men for Ahab's own boats. All races, all creeds, the fire-worship and the sea-worship, are all united to engage in the great disastrous hunt.

When at last the ship is fully in the South Seas, then the

pure beauty comes out. Melville is at his best when moving and working with the waters, and not self-consciously speculating. Yet it is the author's very attempt to get at some mystery behind the show of things which leads him to his highest beauty. The effort is made in a struggle of mystic speculation : then comes the lovely result, in a piece of sheer revelation.

Like Dana, Melville is impressed by the albatross. But he must rather clumsily philosophize, he is in somewhat bad taste—"I remember the first albatross I ever saw. It was during a prolonged gale, in waters hard upon the Antarctic seas. From my forenoon watch below, I ascended to the overcrowded deck; and there, dashed upon the main hatches, I saw a regal, feathered thing of unspotted whiteness, and with a hooked Roman bill sublime. At intervals it arched forth its vast, archangel wings.—Wondrous throbbings and flutterings shook it. Though bodily unharmed, it uttered cries, as some King's ghost in supernatural distress. Through its inexpressible strange eyes methought I peeped to secrets not below the heavens—the white thing was so white, its wings so wide, and in those for ever exiled waters, I had lost the miserable warping memories of traditions and of towns.—I assert then, that in the wondrous bodily whiteness of the bird chiefly lurks the secret of the spell—"

We must remember that Melville's albatross is a prisoner, caught by a bait on a hook. The whole description occurs in a note to the chapter on whiteness. The author dilates upon the whiteness of the whale, Moby Dick, and on the strange, supernatural spell which is cast by pure whiteness. We attribute whiteness to refraction. The sheer mechanical reaction between water and light, or Matter and light, or Matter and fire, causes white incandescence, whether of foam or of burning. In the same way, the utter absorption or drowning of the one element in the other causes blackness, like black flame or black water. The other colors reveal the mysterious degrees of interpenetration between the two.

How lovely it is to be at sea with the Pequod : all the seas are

.here, so wonderful, so utterly sea-like, with barely a grain of
earth interposed : the perfect reality of sea-life.

"It was a cloudy, sultry afternoon; the seamen were lazily
lounging about the decks, or vacantly gazing over into the lead-
coloured waters. Queequeg and I were mildly employed weaving
what is called a sword-mat, for an additional lashing to our boat.
So still and subdued and yet somehow preluding was all the scene,
and such an incantation of reverie lurked in the air that each
silent sailor seemed reselved into his own invisible self.—"

In the midst of this preluding silence came the first cry:
"There she blows! there! there! there! She blows!"—And
then comes the first chase, a marvellous piece of true sea-
writing, the sea, and sheer sea-beings on the chase, sea-
creatures chased. There is scarcely a taint of earth—pure sea-
motion.

" 'Give way men,' whispered Starbuck, drawing still further
aft the sheet of his sail; 'there is time to kill fish yet before the
squall comes. There's white water again!—Close to!—Spring!'
Soon after, two cries in quick succession on each side of us
denoted that the other boats had got fast; but hardly were they
overheard, when with a lightning-like hurtling whisper Starbuck
said : 'Stand up!' and Queequeg, harpoon in hand, sprung to
his feet.—Though not one of the oarsmen was then facing the
life and death peril so close to them ahead, yet with their eyes
on the intense countenance of the mate in the stern of the boat,
they knew that the imminent instant had come; they heard, too,
an enormous wallowing sound, as of fifty elephants stirring in
their litter. Meanwhile the boat was still booming through the
mist, the waves curbing and hissing around us like the erected
crests of enraged serpents.

" 'That's his hump. *There, there,* give it to him!' whispered
Starbuck. A short rushing sound leapt out of the boat; it was the
darted iron of Queequeg. Then all in one welded motion came a
push from astern, while forward the boat seemed striking on a
ledge; the sail collapsed and exploded; a gush of scalding vapour

shot up near by; something rolled and tumbled like an earth-quake beneath us. The whole crew were half-suffocated as they were tossed helter-skelter into the white curdling cream of the squall. Squall, whale, and harpoon had all blended together; and the whale, merely grazed by the iron, escaped. -"

Melville is a master of violent, chaotic physical motion, he can keep up a whole wild chase without a flaw. He is as perfect at creating stillness. The ship is cruising on the Carrol Ground, south of St. Helena.—"It was while gliding through these latter waters that one serene and moonlight night, when all the waves rolled by like scrolls of silver; and, by their soft, suffusing seeth-ings, made what seemed a silvery silence, not a solitude; on such a silent night a silvery jet was seen far in advance of the white bubbles at the bow—"

Then there is the description of brit. "Steering north-eastward from the Crozells we fell in with vast meadows of brit, the minute, yellow substance upon which the Right Whale largely feeds. For leagues and leagues it undulated round us, so that we seemed to be sailing through boundless fields of ripe and golden wheat. On the second day, numbers of Right Whales were seen, secure from the attack of a sperm-whaler like the Pequod, with open jaws sluggishly swam through the brit, which, adher-ing to the fringed fibres of that wondrous Venetian blind in their mouths, was in that manner separated from the water that escaped at the lip. As moving mowers, who side by side slowly and seethingly advance their scythes through the long wet grass of the marshy meads; even so these mon-sters swam, making a strange, grassy, cutting sound; and leaving behind them endless swaths of blue on the yellow sea. But it was only the sound they made as they parted the brit which at all reminded one of mowers. Seen from the mast heads, especially when they paused and were stationary for a while, their vast black forms looked more like masses of rock than any-thing else."

This beautiful passage brings us to the apparition of the squid.

"Slowly wading through the meadows of brit, the Pequod still held her way north-eastward towards the island of Java; a gentle air impelling her keel, so that in the surrounding serenity her three tall tapering masts mildly waved to that languid breeze, as three mild palms on a plain. And still, at wide intervals in the silvery night, that lonely, alluring jet would be seen.

"But one transparent blue morning, when a stillness almost preternatural spread over the sea, however unattended with any stagnant calm; when the long burnished sunglade on the waters seemed a golden finger laid across them, enjoining secrecy; when all the slippered waves whispered together as they softly ran on; in this profound hush of the visible sphere a strange spectre was seen by Daggoo from the mainmast head.

"In the distance, a great white mass lazily rose, and rising higher and higher, and disentangling itself from the azure, at last gleamed before our prow like a snow-slide, new slid from the hills. Thus glistening for a moment, as slowly it subsided, and sank. Then once more arose, and silently gleamed. It seemed not a whale; and yet, is this Moby Dick? thought Daggoo—"

The boats were lowered and pulled to the scene.

"In the same spot where it sank, once more it slowly rose. Almost forgetting for the moment all thoughts of Moby Dick, we now gazed at the most wondrous phenomenon which the secret seas have hitherto revealed to mankind. A vast pulpy mass, furlongs in length and breadth, of a glancing cream-color, lay floating on the water, innumerable long arms radiating from its centre, and curling and twisting like a nest of anacondas, as if blindly to clutch at any hapless object within reach. No perceptible face or front did it have; no conceivable token of either sensation or instinct; but undulated there on the billows, an unearthly, formless, chance-like apparition of life. And with a low sucking it slowly disappeared again."

The following chapters, with their account of whale-hunts, the killing, the stripping, the cutting up, are magnificent records of actual happening. Then comes the queer tale of the meeting of the Jeroboam, a whaler met at sea, all of whose men were under the domination of a religious maniac, one of the ship's hands. There are detailed descriptions of the actual taking of the sperm oil from a whale's head. Dilating on the smallness of the brain of a sperm whale, Melville significantly remarks—"for I believe that much of a man's character will be found betokened in his backbone. I would rather feel your spine than your skull, whoever you are—" And of the whale, he adds: "For, viewed in this light, the wonderful comparative smallness of his brain proper is more than compensated by the wonderful comparative magnitude of his spinal cord."

In among the rush of terrible, awful hunts come touches of pure beauty.

"As the three boats lay there on that gently rolling sea, gazing down into its eternal blue noon; and as not a single groan or cry of any sort, nay not so much as a ripple or a thought, came up from its depths; what landsman would have thought that beneath all that silence and placidity the utmost monster of the seas was writhing and wrenching in agony!"

Perhaps the most stupendous chapter is the one called "the Grand Armada," at the beginning of volume III. The Pequod was drawing through the Sunda Straits towards Java when she came upon a vast host of sperm whales. "Broad on both bows, at a distance of two or three miles, and forming a great semicircle embracing one-half of the level horizon, a continuous chain of whale-jets were up-playing and sparkling in the noonday air." Chasing this great herd, past the straits of Sunda, themselves chased by Javan pirates, the whalers race on. Then the boats are lowered. At last that curious state of inert irresolution came over the whales, when they were, as the seamen say, gallied. Instead of forging ahead in huge martial array they swam violently hither and thither, a surging sea of whales, no longer moving on. Starbuck's boat, made fast to a whale, is towed in amongst this howling Leviathan chaos. In mad career it cockles through the boiling surge of monsters, till it is brought into a clear lagoon in the very centre of the vast, mad, terrified herd. There a sleek, pure calm reigns. There the females swam in peace, and the young whales came snuffing tamely at the boat, like dogs. And there the astonished seamen watched the love-making of these amazing monsters, mammals, now in rut far down in the sea.—"But far beneath this wondrous world upon the surface, another and still stranger world met our eyes, as we gazed over the side. For, suspended in these watery vaults, floated the forms of the nursing mothers of the whales, and those that by their enor-mous girth seemed shortly to become mothers. The lake, as I have hinted, was to a considerable depth exceedingly transparent; and as human infants while sucking will calmly and fixedly gaze away from the breast, as if leading two different lives at a time : and while yet drawing mortal nourishment, be still spiritually feasting upon some unearthly reminiscence, even so did the young of these whales seem looking up towards us, but not at us, as if we were but a bit of gulf-weed in their newborn sight. Floating on their sides, the mothers also seemed quietly eyeing us.—Some of the subtlest secrets of the seas seemed divulged to us in this enchanted pond. We saw young Leviathan amours in the deep. And thus, though surrounded by circle upon circle of con-sternation and affrights, did these inscrutable creatures at the centre freely and fearlessly indulge in all peaceful concernments; yea, serenely revelled in dalliance and delight—"

There is something really overwhelming in these whale-hunts, almost superhuman or inhuman, bigger than life, more terrific than human activity. The same with the chapter on ambergris : it is so curious, so real, yet so unearthly. And again in the chapter called "The Cassock"—surely the oddest piece of phallicism in all the world's literature.

After this comes the amazing account of the try-works, when the ship is turned into the sooty, oily factory in mid-ocean, and the oil is extracted from the blubber. In the night of the red furnace burning on deck, at sea, Melville has his startling experience of reversion. He is at the helm, but has turned to watch the fire : when suddenly he feels the ship rushing backward from him, in mystic reversion.—"Uppermost was the impression, that whatever swift, rushing thing I stood on was not so much bound to any haven ahead, as rushing from all havens astern. A stark, bewildered feeling, as of death, came over me. Convulsively my hands grasped the tiller, but with the crazy conceit that the tiller was somehow, in some enchanted way, inverted. My God! What is the matter with me? thought I."

This dream-experience makes a great impression on him. He ends with an injunction to all men, not to gaze on the red fire when its redness makes all things look ghastly. It seems to him that his gazing on fire had cooked this horror of reversion, undoing.

After some unhealthy work on the ship, Queequeg caught a fever and was like to die.—"How he wasted and wasted in those few, long-lingering days, till there seemed but little left of him but his frame and tattooing. But as all else in him thinned, and his cheek-bones grew sharper, his eyes, nevertheless, seemed growing fuller and fuller; they took on a strangeness of lustre; and mildly but deeply looked out at you there from his sickness, a wondrous testimony to that immortal health in him which could not die or be weakened. And like circles on the water, which, as they grow fainter, expand; so his eyes seemed rounding and rounding, like the circles of Eternity. An awe that cannot be named would steal over you as you sat by the side of the waning savage—"

But Queequeg did not die—and the Pequod emerges from the Eastern Straits, into the full Pacific. "To my meditative Magian rover, this serene Pacific once beheld, must ever after be the sea of his adoption. It rolls the utmost waters of the world—"

In this Pacific the fight goes on.—"It was far down the afternoon; and when all the spearings of the crimson fight were done; and floating in the lovely sunset sea and sky, sun and whale both

died stilly together; then such a sweetness and such a plaintive-
ness, such inwreathing orisons curled up in that rosy air, that it
almost seemed as if far over from the deep green convent valleys
of the Manila isles, the Spanish land-breeze had gone to
sea, freighted with these vesper hymns.—Soothed again,
but only soothed to deeper gloom, Ahab, who had
sterned off from the whale, sat intently watching his final
wanings from the now tranquil boat. For that strange spectacle
observable in all sperm whales dying—the turning of the head
sunwards, and so expiring—that strange spectacle, beheld of
such a placid evening, somehow to Ahab conveyed a wondrous-
ness unknown before. 'He turns and turns him to it; how slowly,
but how steadfastly, his homage-rendering and invoking brow,
with his last dying motions. He too worships fire; . . . ' "

So Ahab soliloquizes : and so the warm-blooded whale turns
for the last time to the sun, which begot him in the waters.

But as we see in the next chapter, it is the Thunder-fire which
Ahab really worships : that livid fire of which he bears the brand,
from head to foot. It is storm, the electric storm of the Pequod,
when the corposants burn in high, tapering flames of supernatural pallor upon the mast-heads, and when the compass is
reversed. After this all is fatality. Life itself seems mystically
reversed. In these hunters of Moby Dick there is nothing but
madness and possession. The captain Ahab moves hand in hand
with the poor imbecile negro boy, Pip, who has been so cruelly
demented, left swimming alone in the vast sea. It is the imbecile
child of the sun hand in hand with the northern monomaniac,
captain and master.

The voyage surges on. They meet one ship, then another. It
is all ordinary day-routine, and yet all is a tension of pure madness and horror, the approaching horror of the last fight. "Hither
and thither, on high, glided the snow-white wings of small un-
speckled birds; these were the gentle thoughts of the feminine
air; but to and fro in the deeps, far down in the bottomless blue,
rushed mighty leviathans, sword-fish and sharks; and these were

the strong, troubled, murderous thinkings of the masculine sea—"
On this day Ahab confesses his weariness, the weariness of his
burden. "But do I look very old, so very, very old, Starbuck:
I feel deadly faint, and bowed, and humped, as though I were
Adam staggering beneath the piled centuries since Paradise—" It
is the Gethsemane of Ahab, before the last fight: the Gethsemane
of the human soul seeking the last self-conquest, the last attainment of extended consciousness—infinite consciousness.

At last they sight the whale. Ahab sees him from his hoisted
perch at the mast-head.—"From this height the whale was now
seen some mile or so ahead, at every roll of the sea revealing his
high, sparkling hump, and regularly jetting his silent spout into
the air.—"

The boats are lowered, to draw near the white whale. "At
length the breathless hunter came so nigh his seemingly un-
suspectful prey that his entire dazzling hump was distinctly
visible, sliding along the sea as if an isolated thing, and continually set in a revolving ring of finest, fleecy, greenish foam. He
saw the vast, involved wrinkles of the slightly projecting head,
beyond. Before it, far out on the soft, Turkish rugged waters,
went the glistening white shadow from his broad, milky fore-
head, a musical rippling playfully accompanying the shade; and
behind, the blue waters interchangeably flowed over the moving
valley of his steady wake; and on either side bright bubbles arose
and danced by his side. But these were broken again by the
light toes of hundreds of gay fowl softly feathering the sea, alter-
nate with their fitful flight; and like to some flagstaff rising from
the pointed hull of an argosy, the tall but shattered pole of a
recent lance projected from the white whale's back; and at intervals one of the clouds of soft-toed fowls hovering, and to and
fro shimmering like a canopy over the fish, silently perched and
rocked on this pole, the long tail-feathers streaming like pennons.

"A gentle joyousness—a mighty mildness of repose in swift-
ness, invested the gliding whale—"

The fight with the whale is too wonderful, and too awful, to be described apart from the book. It lasted three days. The fearful sight, on the third day, of the torn body of the Parsee harpooner, lost on the previous day, now seen lashed on to the flanks of the white whale by the tangle of harpoon-lines, has a mystic dream-horror. The awful and infuriated whale turns upon the ship, symbol of this civilised world of ours. He smites her with a fearful shock. And a few minutes later, from the last of the fighting whale-boats comes the cry, " 'The ship! Great God, where is the ship?'—Soon they through the dim, bewildering mediums saw her sidelong fading phantom, as in the gaseous Fata Morgana; only the uppermost masts out of the water; while fixed by infatuation, or fidelity, or fate, to their once lofty perches, the pagan harpooners still maintained their sinking lookouts on the sea. And now, concentric circles seized the lone boat itself, and all its crew, and each floating oar, and every lance-pole, and spinning, animate and inanimate, all round and round in one vortex, carried the smallest chip of the Pequod out of sight—"

The bird of heaven, the eagle, St. John's bird, goes down with the ship, nailed by Tashtego's hammer, the hammer of the American Indian.

"Now small fowls flew screaming over the yet yawning gulf; a sullen white surf boat against its steep sides; then all collapsed; and then the great shroud of the sea rolled on as it rolled five thousand years ago."

So ends one of the strangest and most wonderful books in the world, closing up its mystery and its tortured symbolism. It is an epic of the sea such as no man has equalled; and it is a book of exoteric symbolism of profound significance, and of considerable tiresomeness.

13.   WHITMAN

13. Whitman

This essay appeared in The Nation and The Athenaeum *for July* 23, 1921. *It was originally written in* 1918 *and re-vised in Sicily in* 1920; *the only time that an essay of the first revision was published. The* 1918 *manuscript (version 1) is lost. Version 2 (the essay below) is only sixty per cent of the length of version 3, published in the book of* 1923. *Version 3 consists of two parts of similar length, part one corres-ponding with the whole of version 2. All quotations in ver-sion 2 occur in the first part of version 3.*

In version 2 Whitman's praise is sung in the highest tones, while in the first part of version 3 Whitman is for the most part subject to derisive criticism. The main charges are against Whitman's belief in comrades and democracy. Law-rence's experiences with J. M. Murry and other "friends" are probably the reasons for his sceptical opinions. While version 2 is appreciative, the corresponding part of version 3 is wholly derisive. Lawrence, realizing this, continued to write the second part of version 3 more appreciatively. Lawrence ardently looked for something good to say about Whitman, which was difficult because, by 1923, *Whitman's theories and feelings were in direct contrast with Lawrence's own. So he projects his own feelings into Whitman: "The soul is a very perfect judge of her own motions, if your mind doesn't dictate to her. Because the mind says Charity! Charity! you don't have to force your soul into kiss-ing lepers or embracing syphilitics. Your lips are the lips of your soul; your body is the body of your soul; your own single, individual soul. That is Whitman's message." This is rather Lawrence's message.*

There is no unity in version 3. The second half is an attempt to improve upon Lawrence's severe judgment of Whitman in the first half. Lawrence is in the dilemma of admiring Whitman both as a person and a poet, yet condemning him because of his ideas. He cannot keep these aspects apart from each other, so he tries, in the second half of version 3, to project his own ideas into Whitman to make him more acceptable to his own conceptions. Version 2, in contrast, is more balanced and loses nothing in value by being much shorter than version 3.

WHITMAN IS THE GREATEST of the Americans. One of the greatest poets of the world, in him an element of falsity troubles us still. Something is wrong: we cannot be quite at ease in his greatness.

This may be our own fault. But we sincerely feel that something is overdone in Whitman; there is something that is too much. Let us get over our quarrel with him first.

All the Americans, when they have trodden new ground, seem to have been conscious of making a breach in the established order. They have been self-conscious about it. They have felt that they were trespassing, transgressing, or going very far, and this has given a certain stridency, or portentousness, or luridness to their manner. Perhaps that is because the steps were taken so rapidly. From Franklin to Whitman is a hundred years. It might be a thousand.

The Americans have finished in haste, with a certain violence and violation, that which Europe began two thousand years ago

or more. Rapidly they have returned to lay open the secrets
which the Christian epoch has taken two thousand years to close
up.

With the Greeks started the great passion for the ideal, the
passion for translating all consciousness into terms of spirit and
ideal or idea. They did this in reaction from the vast old world
which was dying in Egypt. But the Greeks, though they set out
to conquer the animal or sensual being in man, did not set out
to annihilate it. This was left for the Christians.

The Christians, phase by phase , set out actually to *annihilate*
the sensual being in man. They insisted that man was in his
reality *pure spirit,* and that he was perfectible as such. And this
was their business, to achieve such a perfection.

They worked from a profound inward impulse, the Christian
religious impulse. But their proceeding was the same, in living
extension, as that of the Greek esoterics, such as John the Evan-
gel or Socrates. They proceeded, by will and by exaltation, to
overcome *all* the passions and all the appetites and prides.

Now, so far, in Europe, the conquest of the lower self has
been objective. That is, man has moved from a great impulse
within himself, unconscious. But once the conquest has been
effected, there is a temptation for the conscious mind to return
and finger and explore, just as tourists now explore battlefields.
This self-conscious *mental* provoking of sensation and reaction in
the great affective centres is what we call sentimentalism or sensationalism. The mind returns upon the affective centres, and
sets up in them a deliberate reaction.

And this is what all the Americans do, beginning with
Crèvecoeur, Hawthorne, Poe, all the transcendentalists, Melville,
Prescott, Wendell Holmes, Whitman, they are all guilty of this
provoking of mental reactions in the physical self, passions ex-
ploited by the mind. In Europe, men like Balzac and Dickens,
Tolstoi and Hardy, still act direct from the passional motive, and
not inversely, from mental provocation. But the aesthetes and
symbolists, from Baudelaire and Maeterlinck and Oscar Wilde

onwards, and nearly all later Russian, French, and English novel-
ists set up their reactions in the mind and reflect them by a
secondary process down into the body. This makes a vicious
living and a spurious art. It is one of the last and most fatal
effects of idealism. Everything becomes self-conscious and
spurious, to the pitch of madness. It is the madness of the world
of to-day. Europe and America are all alike; all the nations self-
consciously provoking their own passional reactions from the
mind, and *nothing* spontaneous.

And this is our accusation against Whitman, as against the
others. Too often he deliberately, self-consciously *affects* himself. It puts us off, it makes us dislike him. But since such self-
conscious secondariness is a concomitant of all American art, and
yet not sufficiently so to prevent that art from being of rare
quality, we must get over it. The excuse is that the Americans
have had to perform in a century a curve which it will take
Europe much longer to finish, if ever she finishes it.

Whitman has gone further, in actual living expression, than
any man, it seems to me. Dostoevsky has burrowed underground
into the decomposing psyche. But Whitman has gone forward in
life-knowledge. It is he who surmounts the grand climacteric of
our civilization.

Whitman enters on the last phase of spiritual triumph. He
really arrives at that stage of infinity which the seers sought. By
subjecting the *deepest centres* of the lower self, he attains the
maximum consciousness in the higher self : a degree of extensive
consciousness greater, perhaps, than any man in the modern
world.

We have seen Dana and Melville, the two adventurers, setting
out to conquer the last vast *element,* with the spirit. We have
seen Melville touching at last the far end of the immemorial,
prehistoric Pacific civilization, in *Typee.* We have seen his terrific
cruise into universality.

Now we must remember that the way, even towards a state
of infinite comprehension, is through the externals towards the

quick. And the vast elements, the cosmos, the big things, the universals, these are always the externals. These are met first and conquered first. That is why science is so much easier than art. The quick is the living being, the quick of quicks is the individual soul. And it is here, at the quick, that Whitman proceeds to find the experience of infinitude, his vast extension, or concentrated intensification into Allness. He carries the conquest to its end.

If we read his paeans, his chants of praise and deliverance and accession, what do we find? All-embracing, indiscriminate, passional acceptance; surges of chaotic vehemence of invitation and embrace, catalogues, lists, enumerations. "Whoever you are, to endless announcements . . . . " "And of these one and all I weave the song of myself." "Lovers, endless lovers."

Continually the one cry: "I am everything and everything is me. I accept everything in my consciousness; nothing is rejected :—

"I am he that aches with amorous love;
    Does the earth gravitate? does not all matter, aching,
        attract all matter?
So the body of me to all I meet or know."

At last everything is conquered. At last the lower centres are conquered. At last the lowest plane is submitted to the highest. At last there is nothing more to conquer. At last all is one, all is love, even hate is love, even flesh is spirit. The great oneness, the experience of infinity, the triumph of the living spirit, which at last includes everything, is here accomplished.

It is man's accession into wholeness, his knowledge in full. Now he is united with everything. Now he embraces everything into himself in a oneness. Whitman is drunk with the new wine of this new great experience, really drunk with the strange wine of infinitude. So he pours forth his words, his chants of praise and acclamation. It is man's maximum state of consciousness, his highest state of spiritual being. Supreme spiritual consciousness, and the divine drunkenness of supreme consciousness. It is reached through embracing love. "And whoever walks a furlong without sympathy walks to his own funeral dressed in his own shroud." And this supreme state, once reached, shows us the One Identity in everything, Whitman's cryptic *One Identity*.

Thus Whitman becomes in his own person the whole world, the whole universe, the whole eternity of time. Nothing is rejected. Because nothing opposes him. All adds up to one in him. Item by item he identifies himself with the universe, and this accumulative identity he calls Democracy, En Masse, One Identity, and so on.

But this is the last and final truth, the last truth is at the quick. And the quick is the single individual soul, which is never more than itself, though it embrace eternity and infinity, and never *other* than itself, though it include all men. Each vivid soul is unique, and though one soul embrace another, and include it, still it cannot *become* that other soul, or livingly dispossess that other soul. In extending himself, Whitman still remains himself; he does not become the other man, or the other woman, or the tree, or the universe : in spite of Plato.

Which is the maximum truth, though it appears so small in contrast to all these infinites, and En Masses, and Democracies, and Almightynesses. The essential truth is that a man is himself, and only himself, throughout all his greatnesses and extensions and intensifications.

The second truth which we must bring as a charge against Whitman is the one we brought before, namely, that his Allness, his One Identity, his En Masse, his Democracy, is only a half-truth—an enormous half-truth. The other half is Jehovah, and Egypt, and Sennacherib : the other form of Allness, terrible and grand, even as in the Psalms.

Now Whitman's way to Allness, he tells us, is through endless sympathy, merging. But in merging you must merge away from something, as well as towards something, and in sympathy you must depart from one point to arrive at another. Whitman lays down this law of sympathy as the one law, the direction of merging as the one direction. Which is obviously wrong. Why not a right-about-turn? Why not turn slap back to the point from which you started to merge? Why not *that* direction, the reverse of merging, back to the single and overweening self? Why not, instead of endless dilation of sympathy, the retraction into isolation and pride?

Why not? The heart has its systole diastole, the shuttle comes and goes, even the sun rises and sets. We know, as a matter of fact, that all life lies between two poles. The direction is twofold. Whitman's *one direction* becomes a hideous tyranny once he has attained his goal of Allness. His One Identity is a prison of horror, once realized. For identities are manifold and each jewel-like, different as a sapphire from an opal. And the motion of merging becomes at last a vice, a nasty degeneration, as when tissue breaks down into a mucous slime. There must be the sharp retraction from isolation, following the expansion into unification, otherwise the integral being is overstrained and will break, break down like disintegrating tissue into slime, imbecility, epilepsy, vice, like Dostoevsky.

And one word more. Even if you reach the state of infinity, you can't sit down there. You just physically can't. You either have to strain still further into universality and become vaporish, or slimy : or you have to hold your toes and sit tight and practise Nirvana; or you have to come back to common dimensions, eat your pudding and blow your nose and be just yourself; or die and have done with it. A grand experience is a grand experience It brings a man to his maximum. But even at his maximum a man is not more than himself. When he is infinite he is still himself. He still has a nose to wipe. The state of infinity is *only* a state, even if it be the supreme one.

But in achieving this state Whitman opened a new field of living. He drives on to the very centre of life and sublimates even this into consciousness. Melville hunts the remote white whale of the deepest passional body, tracks it down. But it is Whitman who captures the whale. The pure sensual body of man, at its deepest remoteness and intensity, this is the White Whale. And this is what Whitman captures.

He seeks his consummation through one continual ecstasy : the ecstasy of *giving himself,* and of being taken. The ecstasy of his own reaping and merging with another, with others; the sword-cut of sensual death. Whitman's motion is always the motion of *giving himself* : This is my body—take, and eat. It is the great sacrament. He knows nothing of the other sacrament, the sacrament in pride, where the communicant envelops the victim and host in a flame of ecstatic consuming, sensual gratification, and triumph.

But he is concerned with others beside himself : with woman, for example. But what is woman to Whitman? Not much : she is a great function—no more. Whitman's "athletic mothers of these States" are depressing. Muscles and wombs : functional creatures—no more.

"As I see myself reflected in Nature,
    As I see through a mist, One with inexpressible completeness,
        sanity, beauty,
    See the bent head, and arms folded over the breast, the
        Female I see."

That is all. The woman is reduced, really, to a submissive function. She is no longer an individual being with a living soul. She must fold her arms and bend her head and submit to her functioning capacity. Function of sex, function of birth.

"This the nucleus—after the child is born of woman, man is
    born of woman,
    This is the bath of birth, the merge of small and large,
        and the outlet again—"

Acting from the last and profoundest centres, man acts womanless. It is no longer a question of race continuance. It is a question of sheer, ultimate being, the perfection of life, nearest to death. Acting from these centres, man is an extreme being, the unthinkable warrior, creator, mover, and maker.

And the polarity is between man and man. Whitman alone of all moderns has known this positively. Others have known it negatively, *pour épater les bourgeois*. But Whitman knew it positively, in its tremendous knowledge, knew the extremity, the perfectness, and the fatality.

Even Whitman becomes grave, tremulous, before the last dynamic truth of life. In "Calamus" he does not shout. He hesitates: he is reluctant, wistful. But none the less he goes on. And he tells the mystery of manly love, the love of comrades. Continually he tells us the same truth: the new world will be built upon the love of comrades, the new great dynamic of life will be manly love. Out of this inspiration the creation of the future.

The strange Calamus has its pink-tinged root by the pond, and it sends up its leaves of comradeship, comrades at one root, without the intervention of woman, the female. This comradeship is to be the final cohering principle of the new world, the new Democracy. It is the cohering principle of perfect soldiery, as he tells in "Drum Taps." It is the cohering principle of final *unison* in creative activity. And it is extreme and alone, touching the confines of death. It is something terrible to bear, terrible to be responsible for. It is the soul's last and most vivid responsibility, the responsibility for the circuit of final friendship, comradeship, manly love.

"Yet, you are beautiful to me you faint-tinged roots,
    you make me think of death;
Death is beautiful from you (what, indeed, is finally beautiful
    except death and love?).
I think it is not for life I am chanting here my chant of
    lovers, I think it must be for death.
For how calm, how solemn it grows to ascend to the
    atmosphere of lovers;
Death of life, I am then indifferent, my soul declines to

> prefer, (I am not sure but the high soul of lovers welcomes
>   death most),
> Indeed, O death, I think now these leaves mean precisely
>   the same as you mean—"

Here we have the deepest, finest Whitman, the Whitman who
knows the extremity of life, and of the soul's responsibility. He
has come near now to death, in his creative life. But creative
life must come near to death, to link up the mystic circuit. The
pure warriors must stand on the brink of death. So must the men
of a pure creative nation. We shall have no beauty, no dignity,
no essential freedom otherwise. And so it is from Sea-Drift,
where the male bird sings the lost female: not that she is lost,
but lost to him who has had to go beyond her, to sing on the
edge of the great sea, in the night. It is the last voice on the shore.

> "Whereto answering, the sea
> Delaying not, hurrying not,
> Whispered me through the night, and very plainly before
>   daybreak,
> Lisp'd to me the low and delicious word death,
> And again death, death, death, death,
> Hissing melodious, neither like the bird nor like my aroused
>   child's heart,
> But edging near as privately for me rustling at my feet,
> Creeping thence steadily up to my ears and laving me softly
>   all over,
> Death, death, death, death, death—"

What a great poet Whitman is: great like a great Greek.
For him the last enclosures have fallen, he finds himself on the
shore of the last sea. The extreme of life: so near to death. It
is a hushed, deep responsibility. And what is the responsibility?
It is for the new great era of mankind. And upon what is this
new era established? On the perfect circuits of vital flow between
human beings. First, the great sexless normal relation between
individuals, simple sexless friendships, unison of family, and clan,

and nation, and group. Next, the powerful sex relation between man and woman, culminating in the eternal orbit of marriage. And, finally, the sheer friendship, the love between comrades, the manly love which alone can create a new era of life.

The one state, however, does not annul the other : it fulfils the other. Marriage is the great step beyond friendship, and family, and nationality, but it does not supersede these. Marriage should only give repose and perfection to the great previous bonds and relationships. A wife or husband who sets about to annul the old, pre-marriage affections and connections ruins the foundations of marriage. And so with the last, extremest love, the love of comrades. The ultimate comradeship which sets about to destroy marriage destroys its own *raison d'être*. The ultimate comradeship is the final progression from marriage; it is the last seedless flower of pure beauty, beyond purpose. But if it destroys marriage it makes itself purely deathly. In its beauty, the ultimate comradeship flowers on the brink of death. But it flowers from the root of all life upon the blossoming tree of life.

The life-circuit now depends entirely upon the sex-unison of marriage. This circuit must never be broken. But it must be still surpassed. We cannot help the laws of life.

If marriage is sacred, the ultimate comradeship is utterly sacred, since it has no ulterior motive whatever, like procreation. If marriage is eternal, the great bond of life, how much more is this bond eternal, being the great life-circuit which borders on death in all its round. The new, extreme, the sacred relationship of comrades awaits us, and the future of mankind depends on the way in which this relation is entered upon by us. It is a relation between fearless, honorable, self-responsible men, a balance in perfect polarity.

The last phase is entered upon, shakily, by Whitman. It will take us an epoch to establish the new, perfect circuit of our being. It will take an epoch to establish the love of comrades, as marriage is really established now. For fear of going on, forwards, we turn round and destroy, or try to destroy, what lies behind.

We are trying to destroy marriage, because we have not the courage to go forward from marriage to the new issue. Marriage must never be wantonly attacked. *True* marriage is eternal; in it we have our consummation and being. But the final consummation lies in that which is beyond marriage.

And when the bond, or circuit of perfect comrades is established, what then, when we are on the brink of death, fulfilled in the vastness of life? Then, at last, we shall know a starry maturity.

Whitman put us on the track years ago. Why has no one gone on from him? The great poet, why does no one accept his greatest word? The Americans are not worthy of their Whitman. They take him like a cocktail, for fun. Miracle that they have not annihilated every word of him. But these miracles happen.

The greatest modern poet! Whitman, at his best, is purely himself. His verse springs sheer from the spontaneous sources of his being. Hence its lovely, lovely form and rhythm : at the best. It is sheer, perfect *human* spontaneity, spontaneous as a nightingale throbbing, but still controlled, the highest loveliness of human spontaneity, undecorated, unclothed. The whole being is there, sensually throbbing, spiritually quivering, mentally, ideally speaking. It is not, like Swinburne, an exaggeration of the one part of being. It is perfect and whole. The whole soul speaks at once, and is too pure for mechanical assistance of rhyme and measure. The perfect utterance of a concentrated spontaneous soul. The unforgettable loveliness of Whitman's lines!

"Out of the cradle endlessly rocking."
Ave America!

GAYLORD S